SUBTRACTIVE
SCHOOLING

SUNY series, The Social Context of Education
Christine E. Sleeter, editor

SUBTRACTIVE SCHOOLING

U.S.-Mexican Youth and the Politics of Caring

ANGELA VALENZUELA

State University
of New York
Press

Published by
State University of New York Press, Albany

Production by Susan Geraghty
Marketing by Nancy Farrell

Cover photo by Emilio Zamora.

"The teacher was surprised. . ." by Tomás Rivera is reprinted with permission
from the publisher of . . .*y no se lo tragó la tierra*/. . .*And the Earth Did Not
Devour Him* (Houston: Arte Público Press–University of Houston, 1987)

Printed in the United States of America

For information, address State University of New York Press,
194 Washington Avenue, Suite 305, Albany, NY 12210-2384

Library of Congress Cataloging-in-Publication Data

Valenzuela, Angela.
   Subtractive schooling : U.S.
 -Mexican youth and the Politics of Caring / Angela Valenzuela.
     p.   cm. — (SUNY series, the social context of education)
   Includes bibliographical references (p.   ) and index.
   ISBN 0-7914-4321-3 (hc : alk. paper). — ISBN 0-7914-4322-1 (pb. :
alk. paper)
    1. Mexican Americans—Education (Secondary)—Texas—Case studies.
2. Children of immigrants—Education (Secondary)—Texas—Case
studies. 3. Mexican American youth—Social conditions—Texas—Case
studies. I. Title. II. Series: SUNY series, social context of
education.
LC2683.4.V35   1999
371.829′6872073—dc21   98-43568
                                             CIP

11

CONTENTS

TABLES

ACKNOWLEDGMENTS

I am indebted to so many individuals who helped me throughout the various stages of this work. My mentors, Sanford M. Dornbusch, Jerry Herting, John Meyer, Amado Padilla, and Marta Tienda, are a good place to begin. I thank you for encouraging my research interest in both the sociology of education and minority schooling issues, and also for supporting and guiding my career through the years.

Financial support from local and national funders proved critical to bringing this project to fruition. Locally, these include the Rice University Center for Education, Union Texas Petroleum, Price Waterhouse, Towers Perrin, Fulbright and Jaworski, and Andrews and Kurth. Carol Cox of Union Texas Petroleum merits special mention for both supporting me throughout and for facilitating additional support at a critical juncture in my project.

At Rice University, I credit Linda McNeil and Ron Sass, the co-directors of the Center for Education, for their unflagging support. Linda McNeil, in particular, has modeled for me what caring in the professional world looks and feels like: it includes and expands into the realm of the personal. The McNeils—Kenneth, Linda, and their daughters, Kathryn and Carrie—will forever occupy a special place in my, and my family's, heart.

Other Center friends and colleagues whose growth I witnessed and who witnessed mine include Patsy Cooper, Cheryl Craig, Catherine Crawford, Wallace Dominey, Connie Floyd, Debra Gamble, Noni Harcombe, Marvin Hoffman, Bernie Mathes, Doris Robins, Margie Sass, and Richard Smith.

While at Rice University, my writing group—comprised of Elizabeth Long, Anne Klein, Kathryn Milun, Diana Strassmann, and Sharon Traweek—fulfilled the special purpose of helping me to see and feel confident about the power of both my ideas and my writing. Thanks for providing me with a sense of refuge from my intellectual isolation.

Through the Ford Foundation's Minority Postdoctoral Fellowship Program, which granted me time and funding for research during the 1993–94 year, I was able to complete the bulk of my data collection and subsequently, to analyze, write, and in the end, make sense of its many, and often, unwieldy parts. My primary contact at Ford, Christine O'Brien, Program Supervisor of Ford Programs, demonstrated a sincere interest in supporting my work. For this, I am grateful. I also wish to thank Gary Dworkin, my friend and colleague, who agreed to sponsor me locally at the University of Houston during my postdoctoral year.

I wish to thank my friend and colleague Richard Valencia, for consistently providing me with good advice, including his suggestion that I contact Christie Sleeter to see if she would entertain my manuscript as part of her series with the State University of New York Press. Working with Christie has been a rewarding and pleasant experience.

While writing, I also experienced certain, special moments of clarity—or "epiphanies" as we in our writing group referred to them. All of these rare moments coincided with pivotal discussions over my work. I thank Elizabeth Long, George Noblit, Guadalupe San Miguel, and Dennis Shirley for their insightful criticisms and for helping me push my analysis further. Elizabeth, no one could have had a more tireless and devoted mentor than you.

Also worthy of mention are the following individuals who read my manuscript in its developing stages and who provided helpful and invaluable commentary: Bud Mehan, Jonathan Kozol, George Noblit, Nel Noddings, Francisco Rios, Nestor Rodriguez, Ricardo Stanton-Salazar, Henry Trueba, Armando Trujillo, and Olga Vasquez. Olga, in particular, helped me "keep the faith." I wish to thank Kathy Mooney, my editor, for her support and impeccable timing. She not only read my manuscript with a critical eye, she also energized the writing process for me at the exact right moment.

Caring among colleagues conjures up a long list of names of persons to whom I feel indebted: Rodolfo Acuña, Tomás Almaguer, Ed and Laverne Apodaca, José Aranda and Krista Comer, Alicia Arrizón, Luis and Rosanna Arroyo, Inés Hernández-Avila and Juan Avila, Gilda Bloom, Joyce and Bill Bulko, Raymond

Buriel, Diana Bustamante, Norma Cantú, Rick and Maribel Barrera, Sam Barrocas and Teresa Carrillo, Blandina "Bambi" Cardenas, Sylvia Cavazos Peña, Gloria Cuádraz, Lisa Catanzarite and Landon Alexander, Gilbert Cardenas, Jorge Chapa, Regino Chavez and Carol Peterson, Tom Cohen and Lisa Fuentes, Julia Curry-Rodriguez, Roberto deAnda, Arnoldo DeLeón, Fernando deNecochea, Leo Estrada, Roberta Fernández, Estéban Flores, Yolanda Flores Niemann, Doug Foley, Patricia Gándara, the late Letticia Galindo, Juan Gomez-Quiñones, Irma Guardarrama, Victor Guerra, the late Rafael Guzmán, Jackie Hagan, Randy Hansen, Francisca James-Hernández and Rosalía Solórzano, Wayne Holtzman, Toni and Andrew Kennedy, Stephen Klineberg, José Limón, George Lipsitz, José Macías, Alberto Mata, Terry McKenna, Marta Menchaca, Mario Montaño, David Montejano and Jackie Morell, Lorraine and Juan Mora, Victor Nelson-Cisneros, John Ogbu, Michael Olivas, Mary Pardo, Amado Peña and Judy Boles Peña, Irene Peña, Tina Reyes, C.C. and Phil Rhodes, María del Refugio Robledo, Nestor Rodriguez, Mary Romero and Eric Margolis, Ricardo and Harriett Romo, Russell Rumberger, Delia Saldaña, Saúl Sánchez, Inés Talamantez, Javier Tapia, Richard and Jean Tapia, Andrés and Juana Tijerina, Rosario Torres-Raines, Abel Valenzuela, Diego Vigil, Bill Wallauer, Norma Williams, and Devra Weber.

Many of my students supported my work generously. They include Marleni Alvarez, Stela Balderas, Tony Chen, Stella Flores, Michael Fuentes, Laura Vel García, Michael Gomez, the late Theresa Garza, María Garza Lerma, Felicia Martin, Isabel Martinez, Marta Ontiveros, Ann Piper, Gabriella Rivero, Johnny Joseph Rodriguez, Patricia Sanchez, Mark Schoenhals, Manuela Serna, and Laurie Villarreal. I have also derived inspiration from the heart-felt devotion to service among the students in the organization I most enjoyed sponsoring, HACER, or the Hispanic Association for Cultural Enrichment at Rice. *Sigan con la lucha!*

I have acquired a deep respect and admiration for so many of Houston's community leaders that I came across in the course of my research. The following individuals have modeled for me the fierce love of community that we should all possess: Ana Acevedo, Ricardo Aguirre, Marta Almaguer, Carol Alvarado, Yolanda Alvarado, Frank and Sylvia Alvarez, Mary Armendariz,

María Bhattacharjee, Rosemary Blanco, Debbie and Tom Barrera Carrizal, Elias Bongmba, Mayor Lee Brown, Maconda Brown O'Connor, Daniel and Dolores Bustamante, School Board Member Esther Campos, Lorenzo Cano, Dorothy Caram, Leonel Castillo, Councilmember John Castillo and Mary Castillo, Rosemary Covalt, Mary Closner, Robert Cruz, former State Representative Diana Davila, Jaime de la Isla, Ellen de Kanter, Richard Farias, State Representative Jessica Farrar, Councilman Felix Fraga, Eloy Gaitán and Cecilia Pequeño Gaitán, Senator Mario Gallegos, School Board Member Olga Gallegos, Adrián García, Herlinda García, Sylvia García, María (Cris) Garza, Thelma Garza, Alfredo Gavito, Leticia Gloria, Joe Gonzalez, José Angel Gutierrez, Mela Gutierrez, José Hernández, Lisa Hernández, María Theresa Hernández, Norma Hernández, Jessica Hulsey, María Jimenez, Albert Leal, Belia Lopez, Cristóbal López, Betty Maldonado, Marcelo Marini, former State Representative Roman Martinez, Johnny Mata, David Medina, Helen Meza, Gasper and Beckie Mir, Lilly and Benita Morales, Art Murillo, Liz Murillo, Laura Gonzalez Murillo, Elsa Mendoza, Linda Morales, Susie Moreno, W. R. Morris, Yolanda Navarro, Yolanda Navarro Flores, Ana Nuñez, Marcia Olivarez, Laurence Payne, Freddy Porras, Elisama Puente, Alfredo and Diana Santos, Teresa Ramirez, Sylvia Ramos, Frumencio Reyes, Jaime Rivera, Sylvia H. Rodriguez, Manuel Rodriguez, David and Sylvia Rosales, Charles Rotrammel, María Magdalena Rustomji, former Councilmember Gracie Guzmán Saenz and her husband, Eloy Saenz, José Salazar, Guadalupe Sanchez, Yolanda Santos, Eva Silvas, Olga Soliz, Bishop James Tamayo, Adriana Tamez, Patricia Silva-Flores, Kip Tellez, Alfredo P. Tijerina, Alison Torres, Gloria Torres, José Treviño, Lilia Treviño, Rebeca Treviño, Judge Richard Vara, Gracie Vasquez, José Villarreal, Sheila Whitford, Rosie Zamora, and JoAnn Zuñiga. I feel honored to be among you.

I could not have completed this work without the prayers and guidance from the following special individuals: Rev. James and Noelia Benson, Rev. Ananías and Nelly Gonzalez, Rev. Rudy and Ruth Sanchez, and Alfredo and Eva Guel. Thank you all for attending to my family's spiritual well-being.

I also wish to mention a few special friends who will forever hold a special place in my heart. In San Angelo, they include Ben and Linda Escobedo, and my best friend during my teenage years, the late Sylvia "Scooby" Escobedo, and her mother, the late Elena Escobedo. Aside from Scooby and her family, other lifelong friends that have brought me much happiness are Betsy Borremans, Yolanda Zapata Gallichio, and Elva Zepeda. More recently, our family has derived blessings from our friendship with Rodolfo and Yolanda Francisco, Robert and Mary Ann Garcia, Salvador and Amalia Gomez, Jorge and Naomi González, Abel and Kathy Guajardo, Carlos and Rosanna Moreno (*"mi comadre"*), Marta and Arnold Perez, and their respective families.

In our neighborhood, the lines between family, friends, and neighbors have become blissfully blurred. I thank you Wess and Cathy Fryar, María Gonzalez, Lionel and Charek Jellins, Tatcho and Cindy Mindiola, Randy and Kathryn Milun, Guadalupe San Miguel and Alicia Moreno, Marco Piñon and Vangie Vigil for helping us reinforce in our children the importance of social responsibility through your own examples as individuals invested in the creation and maintenance of moral communities. It's deeply gratifying that our many shared moments of enjoyment seamlessly combine having fun with our growing children with intense deliberations over all manner of political, intellectual and spiritual concerns.

My parents, Carlos and Helen Valenzuela, have been a constant source of love, support, and inspiration to me. I am who I am in large part because of them. Thank you for always seeing the best in me and for demonstrating with your lives what it really means to live by God's word. Though my grandparents are deceased, their impact on my life continues into the present. Thank you, Alfredo Camilo Rios and Concepción Haro Rios, for giving me my mother. And thank you, José and Eulalia Valenzuela, for giving me my father. I was conceived in my parents' deep and enduring love for each other.

I wish there were words sufficient enough to express my gratitude to all my family members who have had to put up with our family's many absences from family events because of "the book": on the Valenzuela side is my brother, Alex Valenzuela, and my sister, Valerie Valenzuela Robles, and their lovely families. To my sister-in-law, Jane, my nephews, Nicholas and Jacob, along with my brother-in-law, Rubén Robles, and my new-born baby niece,

Dakota Cristal, *gracias por todo!* To Sandra Hernández, my virtual sister, thank you for your faithful love and support.

Heart-felt thanks also go to my in-laws, Emilio and Eudelia Zamora, as well as to all of my many brothers- and sisters-in-law: Noelia and Orlando Flores, Elia Padrón, Cecilia Amador, Lety and Joseph Sankovet, Norma Alicia and Ramiro Guerra, Rolando and Norma Zamora, Ricardo and Flor Zamora, and Aida and Mario Gonzalez. The Zamoras are uncomplicated in their generosity, loyalty, and kindness.

Giving birth twice during this project were my most exciting and profound experiences. Thanks to Nadia Stein who helped us with both. We will surely make it to the hospital in time if there ever is a next time!

My husband and daughters have kept me sane. Thank you Emilio, Clara, and Luz for loving me unconditionally and for exceeding my prayers and expectations about all that family is supposed to be. Love and affection define much that goes on in my family. Luz often explains what she does with the innocence of a two-year old: "because I love you." At five years of age, Clara says, "It (my love) just keeps going on forever."

FOREWORD

On June 2, 1998, the voters of California passed Proposition 227 in an attempt to eliminate bilingual education and to designate English as not just the dominant language, but the only legitimate language in which academic learning is to occur. Although mainstream media claimed that Latino voters supported Proposition 227 overwhelmingly, other observers reported a different story. According to California Tomorrow (1998), while Proposition 227 was supported by 67% of white voters, it received the support of only 37% of Latinos, 57% of Asians, and 48% of African Americans. The white-Latino gap was striking: two thirds of white voters supported dismantling bilingual education, but two thirds of Latino voters, whose children constitute a majority of the bilingual education students in California, opposed doing so.

In the media blitz preceding the vote, supporters of Proposition 227 maintained that bilingual education hinders language minority children's ability to learn English and ultimately to succeed in society, and that the best way for them to learn English is to be immersed in English-speaking classrooms. Four unstated assumptions undergird this argument. The first is that there is no value in bilingualism, biculturalism, or fluency in a language or culture other than English. I did not see one instance of mainstream media seriously exploring the value of bilingualism or biculturalism for anyone. A second assumption is that fluency in any language except English interferes with education, or at least does not contribute to education in any meaningful way. A third assumption is that research on these issues is irrelevant. In the vast majority of public discussions, arguments were based on personal experiences and opinions; the existence of a research base connecting language programming with academic achievement (e.g., Medina and Mishra 1994; Ramirez et al. 1991; Thomas and Collier 1996) was not acknowledged. A fourth assumption is that monolingual Anglo members of the general public are perfectly capable of deciding what kind of educational programming is best for non–Anglo language minority children—"other people's children" (Delpit 1995)—and are better able to make such decisions than are bilingual education teachers or the communities the children come from.

Yet opposition to bilingual education was often framed around "caring" about language-minority children. I frequently heard educators and non-educators alike express concern that language-minority children will be held back if they do not quickly acquire English, and that anyone who cares about them would not want to see them held back by misguided programming or by a special interest group (i.e., the "bilingual education establishment"). A huge question one needs to ask is: What does it mean to care about children from marginalized communities, given the political and social context in which education takes place? The debates surrounding Proposition 227 are not limited to California; at the time of this writing, several other states, as well as some members of U.S. Congress, are considering similar measures.

In *Subtractive Schooling: U.S.-Mexican Youth and the Politics of Caring*, Angela Valenzuela thoughtfully probes the question of what it means to care about children in a cultural and political context. This book is based on an ethnographic study of a large, inner-city high school in Houston, Texas. Valenzuela takes us into the school and allows us to spend time with the students and teachers. In so doing, she untangles how it is that students experience school as uncaring, while many teachers claim they care about the students. She distinguishes between two very different conceptions of what it means to care about young people: one conception affirms and embraces their culture and community, and the other attempts to divorce young people from their culture and community. This book sensitively examines how the students themselves experienced personal relationships with teachers and a school curriculum that had the goal of mainstreaming them into the dominant society by subtracting their community-based language and culture. In this book, Valenzuela advances a theoretical conception of "care" by situating notions of caring and schooling in a structural and historical perspective.

I would like to contextualize this study within a historical framework for examining racism. In a short but highly useful examination of three thousand years of racism, Merlin Stone (1981) distinguishes between two dimensions of racism, and two stages in the process of constructing and consolidating racism. The two dimensions are economic and cultural racism. Economic racism involves the theft of land, labor, and resources; cultural racism consists of the belief system that is manufactured to legitimate that theft.

The first stage of economic racism consists of violent conquest, accompanied by the construction of a belief system that the conquering group is culturally and intellectually superior to the group it has conquered. In the case of U.S.-Mexico, the United States used military force to claim what is now the southwestern part of the United States, and followed military conquest with forcible measures to overturn Mexican land-ownership claims and to undermine Mexican culture, the Spanish language, and the Catholic religion.

The second stage of racism involves ongoing attempts by the colonizing society to consolidate and stabilize control over the land and people, and to incorporate the people into the labor force in subordinate positions. At the cultural level, the colonizing group proclaims the superiority of its social system. During times of rebellion or instability, the dominant society reinforces its dominance through violence, and through assault on the culture, language, religion, or moral fibre of the subordinate group.

Schools are an instrument of the maintenance of colonial relationships in that they constitute an arm of the state through which belief systems and cultural relationships are taught. Public school curricula proclaim the "triumph of democracy" to the virtual exclusion of any serious analysis of the U.S. conquest (Loewen 1995). Curricula also reflect the degree to which the dominant society tolerates the cultures and languages of subordinate groups. To borrow from Valenzuela, a process of "subtractive schooling" unfolds. That is, policies and practices develop as a part of an ongoing project by Anglo America to consolidate its claim on the southwestern part of the United States, a claim that is continuously rendered unstable as demographics shift, economic security waxes and wanes, and empowerment movements such as the Chicano civil rights movement and school programs such as bilingual education grow. In the 1980s, as demographic shifts in the United States became increasingly visible, and as the economic position of working-class people eroded due to the export of jobs to Third World nations, conservatives stepped up efforts to discredit multicultural education, to establish English as the only official language of the United States, and to dismantle civil rights efforts such as affirmative action. Such efforts can be understood as attempts to consolidate the loyalty of whites of varied social class and ethnic backgrounds, and to squash counterhegemonic discourses that had been developing momentum (Platt 1992). The passage of Proposition 227 is part of an attempt at the cultural level to reestablish stage-two racism.

I do not believe that most Anglo teachers see themselves as colonizers, and that most do care about the students they work with. At the same time, most Anglo teachers do not view racial and ethnic relations within a political perspective, and take for granted beliefs in the superiority of U.S. society, predominance of European and Euro-American culture, and the pragmatic utility of fluency in English only. The alchemy of playing a colonizing role while caring about children can play out in a variety of ways, from disappointment in one's students, to abusive teacher-student relationships, to transformation of teachers' cultural and political awareness. Valenzuela skillfully examines how this care plays out in a school, how students experience and interpret it, and how it interacts with a curriculum that denies students' community-based identities. In so doing, she raises important questions about what it means to educate other people's children.

CHRISTINE E. SLEETER

The teacher was surprised when, hearing that they needed a button on the poster to represent the button industry, the child tore one off his shirt and offered it to her. She was surprised because she knew that this was probably the only shirt the child had. She didn't know whether he did this to be helpful, to feel like he belonged or out of love for her. She did feel the intensity of the child's desire and this was what surprised her most of all.

—Tomás Rivera, *Y No Se Lo Tragó la Tierra*

CHAPTER 1

Introduction

"Listen," [I told my class] "you don't have to be here if you
don't want to be here. No one is forcing you."
—Algebra teacher, Juan Seguín High School

"If the *school* doesn't care about my learning, why should *I*
care? Answer me that. Just answer me that!"
—Ninth-grade student, Juan Seguín High School

When teenagers lament that "Nobody cares," few adults listen.
Whether it is offered as an observation, description, explanation,
or excuse, the charge that "Nobody cares" is routinely dismissed
as childish exaggeration. But what if it were *not* hyperbole? What
if each weekday, for eight hours a day, teenagers inhabited a
world populated by adults who did not care—or at least did not
care for *them* sufficiently?

This book is a field guide to just such a world. It presents the
findings of my three-year ethnographic investigation of academic
achievement and schooling orientations among immigrant Mexican
and Mexican American students[1] at Juan Seguín High School (a
pseudonym) in Houston, Texas. Rather than functioning as a con-
duit for the attainment of the American dream, this large, overcrowded, and underfunded urban school reproduces Mexican youth
as a monolingual, English-speaking, ethnic minority, neither identified with Mexico nor equipped to function competently in America's
mainstream. For the majority of Seguín High School's regular (non-
college-bound) track, schooling is a *subtractive* process. It divests
these youth of important social and cultural resources, leaving them
progressively vulnerable to academic failure.

The progressive nature of academic underachievement among
U.S.-born Mexican students has been documented by comparing
their grades, test scores, dropout rates, and so on with those of
immigrant youth. Studies show that among Mexican and Central

3

American students, generational status plays an influential role in schooling experiences; first- and often second-generation students academically outperform their third- and later-generation counterparts (Vigil and Long 1981; Buriel 1984; Buriel and Cardoza 1988; Ogbu 1991; Matute-Bianchi 1991; Suárez-Orozco 1991; Steinberg et al. 1996). These findings, based primarily on small-scale ethnographic studies, are similarly evident in national-level data (Portes and Rumbaut 1990; Portes and Zhou 1993; Kao and Tienda 1995; Zsembik and Llanes 1996). Rather than revealing the upward mobility pattern historically evident among European-origin groups, research on generational attainments points to an "invisible ceiling" of blocked opportunity for Mexican people (Chapa 1988, 1991; Gans 1992; Bean et al. 1994).

Most scholars have sought to explain the observed generational decline in achievement by comparing the attributes/attitudes of immigrants to those of their later-generation counterparts (Vigil and Long 1981; Matute-Bianchi 1991; Portes and Zhou 1993; Buriel 1984, 1987, 1994). This approach has three major drawbacks. First, it accepts the differences among youth as a priori, rather than as linked to a larger project of cultural eradication in which schools play an important part (Bartolomé 1994). Race/ethnicity are not mere stock that individuals possess, manipulate, and bring to bear on institutional life. Instead, this study of the nexus between generational dynamics and institutional life shows that the latter significantly influences the direction and form that ethnic identities take.

Secondly, generational comparisons that fail to acknowledge schools as key sites for the production of minority status risk an invidious comparison. Contrasting the so-called optimism of immigrant youth with the "antischool" and "subcultural" (Matute-Bianchi 1991; Portes and Zhou 1993, 1994) attitudes of their later-generation counterparts results in a view of U.S.-born youth as "deficient," fundamentally lacking in drive and enthusiasm. DeVillar (1994) cogently argues that U.S.-born, minority youth are seen by schools and society as lacking the linguistic, cultural, moral, and intellectual traits the assimilationist curriculum demands. These students are perceived as requiring ever more cultural assimilation and resocialization—as if the potency of initial treatments somehow systematically fades. This study proposes that the alleged "deficiencies" of regular-track, U.S.-born youth from a low-income community are themselves symptomatic of the ways that schooling is organized to subtract resources from them.

Thirdly, the interrelatedness of immigrant achievement and non-immigrant underachievement gets obscured. Since the framework advanced herein assumes that achievement is a social process whereby orientations toward schooling are nurtured in familiar contexts among those with similar dispositions, then any "politics of difference"—as McCarthy (1994) theorizes—are highly consequential. That is, when immigrant and non-immigrant youth produce invidious "we–they" distinctions, the achievement potential of the entire group gets compromised as windows to the "other's" experience are closed.

Before dismissing urban, U.S.-born youth as lazy underachievers, it behooves researchers and practitioners to first examine the school's role in fostering poor academic performance. Bringing schools into sharper focus, as my study does, reveals that U.S.-born youth are neither inherently antischool nor oppositional. They oppose a schooling process that disrespects them; they oppose not education, but *schooling*. My research suggests that schools like Seguín High are organized formally and informally in ways that fracture students' cultural and ethnic identities, creating social, linguistic, and cultural divisions among the students and between the students and the staff.

As a direct consequence of these divisions, social relationships at Seguín typically are often fragile, incomplete, or nonexistent. Teachers fail to forge meaningful connections with their students; students are alienated from their teachers, and are often (especially between groups of first-generation immigrants and U.S.-born) hostile toward one another, as well; and administrators routinely disregard even the most basic needs of both students and staff. The feeling that "no one cares" is pervasive—and corrosive. Real learning is difficult to sustain in an atmosphere rife with mistrust. Over even comparatively short periods of time, the divisions and misunderstandings that characterize daily life at the school exact high costs in academic, social, and motivational currency. The subtractive nature of schooling virtually assures that students who begin the year with only small reserves of skills, as do most regular-track, U.S.-born youth, will not succeed; and conversely, those who come with more positive orientations or greater skills, as do Mexico-born students, are better equipped to offset the more debilitating aspects of schooling. Thus, what is commonly described as a problem of "generational decline in academic achievement" is much more accurately understood as a problem of *subtractive schooling*—a concept I introduced and developed elsewhere (Valenzuela 1997, 1999).

This chapter briefly describes the quantitative and qualitative aspects of the study I undertook at Seguín (see appendix for a complete description of the research methodology); reviews the literature on immigrant and nonimmigrant achievement; and explains the theoretical framework of the present study. The notion of subtractive schooling that forms the core of my work combines insights from social capital theory (especially Coleman 1988, 1990) and from the academic achievement and educational attainment literature comparing immigrant and U.S.-born youth (i.e., "subtractive assimilation" literature [Cummins 1984; Skutnabb-Kangas and Cummins 1988; Gibson 1988, 1993]). This general orientation is further enriched by existing research on caring and education (Noddings 1984, 1992; Fisher and Tronto 1990; Noblit 1993; Courtney and Noblit 1994; Danin 1994; Prillaman et al. 1994), much of which originally developed out of a concern for the alienating consequences of comprehensive, overcrowded, and bureaucratic schools like Seguín High (Noddings 1984, 1992).

The importance of caring/not caring in the present study also reflects the emphasis accorded to this factor by both students and teachers: explanations for the negative quality of life and schooling at Seguín often involved teachers and students each charging that the other "did not care." Taken together, these three bodies of literature—caring and education, subtractive assimilation, and social capital theory—enable the construction of a more nuanced explanation of achievement and underachievement among immigrant and U.S.-born youth than currently exists.

THE STUDY

My decision to pursue a modified ethnographic approach, one that combined collecting and analyzing both quantitative and qualitative data on generational differences in academic achievement among Mexican youth, was guided by several considerations. First, an exclusive dependence on quantitative data would have precluded my arriving at an in-depth understanding of the meaning of schooling for the study participants. Second, my emergent interest in the quality of interpersonal relationships as well as student groupings and grouping behaviors required my active involvement in the life of the school. Finally, the difficulties of surveying a student population with a large, disaffected segment—many of whom refused to fill out my questionnaire—were overwhelming.

I quickly realized that if I wanted to succeed in my goal of producing a rich, multilayered account of the relationship between schooling and achievement, I would need to gather data from as many sources and through as many means as I could fashion. The key mode of data collection became participant observation, augmented by data gathered from extensive field notes and informal interviews with students, parents, teachers, administrators, and community members and leaders. I did not abandon quantitative measures, however. In addition to questionnaires, I used quantitative data extracted from school and district documents. This kind of information helped direct my attention to important dimensions of schooling, most notably orientations toward school and achievement.

The qualitative component of my study of Mexican youth at Juan Seguín High School began in early fall of 1992. This involved informal, open-ended interviews with both individual students and groups of students, as well as with teachers, and observations at the school site. These encounters alerted me to the importance of human relations to students' motivation to achieve. Relations with school personnel, especially with teachers, play a decisive role in determining the extent to which youth find the school to be a welcoming or an alienating place. Youth, especially the U.S.-born group, frequently expressed their affiliational needs in terms of caring. Each time I reviewed my field notes, I would be struck by how often the words "care," "caring," and "caring for" seemed to leap off the pages, demanding my attention. This naturalistic discourse on caring led me toward the caring literature and a more focused examination of the meanings and uses of caring.

My early qualitative data collection also made clear that how youth group themselves (especially along immigrant/non-immigrant, Spanish-speaking/non-Spanish speaking axes) and the kinds of activities they undertake in those groups (e.g., school-related or non-school-related) bear directly on academic achievement. Students were invested in schooling if their friends were invested in it, or if their teachers were invested in them. In following up on this observation, I found the literature on social capital and on education and caring to be most useful.

I decided that a ground-level, inside look at students' affiliational needs in their schooling context was the optimal approach through which to examine the extent to which school orientations among immigrant and U.S.-born youth were conditioned by affiliational concerns. My interest in teacher-student relations, as well as in student grouping behaviors, translated into consciously seeking out students at times and places where they were likely to congregate. This meant talking to students in groups during their lunch hour, in the halls between classes, in the school library, in the bathroom (girls), during their Physical Education (P.E.) classes, in front of school buildings before and after school, and under the stairwells and in other hiding places favored by students who preferred to skip classes. I also attended numerous school and community functions (see appendix).

I began the quantitative component of my study with a survey of Seguín's entire student body (N = 2,281) in November, 1992. I was primarily interested in determining the extent to which generational status helped explain the varying levels of achievement. Analyzing the data on grades reported in this survey allowed me to establish some basic facts. First, students from Seguín High conform to the general pattern observed elsewhere among first-generation Mexican immigrants and U.S.-born Mexican American youth. The record of achievement among Seguín's immigrant youth is significantly higher than that of their U.S.-born, second- and third+-generation counterparts. Among the generations of U.S.-born youth, however, differences were not statistically significant.[2] Moreover, this difference in achievement is only evident among youth in the regular, non-college-bound track. In other words, as one would expect, being in the college-bound track erases these differences. Romo and Falbo (1996) and Olsen (1997) similarly underscore the importance of track placement as a highly consequential variable that structures the schooling experiences and achievement outcomes of immigrant and Mexican American adolescent youth.

Second, females in every generational group tend to outperform their male counterparts. However, this gender difference is again only evident among youth in the regular, non-college-bound track. Thus placement in the college-bound track has a leveling effect, erasing these differences, as well. Though she did not control for tracking, Matute-Bianchi (1991) reported similar findings on gender in her study of Mexican immigrant and non-immigrant youth. Her statistical analyses pointed not only to females' higher levels of aspirations and hours dedicated to homework, but also to this group's more positive rating of school climate. These findings, coupled with my survey data, led me to consider ways in which gender intersects with generational status to influence schooling orientations and outcomes.

Third, as Matute-Bianchi (1991) found, immigrant youth—regardless of either gender or track placement—experience school significantly more positively than their U.S.-born counterparts. That is, they see teachers as more caring and accessible and they rate the school climate in more positive terms, as well.[3] These students' attitudes contrast markedly with those of their second- and third+-generation counterparts whose responses in turn are not significantly different from one another. Data gathered from interviews and participant observation corroborate this finding of a schooling experience that distinguishes immigrant from U.S.-born youth.

Fourth, the survey showed the students' parents' educational levels to be extremely low, with a "high" average of around nine years attained by the third generation.[4] This information alerted me to the ninth grade as a watershed year, as well as to the idea that parents had little educational "advantage" to confer (Lareau 1989). Accordingly, I tried to talk to as many ninth graders as possible and to incorporate their voices and experience into this ethnographic account. I also pondered the implications of the parents' limited formal education as I recorded the criticisms teachers leveled at students, parents, and the community.

Combining quantitative evidence with my deepening role as a participant-observer helped generate the overarching conceptual frame for this study. I came to locate "the problem" of achievement squarely in school-based relationships and organizational structures and policies designed to erase students' culture. Over the three years in which I collected and analyzed my data, I became increasingly convinced that schooling is organized in ways that subtract resources from Mexican youth.[5]

For theoretical guidance in tracing out the ways in which the schooling experiences and orientations of Mexican high school students affect the range of their schooling outcomes, from achievement through disaffection, psychic withdrawal, resistance, and failure, I turned to the large volume of literature on immigrant/non-immigrant achievement. I review the most relevant aspects of that literature below. To address the issues that my research with Seguín's students identified as most salient, however, it was work in the specific areas of subtractive assimilation, social capital, and caring that proved the most useful. These combined perspectives help explain why schooling is a more positive experience for immigrant than for non-immigrant, U.S.-born youth. They bring to light the ways in which mainstream institutions strip away students' identities, thus weakening or precluding supportive social ties and draining resources important to academic success.

MEXICAN IMMIGRANT AND MEXICAN AMERICAN ACHIEVEMENT

Explanations for differential academic achievement among immigrants and non-immigrants are many and varied. Most offer insights that help explain the gap I observed at Seguín High, but all leave important questions unanswered. Below, I begin by reviewing this literature and noting where it converges with and diverges from my findings. Then, in the theoretical framework section, I discuss the subtractive assimilation, social capital, and caring and education studies that inform and frame my subtractive schooling explanation of underachievement.

Immigrant Achievement

Linguistic and anthropological studies of immigrant academic "success" evident at Seguín point to cognitive and psychocultural factors, respectively, that enhance their adaptability to new school settings.[6] The linguistic literature, in particular, underscores the importance of academic competence in one's own language as a precondition to mastery in a second language (Cummins 1984; Hernández-Chávez 1988; Montaño-Harmon 1991; Lindholm and Aclan 1993; Merino et al. 1993).[7] Immigrant students who possess essential skills in reading, writing, comprehension, and mathematics in their own language (or those who acquire these skills through a bilingual education program) outperform their U.S.-born counterparts. Immigrants' academic competence is further confirmed by findings that students schooled in Mexico tend to outperform Mexican American youth schooled in the United States (Vigil and Long 1981; Buriel 1984, 1987; Buriel and Cardoza 1988; Ogbu 1991; Matute-Bianchi 1991; Steinberg et al. 1996). Findings from my study corroborate the importance of entering cognitive skills to student achievement, often acquired from their previous schooling experiences in Mexico.

The psychocultural domain is a broad category that emphasizes patterns of adaptation and qualities that immigrants possess as explanations for the academic success of immigrant youth. Children from Mexico and other parts of Latin America are strongly driven to succeed and they adhere to traditional enabling values like familism, respect for teachers, and a strong work ethic in their quest for upward mobility (Buriel 1984, 1987; Abi-Nader 1990; Portes and Rumbaut 1990). Valenzuela and Dornbusch (1994) and others (e.g., Buriel 1984; Suárez-Orozco and Suárez-Orozco 1995) add that loyalty to one's homeland culture provides important social, cultural, and emotional resources that help youth navigate through the educational system.[8] Stanton-Salazar and Dornbusch (1995) point out that a bilingual/bicultural network of friends and family helps youth to successfully cross sociocultural and linguistic borders. This in turn may allow them entree to multiple, potentially supportive community and institutional settings.

At Seguín, immigrant students' school-going aspirations are strongly related to their academic achievement, affirming the imagery of their inordinate drive. Qualitative evidence suggests that these aspirations are connected to an esprit de corps achievement orientation coupled with their prior schooling experiences in Mexico that they mostly view as having prepared them well for schooling in the United States. This finding of collectivist orientations resonates with findings from research among adult immigrants (Rodriguez and Nuñez 1986; Keefe and Padilla 1987) and Mexican children (Madsen and Shapira 1970; Kagan and Madsen 1972; Suárez-Orozco and Suárez-Orozco 1995).

An increasingly important topic among scholars of Latino immigrant and non-immigrant youth is the influence of students' peer group associations on their orientations toward school (Mehan et al. 1986, 1994; Matute-Bianchi 1991; Olsen 1997; Vigil 1997). Matute-Bianchi (1991) addresses this concern in her much cited ethnographic study of Mexican immigrant and U.S.-born Mexican youth attending Field High, a school located in a central coast California agricultural community. Corresponding roughly to the generational statuses investigated herein, students fell into one of the five following categories: "Recent Arrivals (or *recien llegados*)," "Mexican-Oriented," "Mexican American," "Chicano," and "Cholos." Whereas the first two categories refer to the immigrant student population, the latter three reference the U.S.-born. Beginning with "Recent Arrivals" and "Mexican-Oriented" students, I address in this and the next section their similarities and differences from the students I came across at Seguín.

At both Seguín and Field High, a key distinction drawn within the immigrant population by school officials and the students themselves is whether one is recently arrived. Having typically arrived in the past three to five years, typical recent arrivals are classified at both schools as "Limited English Proficient" and placed in the English as a Second Language (ESL) program. Most have also attended school in Mexico and they tend to make high grades. A caveat worthy of mention, however, is whether youth emanate from urban centers or rural regions of Mexico (or other rural places in Latin America). A special category of student at Seguín that was not observed in the Matute-Bianchi study is a burgeoning segment of "preliterate" youth, lacking in formal academic training and literacy skills. Socially, these students face difficulties forming friendships among students located outside of their preliterate classes. Because Seguín is ill-equipped to serve these youth, they are at greatest risk among all students of dropping out. These difficulties help sustain their very low representation within the school's immigrant population.

"Mexican-oriented" students at Field High were born in Mexico and came to the United States as small children. They experience U.S. schooling for most of their young lives. They are bicultural and bilingual, often preferring Spanish, and unlike their recently arrived counterparts, they tend to participate in mainstream school activities (like athletic teams, band, choir, etc.). As fluent biculturals, their culturally assimilated status combines with their pride in their Mexican heritage to makes these youth accessible to both their Spanish-dominant and English-dominant peers.

Distinguishing Seguín from Field High is that many such students I met were located in the regular, non-college-bound track.[9] Though ambitious and capable, they often lacked the kind of mentoring that would secure their representation in the privileged rungs of the curriculum; at Seguín, these consist of either honors, magnet, or upper-levels of the Career and Technology Education (CTE) vocational program.[10] Findings from other research (Romo and Falbo 1996; Olsen 1997) suggest that such problems are commonly faced by immigrant youth. Indeed, cross-national data point to a higher dropout rate among first-generation immigrants (National Center for Education Statistics 1992; Rumberger 1995). Notwithstanding these caveats and limitations, immigrant youth still tend to enjoy greater academic success than their U.S.-born counterparts—referred to as "Mexican Americans," "Chicanos," and "Cholos" in the Matute-Bianchi study.

Although Matute-Bianchi did not specifically focus on relationships between the students and their teachers, she infers from her interviews with youth that immigrants' higher success rate is in great part related to their respectful, obedient, and deferential comportment (also see Suárez-Orozco 1991). Students who display these appealing behaviors are rewarded by their teachers. Moreover, Matute-Bianchi suggests, this kind of demeanor may be rewarded because it is consistent with mainstream teachers' expectations of culturally appropriate "Mexican" behavior.

Discussions I had with immigrant youth about their attitudes toward school suggest a need to reconsider the bases of their purported "politeness." While cultural values like respect (*respeto*) encourage deference and docility, a sense of powerlessness or a belief that they are not "entitled" to openly defy school authority just as powerfully explains their comportment, especially for the more recently arrived. Seguín's immigrant students often share their U.S.-born peers' view that learning should be premised on a humane and compassionate pedagogy inscribed in reciprocal relationships, but their sense of being privileged to attend secondary school saps any desire they might have to insert their definition of education into the schooling process.

A final enabling quality highlighted in anthropological research is immigrants' dual frame of reference that allows immigrant youth to compare their present status and attainments to their typically less favorable situation "back home." Because these children's families experience upward mobility at the onset of immigration, a payoff to living in this country is immediately evident (Bean et al. 1991). Thus their interpretation of their deprivation in relative terms undergirds their motivation to succeed in U.S. schools (Ogbu 1991; Suárez-Orozco 1991; Matute-Bianchi 1991). Oppressive economic or political conditions in the homeland make present sacrifices in the United States tolerable (e.g., Suárez-Orozco 1989, 1991; Gibson and Ogbu 1991).

The dual frame of reference also discourages immigrant youth from correlating being Mexican with underachievement or with the social pathologies often ascribed to Mexican Americans and other U.S. minorities. Unlike Mexican American youth, immigrants have had the experience of knowing high-status professionals (e.g., doctors, lawyers, and engineers) who are Mexican. In fact, their key influences were often individuals they had known in Mexico who were themselves professionals. Thus, *Mexicanidad* (or "Mexican-ness") as a *national*, rather than *ethnic minority* identity, contributes to the self-fulfilling expectations evident in both positive school orientations and high academic performance.

Discussions I held with immigrant students at Seguín confirm the reality of a dual frame of reference that contributes to their academic achievement. They noted, for example, that life in Mexico is much more difficult financially than it is in the United States; tight economic conditions make it impossible for most people to pursue schooling beyond the sixth-grade level (the Mexican government subsidizes education through the sixth grade). Evidence from group interviews further reveals a nuance in the concept of the dual frame. It not only informs their aspirations, but also mitigates their critique of schooling since the opportunity for a public education in the United States is "free," however unequal. While their motivation to achieve in U.S. schools appears to win them favor in their teachers' eyes, social pressures to disclaim their critique and express deference also exist.

A peek into the subjective world of immigrant youth at Seguín reveals another paradox. While the quantitative evidence suggests that immigrant youth enjoy more support from their teachers, the qualitative data fail to substantiate this finding. Teachers were scarcely mentioned as pivotal people in their lives. Though this may reflect a limitation of open-ended interviews, another possibility is that this, too, reflects their dual frame of reference that leads them to positively evaluate their situation, including their perceptions of support. This possibility is raised by Stanton-Salazar and Bressler's (1997) quantitative study of adolescents in a southern California high school and Olsen's (1997) ethnographic study of a northern California high school.

Stanton-Salazar and Bressler (1997) find that Spanish-speaking youth score high on perceived measures of support from teachers. However, their low scores on help-seeking behaviors (i.e., the number of times they sought help from a teacher) distinguish them from bilingual and English dominant youth for whom a positive association between the two exists. Since for all other students, help-seeking signals their actual integration and involvement in schooling, immigrant youth appear to infer high levels of support from teachers even against evidence to the contrary.

Olsen (1997) found that despite a lack of trained teachers and a weak academic curriculum for immigrant youth, the latter still had a stronger sense of attachment to school than their U.S.-born peers. Criticizing the school for its limitations was felt as inappropriate and impolite. The combined evidence speaks to the unique subject position of immigrant youth. More generally, they fail to see schooling as subtractive though it begins in earnest with their generation.

In summary, linguistic and psychocultural factors play important roles in the academic progress of immigrant youth at Seguín

High. My data suggest that this list should include other factors, as well: gender and collectivist orientations toward schooling experiences emerge as important factors undergirding a pro-school ethos in the ethnographic account. Qualitative data not only highlight the importance of social ties as enhancing academic performance; in addition, females emerge as key purveyors of social support.

Expanding the list of contributors provides only fleeting satisfaction, however; the longer the list, the more pressing the need to determine the relative weight of each factor. Or are they all equally influential? Existing research provides little guidance. Rather than attempting to evaluate the role of every factor deemed pertinent to immigrant achievement, I offer a ground-level perspective of how schools themselves are organized to perpetuate inequality. This approach broadens the focus to include structural aspects of schooling, such as academic tracking; a curricular bias against Mexican culture, the Spanish language, and things Mexican; and a legacy of (at best) ambiguous relations between the school and the community it serves. Layering upwardly, this study builds on the aforementioned research by developing the view that peer group associations and the schooling orientations that develop within them are themselves influenced by the organization of schooling. Widening the analysis to examine the ways in which schools promote cultural and linguistic subtraction enhances our understanding of why regular-track, immigrant youth tend to outperform their U.S.-born counterparts.

U.S.-Born Underachievement

To date, anthropologist John Ogbu (1974, 1978, 1987, 1991, 1994) has provided the most robust explanation for the underachievement of U.S. minorities, including Mexican Americans. Ogbu's (1991) cultural-ecological framework emphasizes the role of historical racism and institutional oppression in shaping ethnic minorities' opposition to the conventional routes to success available to the dominant group. Ogbu (1991, 1994), Fordham and Ogbu (1986), and Matute-Bianchi (1991) find that African American, as well as "Chicano" and "Cholo" youth adapt strategically to these forces of exclusion in ways that preserve (what remains of) their cultural identities. A chief strategy these scholars have identified involves youth rejecting schooling and underachieving because they correlate academic achievement with "acting white," and because they infer minimal payoff to effort in schooling.[11]

Citing the impact of exclusionary and discriminatory forces in society, Ogbu further argues that a shift from primary to secondary cultural characteristics occurs upon extended contact with, and opposition to, the dominant culture. He categorizes groups with primary and secondary cultural characteristics into the following ideal types: immigrant and involuntary minorities, respectively. The latter group is viewed through the historical lens of their forceful incorporation experience into U.S. society through either slavery, conquest, or colonization.

This discussion on how groups are incorporated into U.S. society is important because it notes the inapplicability of the dominant model of assimilation to the experiences of historically subordinate groups like Mexican Americans. However, because his framework then centers on the differences in perceptions and the adaptational coping strategies that each group uses to negotiate the barriers they face to achieve their goals, the analytical focus gets shifted away from the school site. This analytical move preempts exploration into the interrelatedness of immigrant achievement and non-immigrant underachievement. Ironically, the historical weight he accords to minorities' mode of entry also distances him from the U.S.-Mexican educational experience for whom "forceful incorporation" is arguably an everyday affair.[12]

Bringing the institution of schooling more fully into the analysis of minority achievement, as I do in this work, not only amplifies the concept of oppositionality—as originating in, and nurtured by, schools themselves—but also clarifies the diverse responses to schooling among a group that has historically straddled Ogbu's immigrant and involuntary minority typology. For want of a more dynamic interpretation of students' minority identity development, I turn to McCarthy's (1994) exploration into the "politics of difference" (see chapter 5). That is, immigrant and U.S.-born youth participate in the construction of "otherness" even as they are collectively "othered" by institutional practices that are ideologically invested in their cultural and linguistic divestment. The development of "we-they" distinctions in their social world reinforce achievement patterns and schooling orientations manifest in cross-generational analyses.

Of special relevance is Ogbu's (1991) discussion of societally objectionable secondary cultural characteristics when explaining many of the tensions I observed between students and teachers at Seguín. Urban youth, including Mexican American children, frequently choose clothing and accessories that their teachers interpret as signaling disinterest in schooling. These students also tend to combine withdrawal or apathy in the classroom with occasional displays of aggression toward school authorities. In other words, youth engage in what Ogbu calls "cultural inversion" whereby they consciously or unconsciously oppose the cultural practices and discourses associated with the dominant group (Fordham and Ogbu 1986). As Matute-Bianchi (1991) and others (e.g., Olsen 1997) have similarly observed, appearances do count in the relational dynamics of schooling.

While diverse with respect to their degree of fluency in English and in Spanish, as well as their interests, the majority of regular-track, U.S.-born youth at Seguín fall into Matute-Bianchi's (1991) "Chicano" rubric.[13] As in her study, these students are underachieving, predominantly English-speaking, later- (i.e., second-, third- or fourth-) generation youth. While some do refer to themselves as "Chicano" or "Chicana," more popular self-referents are "Mexican," "*Mexicano*," and "Mexican American." Comparable to their Chicano counterparts at Field High, these youth are marginal to Seguín's curricular and extra-curricular program, and culturally and socially distant from immigrant youth.

The primary distinctions they draw amongst themselves are based on the following, frequently overlapping, categories: race or national origin (e.g., "Black," "White," "Mexican," "Chicana/o," or "Salvadoreño [Salvadoran]"), Spanish or English fluency ("Spanish-speaking," "English-speaking," or "bilingual"), and shared interest (e.g., "Rappers," "New Wavers," "Kickers," "Jocks," "Gangsters" [or "gang-bangers"], or "Wannabes" [i.e., Wannabe gangsters]). "Gangsters" and "Wannabes" come closest to the "Cholo" category identified by Matute-Bianchi (1991).

Like the "Cholos" at Field High, "Gangsters" and "Wannabes" at Seguín are the most disaffected and academically unsuccessful segment of the student body and are identified through their attire by school officials as "gang-oriented." In contrast to the Matute-Bianchi study, however, this group is a quite sizable and growing segment of Seguín's student body, especially among ninth- and tenth-graders for whom gang attire is fashionable (see chapter 3). At Seguín, the lines between "Chicanos," "gangsters," and "Wannabes" are often blurred.

Appearances aside, that Mexican American youth at Seguín High do not equate achievement with "acting white" invites another modification to Ogbu's framework which may better characterize a segment of the African American youth population (Fordham and Ogbu 1986). A strong achievement orientation at Seguín is simply dismissed as "nerdy" or "geeky," suggesting that cultural inversion has greater explanatory value in the realm of self-representation than in attitudes toward achievement. Indeed, the great majority of underachieving, regular-track Mexican Americans at Seguín manifest greater emotional distance from whites than the current literature would predict (Mehan et al. 1994). U.S.-born youth I observed do not oppose education, nor are they uniformly hostile to the equation of education with upward mobility. What they reject is *schooling*—the content of their education and the way it is offered to them.

Unassessed in current scholarship are the academic consequences to many Mexican youth who "learn" perhaps no stronger lesson in school than to devalue the Spanish language, Mexico, Mexican culture, and things Mexican. These biases in turn close off social and linguistic access to their immigrant peers, many of whom possess greater academic competence in this study.

I watched this poisonous cycle play itself out over and over at Seguín High School. U.S.-born and Mexico-born youth routinely mistrust, misunderstand, and misuse one another. The more recent immigrants at Seguín report being appalled by the attire and comportment of their roguish U.S.-born counterparts. They view this group as "*americanizados*" (Americanized), while the more culturally assimilated youth shun their immigrant counterparts as "un-cool," subdued, and "embarrassing" for embodying characteristics they wish to disclaim (Suárez-Orozco and Suárez-

Orozco 1995; Olsen 1997; Vigil 1997). Moreover, they often feel resentful toward immigrants, since the latter frequently outperform or outshine them with their bilingual and bicultural abilities.

These politics of difference are regarded in the existing research literature as incidental to schooling rather than, as I argue, strong evidence of the cultural subtraction that schooling promotes. Besides fueling misunderstandings and intolerance between first and later generations of Mexican youth, the systematic undervaluing of people and things Mexican erodes relations among students, as well as between teachers and students. Cultural distance produces social distance, which in turn reinforces cultural distance.

For additional insight into the effects of schools' structured denial of *Mexicanidad* [Mexican-ness], I consulted the cultural assimilation literature in general, and the subtractive assimilation research in particular. The latter confirms the reality of coercive cultural assimilation but is more concerned with learning than with schooling. Social capital theory and the literature on caring and education, and specifically the work on school-based relationships, provide valuable clues about how cultural subtraction actually occurs in school settings. All three perspectives underpin my explanation of underachievement among Mexican American students.

THE SUBTRACTIVE ELEMENTS OF
CARING AND CULTURAL ASSIMILATION

School subtracts resources from youth in two major ways. First, it dismisses their definition of education which is not only thoroughly grounded in Mexican culture, but also approximates the optimal definition of education advanced by Noddings (1984) and other caring theorists. Second, subtractive schooling encompasses subtractively assimilationist policies and practices that are designed to divest Mexican students of their culture and language. A key consequence of these subtractive elements of schooling is the erosion of students' social capital evident in the presence and absence of academically oriented networks among immigrant and U.S.-born youth, respectively. In other words, within a span of two generations, the "social de-capitalization" of Mexican youth becomes apparent (Putnam 1993, 1995).

Presented below is an optimal definition of caring derived from three sources: caring theory, Mexican culture (embodied in the term, *educación*), and the relational concept of social capital. Although all three share the assumption that individual "progress," loosely defined, is lodged in relationships, their rootedness in diverse perspectives make for differential emphases. Caring theory addresses the need for pedagogy to follow from and flow through relationships cultivated between teacher and student. Although *educación* has implications for pedagogy, it is first a foundational cultural construct that provides instructions on how one should live in the world. With its emphasis on respect, responsibility, and sociality, it provides a benchmark against which all humans are to be judged, formally educated or not. Social capital, on the other hand, emphasizes exchange networks of trust and solidarity among actors wishing to attain goals that cannot be individually attained. The composite imagery of caring that unfolds accords moral authority to teachers and institutional structures that value and actively promote respect and a search for connection, between teacher and student and among students themselves.

Caring and Education

How teachers and students are oriented to each other is central to Noddings's (1984) framework on caring. In her view, the caring teacher's role is to initiate relation, with engrossment in the student's welfare following from this search for connection. Noddings uses the concept of emotional displacement to communicate the notion that one is seized by the other with energy flowing toward his or her project and needs. A teacher's attitudinal predisposition is essential to caring, for it overtly conveys acceptance and confirmation to the *cared-for* student. When the *cared-for* individual responds by demonstrating a willingness to reveal her/his essential self, the reciprocal relation is complete. At a school like Seguín, building this kind of a relationship is extremely difficult—for both parties. Even well-intentioned students and teachers frequently find themselves in conflict. At issue, often, is a mutual misunderstanding of what it means to "care about" school.

Noddings (1984, 1992) and others (Gilligan 1982; Prillaman et al. 1994; Courtney and Noblit 1994; Eaker-Rich and Van Galen 1996) contend, and this study confirms, that schools are structured around an *aesthetic* caring whose essence lies in an attention to things and ideas (Noddings 1984). Rather than centering students' learning around a moral ethic of caring that nurtures and values relationships, schools pursue a narrow, instrumentalist logic. In a similar vein, Prillaman and Eaker (1994) critique the privileging of the *technical* over the *expressive* in discourse on education. Technical discourse refers to impersonal and objective language, including such terms as goals, strategies, and standardized curricula, that is used in decisions made by one group for another. Expressive discourse entails "a broad and loosely defined ethic [of caring] that molds itself in situations and has proper regard for human affections, weaknesses, and anxieties" (Noddings 1984, p. 25).

Thus, teachers tend to be concerned first with form and nonpersonal content and only secondarily, if at all, with their students' subjective reality. At Seguín, they tend to overinterpret urban youths' attire and off-putting behavior as evidence of a rebelliousness that signifies that these students "don't care" about school. Having drawn that conclusion, teachers then often make no further effort to forge effective reciprocal relationships with this group. Immigrant students, on the other hand, are much more likely to evoke teachers' approval. They dress more conservatively than their peers and their deference and pro-school ethos are taken as sure signs that they, unlike "the others," do "care about" school. Immigrant students' seeming willingness to accept their teachers' aesthetic definition of caring and forego their own view of education as based on reciprocal relationships elicits supportive overtures from teachers that are withheld from Mexican American students.

When teachers withhold social ties from Mexican American youth, they confirm this group's belief that schooling is impersonal, irrelevant, and lifeless. Mexican youths' definition of caring, embodied in the word *educación*, forms the basis of their critique of school-based relationships. *Educación* has cultural roots that help explain why authentic, as opposed to aesthetic, caring is particularly important for Mexican youth (Mejía 1983; Reese et al. 1991). *Educación* is a conceptually broader term than its English language cognate. It refers to the family's role of inculcating in children a sense of moral, social, and personal responsibility and serves as the foundation for all other learning. Though inclusive of formal academic training, *educación* additionally refers to competence in the social world, wherein one respects the dignity and individuality of others.

This person-, as opposed to object-, orientation further suggests the futility of academic knowledge and skills when individuals do not know how to live in the world as caring, responsible, well-mannered, and respectful human beings. Accordingly, Quiroz (1996) finds that Latino students' sentiments toward schooling are strongly related to experiences with teachers. Darder (1995) also finds that Latino teachers' expectations tend to focus strongly on the notions of repect, discipline, and social responsibility. *Educación* thus represents both means and end, such that the end-state of being *bien educada/o* is accomplished through a process characterized by respectful relations. Conversely, a person who is *mal educada/o* is deemed disrespectful and inadequately oriented toward others.

Non-Latino teachers' characteristic lack of knowledge of the Spanish language and dismissive attitude toward Mexican culture makes them unlikely to be familiar with this cultural definition of *educación*. Thus, when teachers deny their students the opportunity to engage in reciprocal relationships, they simultaneously invalidate the definition of education that most of these young people embrace. And, since that definition is thoroughly grounded in Mexican culture, its rejection constitutes a dismissal of their culture as well. Lost to schools is an opportunity to foster academic achievement by building on the strong motivational force embedded in students' familial identities (Suárez-Orozco 1989; Abi-Nader 1990; Valenzuela and Dornbusch 1994).

Misperceptions about caring are not confined to the student-teacher nexus. Immigrant and Mexican American youth at Seguín, despite a shared understanding of the meaning of *educación*, define their own schooling experiences differently. For example, despite feeling "invisible" in mainstream, regular-track classrooms, immigrant students rarely share U.S.-born youth's perception of U.S. schooling as fashioned to promote the ascendancy of some students more than others. Immigrants experience more overt discrimination—including at the hands of many insensitive Mexican American youth—than any other group in this Mexican-origin community. Nevertheless, their sense of progress and family betterment and their commitment to a pro-school ethos propel them onward. Whatever complaints they might have about their schooling experiences in the United States, these are blunted and silenced by their appreciation of the opportunity to pursue an education beyond what would have been available to them in Mexico. U.S.-born youth, in contrast, demonstrate their sense of entitlement to *educación* when they demand, either with their voices or their bodies, a more humane vision of schooling. Most often, school officials fail to interpret these challenges correctly, partly because they are unaware that despite their acculturated, English-dominant status, Mexican American students at Seguín retain an understanding of education that is eminently Mexican in orientation.

Differences in the ways in which Mexican American and immigrant students perceive their schooling experiences color each group's response to the exhortation that they "care about" school. Immigrant students acquiesce. Their grounded sense of identity combines with their unfamiliarity with the Mexican minority experience to enable them to "care about" school without the threat of language or culture loss, or even the burden of cultural derogation when their sights are set on swiftly acculturating toward the mainstream. U.S.-born youth, who hear in the demand to "care about" school an implicit threat to their ethnic identity, often withdraw or rebel.

Thus, an obvious limit to caring exists when teachers ask all students to care about school while many students ask to be cared for *before* they care about. With students and school officials talking past each other, a mutual sense of alienation evolves. This dynamic is well documented in thinking about caring and education. Less obvious to caring theorists are the racist and authoritarian undertones that accompany the demand that youth at places like Seguín High "care about" school. The overt request overlies a covert demand that students embrace a curriculum that either dismisses or derogates their ethnicity and that they respond caringly to school officials who often hold their culture and community in contempt.

Misunderstandings about the meaning of caring thus subtract resources from youth by impeding the development of authentic caring and by obliging students to participate in a non-neutral, power-evasive position of aesthetic, or superficial, caring. The widespread disaffection with schooling among U.S.-born youth should thus be attributed to their experience of schooling as subtractive or as an implicit threat to ethnic identity that accompanies the demand that youth care about school. Rather than building on students' cultural and linguistic knowledge and heritage to create biculturally and bilingually competent youth, schools subtract these identifications from them to their social and academic detriment.

Conceptualizations of educational "caring" must more explicitly challenge the notion that assimilation is a neutral process so that cultural- and language-affirming curricula may be set into motion. The definition of authentic caring that evolves in this work thus expands on caring theory to include a pedagogical preoccupation with questions of otherness, difference, and power that reside within the assimilation process itself (Portes and Rumbaut 1990; Darder 1991; Spring 1997). In such a world, "difference is seen as a resource, not as a threat" (Flores and Benmayor 1997, p. 5). While issues of class, race, and gender are of increasing concern to caring theorists (e.g., Webb-Dempsey et al. 1996), the curriculum, and its subtractive elements therein, remains a sacred cow, powerful and unassessed.

Subtractive Assimilation

As advanced by Cummins (1984, 1986) and Gibson (1993), the concept of "subtractive assimilation" is predicated on the assumption that assimilation is a non-neutral process and that its widespread application negatively impacts the economic and political integration of minorities.[14] Even bilingual education programs that explicitly attend to the linguistic needs of minority youth can be, and typically are, subtractive if they do not reinforce students' native language skills and cultural identity (Cummins 1988). The very rationale of English as a Second Language (ESL)—the predominant language program at the high school level—is subtractive. As ESL programs are designed to transition youth into an English-only curriculum, they neither reinforce their native language skills nor their cultural identities.[15] Although there are many other aspects of schooling that are subtractive (see chapter 5), it is important to emphasize how the organization of schooling has been historically implicated in the devaluation of the Spanish language, Mexico, Mexican culture, and things Mexican (Lopez 1976; Hernández-Chávez 1988).

Merino and coworkers (1993) note that American institutions have responded *additively* to immigrant groups who come to the United States either as members of an educated class or as speakers of high-status languages. For newcomers who speak a nonstandard linguistic variety, emanate from rural backgrounds, or are nonliterate, U.S. society has been much less welcoming (see Sanchez [1993] and Galindo [1992] for a discussion of linguistic varieties of the Spanish language in the Southwest). While possessing an accent in a high-status language is perceived positively and may even constitute an advantage, the same does not hold true for members of historically subordinate groups. Working similarly to color and personal appearance, Lopez (1976) notes how language is a marker for ethnicity that can serve as a basis for exclusion or even "de-ethnicization" through the schooling process (see Lucas et al. 1995, for counterexamples in non-mainstream schools and classrooms).

Conveying a meaning similar to that of Lopez's (1976) "de-ethnicization," Spring (1997) characterizes the political context in which U.S. minorities have had to struggle for educational equality as one of "deculturalization." Spring notes correctly how struggles over educational policy reflect deeper ideological debates about cultural forms that define, or should define, America. Though short of opening the "black box" of schooling, Spring's historical framework nevertheless underscores its politicized nature in the case of minority youth.

Because of its focus on how immigrants and non-immigrants *learn* rather than how they are *schooled*, the subtractive assimilation literature accords insufficient attention to how the organization of schooling can be just as consequential to the academic progress of minority youth. To communicate this broader structural principle, I use the term "subtractive schooling." This brings the school into sharper focus and suggests that schools may be subtractive in ways that extend beyond the concept of subtractive cultural assimilation to include the content and organization of the curriculum. Subtractive schooling thus widens the analytical scope to examine other ways that schools subtract resources from youth. One critically important route that the cultural assimilation literature does not address involves school-based relationships. Research into the effects of caring and the role of social capital provide guidance in evaluating the significance of social ties at school.

Social Capital

Emanating from an exchange theory perspective in sociology, social capital is especially appropriate for addressing the structure of relationships among immigrant and non-immigrant youth, as well as highlighting the effects of breakdowns or enhancements in the flow of school-related information and support. In contrast to other forms of capital (i.e., human, physical, and cultural), social capital is neither a single entity nor reflective of individuals' attributes. Social capital is defined by its *function* in group or network structures. Coleman (1988) posits an interaction between human and social capital variables to communicate the view that social capital is not an intrinsic feature of social networks. Rather, *it comes into being* whenever social interaction makes use of resources residing within the web of social relationships. Exchange relationships thus constitute social capital when they enable the attainment of goals that cannot be attained individually. In this view, academic achievement is best understood not as an individual attribute but as a collective process; and, specifically, one that issues from nonrationalistic, emotional commitments among individuals who are embedded in supportive networks.

Coleman's (1988, 1990) formulation reveals the extent to which school and socioeconomic success are predicated on constructive social ties characterized by reciprocal relationships (also see Valenzuela and Dornbusch 1994; Stanton-Salazar 1995,

1996). Positive social relations at school are highly productive because they allow for the accumulation of social capital that can then be converted into socially valued resources or opportunities (e.g., good grades, a high school diploma, access to privileged information, etc.). Beyond helping individuals attain such human capital as education and skills, social capital fosters the development of trust, norms, and expectations among youth who come to share a similar goal-orientation toward schooling. Exchanges of various kinds—like having access to another's homework or word-processor, or belonging to a study group—enable youth to create and recreate a pro-school ethos.

At Seguín, the scholastic support networks that generate social capital are most often associated with immigrant youth. Such networks may consist of two or more students who share school-related information, material resources, and school-based knowledge. These groups may or may not continue over time and they often shift in composition from one semester to the next. Though uncommon, especially for youth who are peripheral to the school's academic program, these groups may also include school personnel. Immigrants' collective achievement strategies, when combined with the academic competence their prior schooling provides, directly affect their level of achievement. Academic competence thus functions as a human capital variable that, when marshaled in the context of the peer group, *becomes* a social capital variable. This process is especially evident among females in Seguín's immigrant student population. The qualitative data reveal that females' higher average levels of academic competence enables them to contribute significantly to their friendship networks as purveyors of social capital and academic support. Evidence that male friends and boyfriends often exploit young women's social skills and resources is also provided.

The acquisition of social capital is not automatic, however, nor is its accumulation over time assured. The productive potential of social relationships may be undercut in a variety of ways. Although Coleman notes that ideology and social structure may work against or even destroy the formation and maintenance of social capital, he does not address the most significant ways in which social capital may be offset or eroded at the microlevel.

From an ideological standpoint, a pro-school ethos among

socially capitaled youth is no match against an invisible system of tracking that excludes its vast majority. Strategizing for the next assignment or exam does not guarantee that the exclusionary aspects of schooling will either cease or magically come to light. So while an esprit de corps among immigrant youth may bode well for specific achievement goals within the regular track, immigrants' ascendancy into the privileged rungs of the curriculum does not automatically follow (Olsen 1997). Conversely, the lack of an esprit de corps among U.S.-born, regular-track youth signifies not only their "socially de-capitalized" status—evident in a paucity of academically oriented networks among them—but also their disaffection from a highly unequal system of rewards and privileges.

Under conditions of institutionalized oppression, Ogbu (1991) observes that students' ethnic minority identities become collective expressions that help buffer them against the potentially psychologically damaging elements embedded within the dominant, individualistic model of mobility. Willis's (1977) ethnography of working-class, British youth similarly finds that students defy the dominant achievement ideology by producing contrary ways of being that oppose dominant cultural practices and discourses. Hence, Seguín students' de-identification from Mexican culture meshes with an experientially rooted understanding of their own prospects for mobility to make "be[ing] like an immigrant," as one Seguín school official admonished, an undesirable, if not impossible, alternative for most U.S.-born youth.

Finally, students' social capital may get thwarted through subtle yet pervasive forces of exclusion lodged in divergent perspectives in human relationships (Stanton-Salazar 1997). Differences in the meaning of caring at Seguín alongside the social and cultural distance that characterizes most relations embody this concern. Finally, the maintenance and elaboration of students' social capital is jeopardized by institutional policies and practices which subtract resources from them. The concept of "social de-capitalization" invites a more historical application of the concept of social capital to more accurately convey the experience of schooling for U.S. minorities. In the school setting, the social and cultural distance that characterizes most relations combine with subtractive schooling to call into play all of these aspects of social ties.

UNMASKING BARRIERS TO PROGRESS

Combining the concept of subtractive assimilation with Coleman's (1988) concept of social capital and the caring literature produces a revised theoretical formulation. The subtractive assimilation and social capital frameworks cover the "blind spot" in the caring and education literature that overlooks the connected issues of race, power, and culture. Merging insights from all three perspectives explains variation in schooling experiences between immigrant and U.S.-born youth by directing attention to the ways in which the formal and informal organization of schooling divests Mexican students of essential resources. The operant model of schooling for acculturated, U.S.-born youth structurally deprives them of social capital that they would otherwise enjoy were the school not so aggressively (subtractively) assimilationist. Stated differently, rather than students failing schools, schools fail students with a pedagogical logic that not only assures the ascendancy of a few, but also jeopardizes their access to those among them who are either academically strong or who belong to academically supportive networks.

While relationships with teachers exert a tremendous impact on the kinds of schooling orientations that develop in school, the social capital embedded in youths' networks also play a clear, productive role. Productive relations with teachers and among students make schooling worthwhile and manageable. In so doing, the potential for higher academic achievement increases. However as mentioned above, whether real educational mobility occurs, remains a nagging concern.

To the extent that relationships with teachers affect students' schooling orientations and achievement, this study provides new information on barriers to progress that are lodged in assumptions about education. To the extent that relations among youth affect their schooling orientations and achievement, differing levels of social capital between immigrant and U.S.-born youth are presented here as an artifact of subtractive schooling. Academic success and failure are presented more as products of schooling rather than as something that young people do.

Schools wishing to embark on a project of authentic caring would do well to consider the "social de-capitalization" or limited presence of academically oriented networks among U.S.-born youth as, in large part, a creation of current configurations of schooling. The social and linguistic cleavages that develop among youth become yet another overlay to the major institutional cleavage already engendered by curricular tracking. At Seguín High, the major cleavage is between the small numbers of college-bound youth (10–14 percent annually) and the overwhelming majority located in the regular track program (86–90 percent annually). This division deprives the regular-track, "middle majority"—as expressed to me by Seguín's career counselor—of the resources and the pro-school ethos that exist among college-bound youth.

The "track" within the regular track program subdivides ESL and non-ESL youth, creating a "cultural track" that separates Spanish- from English-speaking students. Youth in the former program are destined to be shunted into regular-track classes; ESL honors courses do not exist. Thus, after acquiring fluency in the English language, ESL youth typically experience only horizontal mobility. Since many immigrant youth have been schooled in Mexico and they demonstrate extraordinary potential to achieve in school, a system that is insensitive to their cognitive and linguistic competencies unfairly narrows their educational opportunities.

The practice of cultural tracking is consequential to U.S.-born youth, as well. This separation encourages and legitimates, on the one hand, a status hierarchy that relegates immigrant youth to the bottom. On the other, it nurtures in student groups the kind of distinct and distorted identities that sabotage communication and preclude bridge-building. Structural distance and de-identification from immigrants push U.S.-born youth who are not located in the more privileged rungs of the curriculum even further into the academic periphery, where they are deprived of access to social capital manifest in the more academically supportive environment enjoyed by immigrants. The solution is not to deprive immigrants of much-needed language support systems, but rather to restructure academic programs so that they enhance learning opportunities for all (see Valdés 1998 who also makes this argument).

Curricular divisions between student populations not only reinforce each group's misperceptions of the other; they also deprive U.S.-born students of potentially positive school experiences, including enhanced social ties. The pervasive view among U.S.-born youth—that no one around them is genuinely interested in school—underscores the extent to which they are alienated from schooling generally and from the social environment experienced by Spanish-dominant, Mexican-oriented, immigrant youth, specifically. Such alienation involves an impoverished definition of one's social world—a world so narrow and rigidly bounded that it does not include immigrants.[16] Ironically, the stigmatized status that immigrants—especially the more "Mexicanized"—endure vis-à-vis their Mexican American peers enhances their peer group solidarity and protects many from the seductive elements of the peer group culture characteristic of their U.S.-born counterparts.

Disassociation and de-identification with immigrant youth and Mexican culture has no such hidden advantage for Mexican American youth. The English-dominant and strongly peer-oriented students who people this book walk Seguín's halls vacillating between displays of aggressiveness and indifference. They are either underachieving or psychically and emotionally detached from the academic mainstream. While this representation of self is fueled by its compatibility with being in style under conditions of poverty, it also constitutes the basis for teachers' and administrators' negative appraisals and attention. Rather than seeing urban youths' bodies as the site of agency, critical thinking, and resistance to the school's lack of connectedness to them, school officials see hapless, disengaged individuals who act out their defiance through their strut-and-swagger attitude toward school rules (Giroux 1992). As I intend to show, beneath that facade are youth who seek unconditional acceptance and caring relationships as the fundament of the teacher-learning exchange.

This study suggests that differences in school orientation among the middle majority of immigrant/non-immigrant youth located in the culturally fragmented regular track are better read as products of a larger schooling context. Despite ample evidence that U.S.-born youth are achieving at a much lower rate in comparison to their immigrant peers, the theoretical question that emerges from the framework I have elaborated is not whether achievement declines generationally but rather how schooling subtracts resources from youth.

CHAPTER 2

*Seguín High School
in Historical Perspective:
Mexican Americans' Struggle for
Equal Educational Opportunity
in Houston*

Seguín High School is located in the "East End," an inner-city community of Houston.[1] The area spans twenty-five square miles, stretching east from the shadows of downtown to the banks of the turning basin of the city's ship channel. Once virtually all white and middle class, the East End has changed rapidly since the 1970s. Today it is a virtually all-brown (predominantly Mexican), working-class area zoned for both industry and residence. The roads entering the East End closest to where Seguín is located lead to rows of industrial warehouses, junk yards, auto repair shops, wrecked-car yards, trucking businesses, furniture warehouses, liquor stores, and a handful of mom-and-pop convenience stores. Nearby, a colossal industrial plant, Maxwell House Coffee, emits an intense odor of roasted coffee beans that pervades the entire community.

The boundaries of the East End almost fully overlap those for the geographical attendance zone for Seguín; and the high school's student body mirrors the community's demographic transformation. Seguín's predominately white student population shifted to a nearly "all Mexican" composition by 1983–84. As the student body changed, so did the school's academic profile. Once a model institution, Seguín is now one of the poorest-performing schools in the Houston Independent School District (HISD).

Another trend that joins the histories of Seguín and its community is the emergence of an ethnic brand of politics that has focused on problems in the school. Activists have supported numerous causes, including legal challenges against segregation, a student walkout, and school reforms aimed at both the physical plant and the core curriculum. Community and school changes, as well as these political struggles, form the backdrop for the day-to-day contestations that my study addresses.

This chapter places the East End's transformations and their consequences for Seguín High School in historical perspective. The story of Seguín necessarily begins with a review of key historical developments that have given the school and its community its distinctive underachieving, working-class, ethnic character. The discussion then focuses on events that led up to the 1989 student walkout; the walkout itself; and the reform efforts that have followed in its wake. At issue throughout is the Mexican American community's desire for inclusion and equal educational opportunity, even despite the institutionalized forces of educational neglect.

THE EARLY YEARS

Although Mexicans were present when Houston was formally established (in 1836), their population did not show appreciable increases until the early 1900s.[2] At that time, the growth of major railroad lines around Houston opened up laboring jobs, luring thousands of workers from Mexico and deep South Texas who were eager to escape economic impoverishment at home. This northward flow of workers continued as new sources of low-skill employment, such as warehouses, railroad yards, and ship channel construction work, emerged. The first major Mexican neighborhood took shape during the first ten years of the century in the Second Ward east of downtown; other communities appeared during the second decade of the 1900s, in such nearby neighborhoods as Magnolia Park. Gradually, Mexicans transformed these previously all-white communities into ethnic, working-class districts.[3]

White workers, fearing wage depression or job displacement as a result of the steadily increasing supply of Mexican labor, closed ranks. In the 1920s, anti-Mexican campaigns by unions and Ku Klux Klan chapters seeking to preserve higher-skilled and better-paying jobs for whites were commonplace.[4] The advent of the Depression stirred nativists to urge government intervention, as well; more than one thousand Mexicans from the Houston area were repatriated during the early 1930s. The end of the Depression and the wartime expansion of the economy reversed this enforced exodus. By 1940, Houston's Mexican population stood at twenty thousand—the third largest congregation of Mexicans outside the border region. Mexican workers made occupational as well as numerical gains during the war period; many left behind the lower-skilled and lower-paying jobs they were typically assigned and made inroads into higher-level, blue-collar positions in the industries they had already penetrated—railroads, dockyards, construction, and oil fields and refineries. These occupational gains did not, however, match those of white workers during the same period.[5]

The growth and dispersal of the city's Mexican population during the postwar period represents one of Houston's most significant demographic developments. The population had doubled by 1950 and increased to 75,000 in 1960. By 1970, the population had doubled again, nearing the 150,000 mark. Dramatic increases were also evident through the 1980s and into the 1990s, when the population grew from 280,691 to 442,943. During most of these decades, Mexicans have lived throughout the city and even in the suburbs, but they have always been concentrated in the poorer sections of the inner city, particularly in the early settlement areas east and southeast of the downtown area. According to the 1990 U.S. Census, 65,273 people live in the fourteen census tracts surrounding Seguín. Of these residents, 85 percent are Latino; whites (10 percent), blacks (4 percent), and others (1 percent) make up the remainder.

Occupational stagnation, health hazards, poor housing conditions, general poverty, and in some cases, impoverishment characterize Houston's older communities (Lipsitz 1995). The East End is no exception. The area's occupational profile has shown little change. Residents sixteen years of age and over typically concentrate in the technical, sales, service, production, repair, operator, and laborer categories. Over the decade between 1980 and 1990, there was a slight decline (from 34 to 30 percent) in the numbers of Mexicans in the laboring/operators occupations; in all other occupational categories, East End residents' proportions remained the same (U.S. Census Bureau 1990). Qualitative data show that Seguín parents tend to hold sales, service, and manufacturing sector jobs. Working mothers are often employed as domestics, janitors, seamstresses, and waitresses. Fathers are apt to work as truck drivers, machine operators, construction workers, landscapers, painters, or as other unskilled or semi-skilled laborers.

Of all East End Latino households, 21.7 percent are female-headed, with no father present (U.S. Census Bureau 1989). Among Latino "East Enders," married couples with children eighteen years of age or younger registered an average family income of $23,962 in 1989. Latino families with children under eighteen years, and without a husband, claimed a mean family income of $12,782. The comparable figures for whites in the same area were $54,672 and $23,951.

CHANGING DEMOGRAPHICS AND THE "MEXICANIZATION" OF THE EAST END AND SEGUÍN HIGH

Seguín High School was built in 1936 as part of Franklin D. Roosevelt's Works Progress Administration program. Besides providing jobs for the unemployed, the construction of the new school was intended to relieve crowding in the three other schools then serving the East End. The largely white community had been inundated with new residents in the early 1930s when work on the Houston ship channel began. That new source of employment, coupled with expanding wartime job opportunities, proved a boon for the community. Neat, grassy lawns, Victorian homes, and tree-shaded parks and avenues announced the arrival of a new middle-class prosperity to the East End. The surrounding communities, extending westward to the downtown area and eastward to the ship channel, were more industrial and working class. They were also increasingly less white, thanks to a rapidly expanding Mexican American population.

Seguín High School reflected the white, middle-class character of its more immediate community until the late 1960s. From the beginning, the school's administration, staff, and student body had been predominantly white and solidly middle class. As late as the 1950s, the school's educational record was unblemished. A survey of graduates who attended Seguín during the 1949–50 academic year showed that close to half (43.8 percent) had enrolled in colleges and universities in pursuit of bachelor's degrees. A quarter (25.9 percent) worked in clerical or sales jobs; none reported being in agriculture or manual labor; and none reported being unemployed (HISD Board Member Services 1951).

Negligible numbers of Mexican students attended Seguín during the early years (e.g., only one Spanish-surnamed student appeared among the 382 seniors depicted in the school's 1945 yearbook). Although the school-age Mexican American population in the area was growing, few attended school beyond the elementary and middle grades (DeLeón 1989; San Miguel 1997).[6] By the mid-1970s, however, Seguín's student body had come to reflect a more Mexican identity and by 1983–84, had become virtually "all Mexican." The 1990s student population continues to be predominantly Latino (95 percent) comprised mostly of Mexicans and a small but growing percentage of *Salvadoreños*. In contrast, African Americans (3 percent) and whites (2 percent) trail far behind. Meanwhile, the faculty is disproportionately white.

The first appreciable change in the makeup of the school's faculty occurred in 1972 when African American faculty representation increased to 25 percent. Despite rising Latino student enrollments, no equivalent change in the composition of the faculty took place until 1990, when the district hired a Mexican American principal who actively recruited Mexican American teachers. During this principal's administration (1990–1993), Mexican American representation expanded to an unprecedented 15 percent of the staff. By 1994–95, the school increased this number slightly and boasted the highest percentage of Latino faculty of any high school in the district. Currently, out of 154 teachers, 29 (or 19 percent) are Latino and predominantly Mexican American. Whites, African Americans, and Asians represent 81 (52 percent), 45 (27 percent), and 3 (1 percent), respectively. These figures do not come close to approximating the virtually all-Mexican student population.

One third of the Latino faculty are located in the English as a Second Language (ESL) Program, which serves immigrant youth. The remaining two thirds are spread thinly throughout the remainder of the academic program. According to Seguín's current principal, Mr. Cedillo, this translates into adolescents' limited exposure to Latino role models and vexed relations between teachers and parents. "Unwritten rules get broken all the time," he says. He suggests, for instance that Mexicans are a lot more "people-oriented" than Anglos who are more private and who appear cold and withdrawn from a Mexican perspective. Since white faculty comprise over half (52 percent) of his faculty, cross-cultural issues invariably surface. In response to a question that I asked him about African American teachers' abilities to relate to youth, he said that some are very sensitive though they, too, are removed from the Mexican community.

A district-wide pattern of hiring out-of-state teachers also exacerbates social and cultural distance. That is, in a staff that is 50 percent veteran (at Seguín eleven years or longer) and 50 percent nonveteran, half of those in the latter category frequently emanate from states like Iowa or Wisconsin where few, if any, have had any experience with urban Mexican youth. Since most of these within a three- to five-year time span eventually leave for other teaching jobs outside of the district, an unstable situation of disaffected, turnstile faculty prevails. Mr. Cedillo sarcastically refers to this vexed, districtwide hiring practice as the "Wisconsin Model."

Of the veteran staff, Mr. Cedillo sees most of them as "not very good teachers" who remain mostly because they cannot get jobs in suburban schools outside of the district. "There are some exceptions, of course," he adds. Most disappointing to Mr. Cedillo is the fact that though hundreds of teachers descend daily upon Seguín and other East End area schools (of 17 elementary, 2 middle, and one other high school), few invest their time, money, and resources in the community. Veterans and nonveterans are no different in this regard.

Although Seguín faculty are not paid well, socioeconomic disparities between them and their students nevertheless reveal their distinctiveness from the community they serve. The lowest average salary made by beginning teachers ($24,499) is still higher than the average annual income of East End married couple families with children eighteen years or younger ($23,962). When compared to his staff of eighty-seven faculty (or 56.5 percent) with eleven or more years of experience whose average earnings approximate $40,000 annually, the economic disparity increases significantly (HISD Academic Excellence Indicator System Report 1995–96).

The browning, or "Mexicanization," of East End schools reflects demographic changes districtwide. During the 1980s, Mexicans represented over 98 percent of the district's total Latino population. High birthrates among the Latino population contributed to this demographic growth: the Latino population grew 75 percent between 1970 and 1980. The infusion of South and Central American immigrants into the Mexican community gave added weight to changing population trends in the schools (Tomás Rivera Center 1994).

Table 2.1 captures the direction and magnitude of these changes. In the 1969–70 school year, the Latino school population constituted approximately 14 percent of the Houston district total, while whites registered a majority (slight) for the last time. By the 1995–96 school year, this relationship was inverted: the Latino school population reached 51 percent and white representation plummeted to 11.3 percent. The upward trend in proportional representation is similar when minority groups are combined. By 1980–81, the combined minority student population had surpassed white proportional representation, to stand at 73 percent. A decline in African American student representation during the late 1980s was offset by a more impressive Latino increase, giving minority students a still greater proportion— almost 87 percent (HISD Pupil Accounting Department 1993).[7]

Table 2.2 shows that by the year 2000, Latinos will comprise 55 percent of the total HISD population. Comparable figures for whites and African Americans are 10 and 32 percent, respectively (HISD Attendance Boundaries and Transfer Department 1996). While the projections for other ethnic groups reveal either stagnation or decline, Latinos are expected to add to the enrollment rolls an average of four thousand students per year until the year 2000. Mexicans will also continue to predominate among Latinos.

TABLE 2.1
Membership Comparisons by Ethnicity, 1968–1997

Year	Other* Mem.	%	African American Mem.	%	Latino Mem.	%	White Mem.	%	Grand Total
1968–69	1,227	.50	81,759	33.41	30,724	12.55	131,032	53.54	244,742
1969–70	1,106	.47	78,893	33.42	31,605	13.39	124,451	52.72	236,055
1970–71	1,234	.51	85,964	35.65	34,759	14.42	119,181	49.42	241,138
1971–72	1,147	.49	87,104	37.56	36,111	15.57	107,560	46.38	231,922
1972–73	976	.43	88,864	39.43	37,275	16.54	98,282	43.60	225,397
1973–74	1,038	.48	88,792	41.07	38,625	17.86	87,749	40.59	216,204
1974–75	983	.47	88,477	42.01	39,734	18.86	81,430	38.66	210,624
1975–76	1,194	.57	90,034	42.59	42,963	20.32	77,217	36.52	211,408
1976–77	1,853	.88	90,635	43.16	45,743	21.78	71,794	34.18	210,025
1977–78	2,274	1.10	91,157	44.04	47,127	22.76	66,440	32.10	206,998
1978–79	2,803	1.39	90,872	44.99	48,877	24.20	59,408	29.42	201,960
1979–80	3,384	1.75	87,797	45.28	49,639	25.60	53,086	27.37	193,906
1980–81	4,218	2.17	87,102	44.89	53,917	27.79	48,806	25.15	194,043
1981–82	5,262	2.71	85,834	44.31	57,558	29.72	45,048	23.26	193,702
1982–83	6,431	3.30	85,679	44.07	60,193	30.96	42,136	21.67	194,439

(continued on next page)

TABLE 2.1 (continued)

Year	Other*		African American		Latino		White		Grand Total
	Mem.	%	Mem.	%	Mem.	%	Mem.	%	
1983-84	5,970	3.15	83,592	44.12	61,424	32.42	38,481	20.31	189,467
1984-85	5,984	3.20	81,493	43.57	63,950	34.19	35,604	19.04	187,031
1985-86	6,481	3.34	83,423	43.03	69,874	36.04	34,111	17.59	193,889
1986-87	6,011	3.09	82,763	42.54	72,856	37.44	32,937	16.93	194,567
1987-88	5,627	2.93	80,274	41.85	74,608	38.89	31,322	16.33	191,831
1988-89	5,283	2.78	77,828	40.88	77,701	40.81	29,569	15.53	190,381
1989-90	5,044	2.64	75,715	39.58	81,522	42.62	29,003	15.16	191,284
1990-91	5,252	2.70	74,220	38.15	87,304	44.88	27,772	14.27	194,548
1991-92	5,466	2.77	73,211	37.08	91,818	46.51	26,918	13.64	197,413
1992-93	5,544	2.79	71,982	36.26	95,402	48.05	25,608	12.90	198,536
1993-94	5,658	2.82	71,605	35.69	98,786	49.24	24,564	12.24	200,613
1994-95	5,651	2.80	71,989	35.60	101,116	50.0	23,607	11.70	202,363
1995-96	5,781	2.80	72,247	34.90	105,523	51.0	23,385	11.30	206,936
1996-97	5,857	2.80	72,003	34.40	108,773	52.0	22,742	10.9	209,375

Source: Houston Independent School District Pupil Accounting Department.

*"Other" combines Native Americans and Asian or Pacific Islanders.

Despite a long period of dramatic growth in the size of Seguín's student body (by 1983–84, there were an unprecedented 2,458 students; more recently, the numbers have hovered between 2,900 and 3,400), there has not been a proportional increase in the numbers of graduating seniors. Table 2.3 shows how the number of graduates declined significantly in absolute and proportional terms during this twenty-six-year period.

The declining numbers of graduates reflect a serious dropout problem at Seguín. In any given year, between twelve and fifteen hundred Seguín students enter the ninth grade; at the end of any given year, only four to five hundred students graduate. Thus, more than 70 percent of Seguín's ninth-graders never graduate. This figure further exceeds an already abysmal situation districtwide: if measuring twelfth-grade enrollment as a percent of ninth-grade enrollment, official statistics minimally suggest a 48 percent dropout rate for the district as a whole (District and School Profiles, 1996–97). This statistic is conservative, however, since it includes neither seniors who fail to graduate from high school nor those who drop out during the summer months.[8]

The high dropout rate at Seguín has a profound effect on the composition of the student body. One of the most obvious results is that the number of students progressively declines with each succeeding year. Another way to state this is that in any given year more than half of the school population is composed of freshmen, or ninth-graders. A full quarter of them are usually repeating the

TABLE 2.2
Forecast to Year 2000 of
Houston Independent School District Membership by Ethnicity

Ethnicity	1995		2000	
	N	%	N	%
American Indian or Alaskan	116	<1	116	<1
Asian or Pacific Islander	5,645	3	6,233	3
Black, not of Latino Origin	72,059	35	73,145	32
Latino	105,923	51	125,803	55
White, not of Latino Origin	23,255	11	24,312	10
Total	206,998	100%	229,610	100%

Source: HISD Attendance Boundaries and Transfer Department, 1996.

ninth grade for at least a second time. Clearly, this suggests that the dropout problem is directly associated with low levels of achievement that are especially evident among the ninth-graders. School officials often refer to these students as "career ninth-graders."[9]

Despite a growing school-age population and community initiatives such as public support for school reforms, "Back-to-

TABLE 2.3
Number and Percent of Graduates, 1970–90*

Year	Enrollment	No. of Graduating Seniors	Share of Total
1970–71	2,320	521	.23
1971–72	2,288	505	.22
1972–73	2,360	607	.26
1973–74	2,173	591	.27
1974–75	2,122	648	.31
1975–76	2,048	501	.25
1976–77	2,104	563	.27
1977–78	2,034	528	.26
1978–79	2,000	503	.25
1979–80	2,048	494	.24
1980–81	1,973	582	.29
1981–82	1,758	472	.24
1982–83	2,300	453	.20
1983–84	2,458	368	.15
1984–85	2,584	406	.16
1985–86	2,833	440	.16
1986–87	2,904	487	.17
1987–88	2,910	299	.10
1988–89	2,881	392	.14
1989–90	2,939	448	.15
1990–91	2,506	395	.16
1991–92	3,145	385	.12
1992–93	3,101	410	.13
1993–94	2,995	350	.11
1994–95	3,062	345	.11
1995–96	3,108	415	.13

Sources: Through 1990, adapted from "Special Report to the Board of Education, March 1, 1990." After 1990, from the Seguín High registrar.

*Pre-1970 data not available.

School Drives," and preschool campaigns, the poor educational record of East End residents persists. Sixty-eight percent of East End parents have completed fewer than eleven years of education, while only 18 percent have completed high school. Immigrant parents of Seguín High School students average a little over six years of education, while parents of third-generation, U.S.-born youth average around nine. The low attainment level among the third generation and beyond reflects statewide trends.[10] Moreover, it suggests that the problem is not driven by the presence of immigrants, who might be expected to significantly lower the aggregate figures. In any case, only 36.2 percent of East End residents are immigrant Mexicans.

Perhaps because of a U.S. Census undercount in 1990, this figure is at variance with immigrant representation at Seguín. Currently, they comprise 45 percent of the entire student body with varying lengths of residency and a median number of ten years living in the United States. The U.S.-born children of immigrant parents, or the second generation, constitute 32 percent of the total. Third- and fourth-generation youth follow with a proportionately lower representation of 14 and 9 percent, respectively. Despite this generational diversity, I designed this study to compare the schooling experiences of first-generation immigrants with those of U.S.-born youth because of the similarities across all members of the second and later generations and because of these adolescents' distinctiveness from their immigrant counterparts.

There is no doubt that demographic changes reconfigured the East End as a whole and Seguín, in particular. Much as the community lost its white, middle-class affluence, the high school lost its academic luster. But demographics were not the only source of this downward spiral.

ROSS V. ECKELS AND THE STRUGGLE FOR JUST INTEGRATION

The Court Order

Public protests against court-ordered integration wrought far-reaching changes at Seguín and in its surrounding community beginning in the 1970s. In a June 1, 1970, desegregation ruling,

Ross v. Eckels, Judge Ben C. Connally began the political process that eventually completely eroded Seguín's white, middle-class base. Judge Connally based his decision on a case initiated by African Americans fourteen years earlier, in response to *Brown v. The Board of Education* (1954) decision (DeLeón 1989; San Miguel forthcoming).[11] His plan called for the integration of African Americans and Mexican Americans—on the presumption that the latter were "white." Connally's ruling constituted an outright denial of a Mexican American ethnic minority identity. It was also an official acceptance of the status quo, which separated minority and white youth.

The NAACP and Mexican American groups, including the Mexican American Legal Defense and Education Fund (MALDEF), opposed the plan. MALDEF filed an *amicus curiae* (friend of the court) brief with the Fifth Circuit Court of Appeals in New Orleans, requesting that Connally's plan be amended to consider Mexican Americans an "identifiable ethnic minority." This request was based on the *Cisneros v. Corpus Christi ISD* decision in June 1970, which established the legal framework for such a challenge against desegregation. According to *Cisneros*, the equal protection clause of the Fourteenth Amendment accorded Mexican Americans minority status and protected them against the widespread practice of designating them "white" in order to either integrate or refuse to integrate schools (San Miguel 1987, forthcoming).

In August 1970, the Court of Appeals overruled Connally's order, but it rejected the argument that mixing Mexican Americans and African Americans did not provide equality of opportunity. It further proposed that HISD implement a pairing plan at the elementary school level to desegregate predominantly minority schools. The integration plan allowed school authorities to treat Mexican Americans as "white" for desegregation purposes. This resulted in the pairing of African American and Mexican American children enrolled in twenty-five Houston elementary schools. Among these, fifteen were predominantly African American, nine were mostly Mexican American, and one was largely white.[12]

Although the focus on integration occurred mostly at the elementary school level, middle and high schools were also affected.

At the high school level, school officials redrew school boundaries to join African American and Mexican American schools and to facilitate "integration."[13] Ironically, while HISD was implementing this new segregationist policy, school districts in other parts of the state were complying with *Cisneros* (DeLeón 1989).

The Boycott

The Mexican American community of Houston organized against the Court of Appeal's ruling. A newly formed, loose confederation, the Mexican-American Education Council (MAEC), orchestrated protests that involved public school students, parents, university students, and community leaders. This action was the first step in a long process that eventually led to the 1989 student walkout, one of the most significant student protests in HISD history.

On the first day of school, August 31, 1970, hundreds of students boycotted Houston schools and picketed either the school to which they had been assigned or the district administration building. In the East End area, approximately 75 percent of the students did not attend school on the first day. The boycott lasted three weeks and involved 60 percent of the 5,831 students affected by the pairing order. Intense picketing and boycotting of elementary schools spread to the secondary level by the end of the first week. Parents encouraged protesting students to attend *huelga* (or strike) schools that the MAEC had established. Approximately 2,000 students attended these schools, which were staffed by volunteers from city schools and area universities; another 3,500 children stayed at home (DeLeón 1989).

Mexican American students and parents were the primary actors in the protests at the various school sites. However, community and university students were also involved. Over one hundred people marched in front of the district administration building chanting, "Brown, Brown, We're not White, We're Brown!" (San Miguel forthcoming, p. 144). This activism was part of a larger movement taking place among Mexican Americans in the Southwest known as the "Chicano Movement." It represented a departure from the politics of the earlier assimilationist-oriented generation of Mexican Americans. As a former Seguín teacher who taught as a volunteer in a *huelga* school recalled:

You know, we took the district by surprise. They were shocked
at our massive protest. We blew the stereotype of the meek, passive *Mexicano*. They didn't know what hit them. . . . I have
never seen such unity among *Mexicanos* since.

The older generation had preferred working through the system, sought recognition as white or Caucasian, and pursued integration. In contrast, the new generation was radical, vocal, and
ideological. It advanced a critique of the public school system as
dismissive of the needs of Mexican American youth. These kinds
of differences in perspectives and strategies kept the middle class
and old-guard political elite (e.g., the League of Latin American
Citizens, the Political Association of Spanish-Speaking Organizations, and the American G.I. Forum) from participating in the
boycott.

During the boycott, MAEC developed a list of twenty
demands for achieving racial integration, greater ethnic representation in faculty and staff, and curricular reform in Houston's
public schools.[14] Key among the demands for racial integration
were that Mexican Americans be accorded ethnic minority status
and that the district appeal the pairing decision to the Supreme
Court. Fearing an escalation in boycott activity already in its third
week, the superintendent invited Mexican American leaders to
discuss their grievances. The district promised to meet seventeen
of the twenty demands, including the call for an appeal to the
Supreme Court. The district's subsequent appeal requested the
Fifth Circuit Court of Appeals to issue a stay in the pairing plan
until the Supreme Court had the opportunity to resolve the equal
protection argument. MAEC responded to this show of good
faith by ending the boycott. Most students returned to their regular schools.

In December, without waiting to hear from the Supreme
Court, the Fifth Circuit Court refused to grant the district's
request for a delay in implementing the pairing decision. The
court construed the equal protection argument achieved in *Cisneros* as a lower court decision that did not apply to Houston.
This forced district officials to move forward with integration,
putting into action a plan they maintained was less disruptive,
since it involved only twenty-one of the original twenty-five

schools. Nineteen of these schools, however, were predominantly minority. In late January, MAEC adopted a policy of noncooperation. Parents resurrected the picketing and boycotting. The Ross appeal to the U.S. Supreme Court was eventually turned down, leaving the entire question of desegregation unresolved.

Impact on Seguín

Seguín did not figure prominently in the boycott, partly because the high school had relatively few Mexican American students, and partly because most of the pairing plans involved elementary, not secondary, schools. Rezoning at the secondary level, however, did contribute to a surge in enrollment at Seguín. With the addition of large numbers of African Americans and Mexican Americans, the size of the student body ballooned from 1,632 during the 1969–70 academic year to 2,320 the following year. A former Seguín teacher commented on the "strange situation" that developed as a result of desegregation:

> In 1970, when school started, Seguín was about twenty percent Mexican American. Then . . . it was about 80 percent because of desegregation, rezoning, that sort of thing. So the teachers at Seguín High School, the Anglos, went through sort of a cultural shock because on Friday when they left school, the majority of their kids were white. On Monday when they returned to work, 80 percent of their kids were Mexican American, through rezoning.

This former teacher also noted that the increased presence of Mexican Americans at Seguín was only partly attributable to rezoning. He recalled that a large number of youth gave false addresses in order to attend Seguín rather than the predominantly African American school to which they had been assigned by the rezoning. This action may have represented a silent protest against integration with African Americans at the high school level.

The boycott continued through 1971–72, but the number of individuals actively protesting and attending *huelga* schools waned considerably. In 1973, long after the crisis atmosphere in the Houston schools had lifted, the Supreme Court, reviewing the Denver case, *Keyes v. School District No. 1*, decreed that Mexican Americans were an identifiable minority group. By this time, Houston district officials had discovered that their integration plan was encouraging "white flight" to the suburbs. To stem this flow, HISD piloted new approaches to integration.

Magnet Schools

Despite criticism by spokespersons from the Mexican American community, further integration was attempted through the "Magnet School Plan," which created districtwide specialty schools and specialty programs within schools. These "magnet schools" were designed to attract students across neighborhood lines for the purpose of improving the quality of education and promoting integration, as well as to stem white flight. Mexican American activists opposed the magnet plan on the grounds that it would create a two-tiered system, providing top-quality educational opportunity for some students, but leaving the majority to make do with less. The community's apprehension did not deter the district; the magnet school plan became a reality (DeLeón 1989; San Miguel 1997).

A tri-ethnic task force composed of twenty-one citizens and HISD staff promoted the magnet school concept beginning in November 1974. The district's 104 magnet schools were created either as separate and unique schools or as programs located within "regular" schools. Small pupil/teacher ratios combine with a strong basic academic program and a specialty enrichment program to provide youth with a high-quality education. Each school's (or program's) particular specialty (e.g., health, science, art, teaching, etc.) further prepares students for specialized careers.

Enrollments within magnet schools/programs are meant to mirror Houston's ethnic population distribution. In 1976, approximately 40 percent were African American, 40 percent white, and 20 percent Mexican American (Brandstetter and Foster 1976). Seguín has a magnet program that directs youth toward the teaching profession. The program accommodates approximately 170 students. Overall, the magnet program is considered a success. Although white flight has not ended, magnet schools have encouraged many families to stay in the district. Ironically, however, though magnet schools/programs have accomplished a modicum of integration, whites have still disproportionately benefited from them. Despite this disparity, conservative forces launched a successful challenge against the historic goal of integration in 1997. In the interest of eliminating alleged racial "preferences," race can no longer be used as a basis for admissions.

THE SEGUÍN SCHOOL WALKOUT

The protests of the early 1970s had mainly addressed issues of access, opposing the courts' and the district's persistence in maintaining a segregated system that privileged white students. With desegregation adopted as official policy and much larger numbers of Mexican students in the schools, students and community activists gained confidence and began to speak to parity issues such as equal treatment. This new focus eventually gave impetus to one of Seguín's most significant student actions: a walkout by at least 1,000 students—one third of the entire student enrollment of 2,939 students—on October 20, 1989.[15]

The walkout gave dramatic visibility to many grievances that had been building for years among Mexicans in the district as a whole, as well as at Seguín. From the mid to late 1980s, parents and community leaders had publicly criticized the high school's record of poor academic achievement, its culturally insensitive administration, and its tolerance of high dropout rates. Several district-sponsored task force investigations had confirmed that Seguín was riddled with problems. Some of the most frequently cited include the following: teachers hold low expectations for youth; youth feel that teachers do not care whether they stay in school or leave; communications between the school and families typically include no Spanish translation; an insufficient number of bilingual counselors, coupled with inadequate counseling and course scheduling; scheduling problems that have left as many as 40 percent of the students without the correct number of classes or with incorrect classes; improperly certified or noncertified ESL teachers; a shortage of teachers available to sponsor clubs and extracurricular activities; an outdated textbook record-keeping system; an unclean and poorly maintained physical plant; and an inadequately funded ESL program. The magnitude and systemic nature of many of these problems made them impervious to the kind of quick-fix, cosmetic repairs favored by the district. Thus, although sporadic attempts to correct problems were undertaken, no long-term solutions evolved.

The 1989 Seguín walkout exposed the broader structure of institutionalized, educational neglect. One of the most striking aspects of the complaints voiced by the students was how often they were couched in terms of caring. Community activists involved in the tumultuous period of the late 1980s and early 1990s also remember problems at Seguín as issues of caring created by indifferent and culturally insensitive school officials. The final straw for the students in the fall of 1989 was a monumental course scheduling problem—one that was still unresolved seven weeks into the school year. Course scheduling is typically a charged issue at the beginning of each year, in part because of students' high mobility rates within the district, and in part because the school's counseling staff is far too small for the size of its student body. Still, even by Seguín's standards, this particular year's problems were overwhelming.

Students were assigned to wrong classes, as well as to classes they had already taken and passed. Some were assigned to classes in the girls' bathroom and in broom closets. One sophomore described her first six weeks of school this way:

> I remember I was in a classroom without a teacher for the whole first six weeks. I showed up every day and hanged out or did my homework but half the class dropped out. I ended up getting a grade for just showing up. This was the first time I really saw how the school didn't care for me or any of us. If I learned or if I didn't learn, so what? I remember feeling very depressed about that. Then I got angry. [Sophomore female student who walked out and eventually graduated.]

Other problems aggravated an already bad situation. The bathrooms were in need of repair, with toilets that did not flush and stalls without doors. Some classrooms had no seats or books; others were overcrowded; and still others had scarcely any students in them. Computer classrooms either had no computers or lacked electrical outlets. Cafeteria overcrowding created a negative dynamic all its own. To accommodate the bloated student body, the cafeteria operated in three shifts—of nine hundred students (in a space designed for 750) each. This arrangement resulted in too little time for the students in each shift to go through the food lines. And, according to the students, the cafeteria food was definitely not worth the wait: it tasted "bad."

The demands the students made when they walked out point to additional problem areas at the school. They called for bilingual counselors, computerized schedules, and more books and resources, including computers (the ones they had were either obsolete or malfunctioning). The students also asked for dropout prevention and retention programs, an expansion of their honors, magnet, and special education programs, and equal funding across all district schools.[16]

Each of these demands revealed a serious problem, worthy of action. Still, it was scheduling that proved crucial. The mishaps over class assignments had a special effect on the honors program students. Privileged and "protected," this group had never experienced the curricular mishandling to which the regular-track students had been subjected on a regular basis. Now, however, the lack of even a tolerable master schedule created waves large enough to wash over all of Seguín's students, including those certified as its best and brightest. The honor students' involvement as leaders and participants ensured the success of the walkout. As an English teacher whose "regular" students walked out explained:

> They [the honors students] gave the walkout legitimacy. They could articulate their grievances knowing that people would listen to them. If it had been my kids, they might have been seen as just a bunch of troublemakers—if they could have even pulled it off in the first place.

This issue of legitimacy and recognition may account for why a walkout had not occurred earlier. A community member who supported the students at the time of the walkout expressed a related opinion:

> When you're a student with low grades, in "dumbed-down" courses, your opinion doesn't matter much even if you're right in your criticism about the school. Dropping out is what you do. And that's the same as walking out. You just do it alone.

Some of the honors students traced their willingness to orchestrate a walkout to the galvanizing effects of a history class discussion on the First Amendment right of free speech and peaceful assembly that had been a part of a more general discussion of the Civil Rights Movement and Martin Luther King's strategy of peaceful, nonviolent protest. An episode from the television show "21 Jump Street" a week earlier provided added impetus. That episode focused on a walkout students had organized to protest what they deemed to be the unreasonable demands of their principal. Thus, the idea that protesting the conditions of one's schooling was acceptable as long as it was peaceful, took root.

On a Tuesday, four days before the walkout, student leaders moved quickly to announce the planned walkout. They relied on a combination of word-of-mouth and fliers they had reproduced on the school copy machine. On Thursday, the principal, who by now had gotten wind of the students' plan, announced over the intercom that anyone involved in the walkout would "pay the full price" (*Houston Chronicle*, October 29, 1989). This threat backfired. Rather than deterring students, it galvanized them; many grew even more determined to walk out. At 8:45 on the morning of the walkout, leaders opened classroom doors and shouted "WALKOUT!" into the rooms. At this signal, the students poured out onto the school's front lawn. The principal ordered campus security to lock building doors and to arrest participating students. The presence of tipped-off television crews and news organizations, however, prevented either of these orders from being carried out.

Among the nine or so walkout leaders was the son of a city councilman. This student made the following statement to the local press:

> It's a shame we had to go to such extremes to get them to listen to us. . . . You really can't blame everything on her [the new school principal]. Every year I've been there, it takes two to three weeks to get scheduling done for everyone. That has been going on for years. (*Houston Chronicle*, October 23, 1989)

Other newspaper accounts included quotes from students who expressed deep satisfaction with having attained some measure of "respect" and empowerment as a result of the walkout (see, for example, comments by students in the *Houston Post,* October 22, 1989). In the October 29 report of the walkout in the *Houston Chronicle,* the senior class president—who had gone to class instead of walking out—indicated surprise at the participation of honors students in the walkout. "When I saw them out there, I thought, 'They are really serious. They really want to stand up for their rights.'"

Combined with parent and community pressure, the walkout sparked immediate action on the district's part. A number of community meetings were held, at least one of which involved the district superintendent. Passions ran high. Community representatives made it clear that they would settle for nothing less than an immediate response to the students' demands—and a full investigation of the school. And student leaders continued to publicly criticize the quality of the education they were receiving. Former Seguín graduates came forward to express their grievances, as well. At one October evening meeting, for example, a female college student attending the University of Houston stood to speak before an audience of approximately two hundred students, faculty, and community activists. She noted bitterly that she had graduated at the top of her class, and yet she had found herself poorly prepared for college. She denounced Seguín for sending her off academically disadvantaged vis-à-vis her college peers.

In addition to holding public meetings, the district responded in several other ways, including appointing a task force comprised of students, parents, teachers, and civic leaders. This group was charged with the responsibility of conducting a full investigation of conditions at Seguín. The task force worked for four-and-one-half months interviewing staff, students, and community members; examining school records, files, and procedures; and auditing financial and bookkeeping records. The interviews elicited a common complaint: the teachers and administrators at Seguín do not care about the students.

What made this long-standing student grievance especially powerful was that this time it came from the whole community. Parents and community leaders joined students in expressing their frustration and alienation. Using the language of caring, they addressed all aspects of schooling, including distance from teachers, scheduling and transcript errors, and cultural insensitivity. Major complaints were the school's lack of Spanish-speaking counselors, teachers, and administrators. Lack of communications between the school and home left parents feeling dismissed by the school. The PTA parents noted how few faculty members bothered to participate in the organization and viewed this as another expression of noncaring.

The students' examples of their teachers' lack of care went to the heart of their daily experiences at Seguín. A faculty member who interviewed students as part of her responsibilities as a task force participant indicated to me that teachers' lack of caring "was at the top of their [students'] list of concerns." In a letter submitted to the task force, she included the following student complaints:

> There is a general lack of respect of students' dignity and cultural differences. For example, some teachers still continue to tell students not to speak "Spanish." This goes on even in the halls when the students are passing. Some teachers call students "wetback"—although the teachers may do it jokingly or have that type of rapor [sic] with the student, the fact that a teacher uses any derogatory remarks contributes to a student's disrespect for teachers.

> Some teachers also curse in the classroom or cuss students out in the classroom and that is a lack of respect for students. This type of attitude and behavior demonstrated by some teachers is an obvious contradiction to the school's mission and the educational goals of the school.

> Some teachers openly criticize the administration and the school, so how can the students be expected to respect authority and feel pride in their school.[17]

Finally, in recalling the fleeting sense of recognition that the students drew from their participation in the walkout, one senior offered this description of the contrast between that event and normal life at Seguín:

> It was like they [students] felt that for once in maybe their whole lives they were really being shown respect and being shown like somebody really cared and wanted to listen. (Student member of the task force, investigative team; senior male at the time of the walkout)

Other actions by HISD officials after the walkout included the superintendent's speedy replacement of Seguín's principal; the appointment of a school counselor to deal exclusively with the dropout problem, and the addition of three bilingual teachers to handle the needs of bilingual students. The district also established a social service organization, Communities in Schools, to better address students' personal needs. Though understaffed with two to three counselors, this organization has provided the most help to troubled youth. They provide direct counseling and refer students and their families whenever appropriate to community-based programs and services better equipped to meet their needs.

Changes that were especially popular with the students addressed their complaints about the cafeteria. The task force's recommendations for physical changes to the school plant were taken seriously. Too many students in too small a space was more than a serious inconvenience for those students who waited in long lines for lunch. It was a safety hazard. In a matter of months, more doors were added to the cafeteria and the number of eating spaces were expanded. And, while officials explored ways to improve the school's menu, catering services were brought in.

The district's quick response on several fronts—including ordering books, fixing schedules, adding counselors, expanding the campus security staff, hiring a dropout prevention coordinator, enlisting a corporate sponsor, and supplying better cafeteria food—satisfied many of the student leaders, who interpreted these actions as evidence that the district was acting in good faith. Satisfaction across the student body as a whole was uneven, however. Problems persisted and tensions continued to run high for months. Students played out their frustrations by engaging in several food fights. The largest of these incidents was reported on October 26 in the *Houston Chronicle*, under a column headed, "Cafeteria Woes at Seguín." The paper reported that around six hundred students had agreed to throw their trays in the air, but that their actions seemed not to constitute any organized form of protest. Teachers remembering the incident concur with the paper's account.

The food fights, which may have begun with two feuding groups, rapidly escalated. The teachers' response to the free-for-all atmosphere at lunch time was to avoid the cafeteria altogether. Students had to crawl under tables to protect themselves from airborne food, trays, and utensils. These incidents starkly reveal the administration's loss of control over a restless and frustrated student body.

Continuing dissatisfaction and discontent among the students reflected their impatience with the lack of resolution of many of the problems that had originally impelled them to walk out. These included incorrect schedules, poor test preparation for the state standardized examination, and no improvement in the dropout rate. And, finally, the instability wrought by the changes and proposed changes left many students chronically ill at ease. Shortly after the walkout, many of the students interviewed by the investigative team were highly critical of the teachers. One student leader indicated to me that the results of this investigation, embodied in the "Special Report to the Board of Education," made many students feel vulnerable. Rumors shot through the school that the teachers planned to retaliate.[18]

Conspicuously absent from the discussions about how to improve the school that took place in the tumultuous months following the walkout was the topic of the school's core curriculum—despite its perennial importance to the majority of Mexican American faculty. That these critical voices from within the school were (and continue to be) scarcely audible attests in part to the level of crisis in the school. As one white ESL teacher expressed: "How could we even begin talking about methodologies, approaches, and restructuring the curriculum when we didn't even have books?" This teacher further qualified her statement by suggesting that even without the distraction of no books, this kind of discussion was unlikely to occur: her white and African American colleagues found the prospect of changing the core curriculum simply too threatening. "They'd just rather wish this problem of more and more immigrants away. It is much too inconvenient to really sit down and deal with," she observed, cynically. Thus, the (subtractive) curriculum—addressed more fully in chapter 5—remains a sacred cow; even the walkout could not inspire any meaningful change in this area. What the students' and community's protest did accomplish was a thorough disruption of the harmful isolation that had characterized Seguín up to that point.

CONCLUSION

Despite the community's lofty hopes, inspired by the hiring of two consecutive Mexican American principals during the 1990s and by the heroic attempts toward positive change spearheaded by a small cadre of committed teachers and at least one assistant principal who rigorously evaluated and attempted to help faculty improve their teaching (see chapter 3), systemic problems prevail at Seguín. Also promising was the HISD's implementation of site-based management in 1992 to afford schools greater autonomy. This decentralization effort involved the establishment of a Shared Decision-Making (SDM) committee process on every campus that assumes responsibility for the school's budget and that seeks waivers from the district for unnecessary rules and regulations. While these committees are inclusive with administrative, teacher, parent, community, and student representation, they have done little to alter unwieldy, problem-plagued institutions like Seguín. Ineffective leadership, turf conflicts—mainly between teachers and counselors—limited funding, distance from the surrounding community, and institutional inertia are reasons for Seguín's limited positive impact through its SDM Committee.

Hence, the academic well-being of most Seguín students has been unaffected by the walkout and districtwide decentralization: low achievement, high dropout rates, cultural insensitivity, and severe scheduling problems continue. When they seek to explain the persistence of underachievement and high dropout at the high school, students, parents, and community members inevitably return to the language of "caring." For them, "caring" connotes concerns over inequitable schooling resources, overcrowded and decaying school buildings, and a lack of sensitivity toward Spanish-speakers, Mexican culture, and things Mexican.

Even in the more objective, less ideological realm of resources, Seguín spends 599 fewer dollars per student than the district average. According to the Academic Excellence Indicator System Report (1995–96), Seguín students receive $2,859 while the district averages $3,458 per student. This disparity is attributable to Seguín's poor motivation as well as a lack of talent and experience in writing proposals and generating funds for their youth. It is this lack of caring that underlies Seguín's dismal record of academic failure. The insidiousness of the school's non-caring atmosphere is captured in this student's reflections on the conditions that led to the October 1989 walkout:

> In the honors classes it was okay, but in the regular classes, there wasn't very much support. There were a few teachers that were genuinely concerned about where you were going from their classes, what you were going to do in the future . . . but a lot of them they seemed like they were tired. They didn't want to be at this school, you know, they didn't hear your complaints. They just wanted you to do their work or get out. (Freshman female student who helped distribute posters during the walkout)

Students and community members I interviewed saw the October 1989 walkout (retrospectively) as inevitable. In a span of two decades, the school's size and demographic makeup had changed so dramatically that corresponding changes in the content and structure of schooling should have occupied center stage. Mr. Cedillo, Seguín's current principal, summed up Seguín's situation simply, observing, "They [school and district officials] knew where this school was headed and you know, they just let it happen." Cedillo's remark encompasses the paucity of Latino faculty, the white bias of the curriculum, the lack of Spanish-speaking staff, and the harmful consequences to youth schooled under such conditions.

Mr. Cedillo shares the critique of schooling presented in my work. However, he feels that his "hands are tied" with respect to bringing about progressive change. He cites the low number of Latino faculty in his school, the small number of Latino high school principals in the district, and the low representation of Latinos on the school board and the upper levels of the central district administration as practical limitations on the likelihood of real reform. He feels that he cannot be the leader that he would like to be because the political infrastructure is not in place to protect him.

Viewing Seguín's problems from the top may give Mr. Cedillo the distance he needs to limit his energies to only those areas he thinks he may be able to change. The students' view from the bottom affords no such distance and no such comfort:

It almost seemed, maybe I'm wrong, like the teachers didn't want to know us, or too much about us. I try to be fair. Maybe it was like the more they knew us, the more they'd be responsible and their problems were so big, big! What would it mean in that situation to genuinely care for us? It would mean caring for big problems. And, not to let anybody off the hook, but who of all of them was ready or willing to take on a cause for *raza* [the Mexican American people]? (Junior female who walked out and eventually graduated from another high school)

The walkout was about caring. We cared for our education though the teachers and administration didn't care for us. Even if they said they cared, talk is cheap. If it wasn't their fault the school was in such trouble—and they'll tell you that, clean their hands—it was their responsibility no matter what. *Todos, toditos* [All, all], they were all to blame. (Freshman male student who walked out and eventually dropped out of school, took his G.E.D. and enrolled in a community college)

CHAPTER 3

Teacher-Student Relations and the Politics of Caring

This chapter examines competing definitions of caring at Seguín. The predominantly non-Latino teaching staff sees students as not sufficiently *caring about* school, while students see teachers as not sufficiently *caring for* them. Teachers expect students to demonstrate caring about schooling with an abstract, or *aesthetic* commitment to ideas or practices that purportedly lead to achievement. Immigrant and U.S.-born youth, on the other hand, are committed to an *authentic* form of caring that emphasizes relations of reciprocity between teachers and students.

Complicating most teachers' demands that students care about school is their displeasure with students' self-representations, on the one hand, and the debilitating institutional barriers they face on a daily basis that impede their abilities to connect effectively with youths' social world, on the other. From these adults' perspective, the way youth dress, talk, and generally deport themselves "proves" that they do not care about school. For their part, students argue that they should be assessed, valued, and engaged as whole people, not as automatons in baggy pants. They articulate a vision of education that parallels the Mexican concept of *educación*. That is, they prefer a model of schooling premised on respectful, caring relations. As discussed in chapter 1, *educación* closely resembles Noddings' (1988) concept of authentic caring which views sustained reciprocal relationships between teachers and students as the basis for all learning.

Noddings (1984, 1992) argues that teachers' ultimate goal of apprehending their students' subjective reality is best achieved through engrossment in their students' welfare and emotional displacement. That is, authentically caring teachers are seized by their students and energy flows toward their projects and needs.

The benefit of such profound relatedness for the student is the development of a sense of competence and mastery over worldly tasks. In the absence of such connectedness, students are not only reduced to the level of objects, they may also be diverted from learning the skills necessary for mastering their academic and social environment. Thus, the difference in the way students and teachers perceive school-based relationships can bear directly on students' potential to achieve.

The landscape of caring orientations among teachers and immigrant and U.S.-born students at Seguín is presented in the following pages. A mutual sense of alienation evolves when teachers and students hold different understandings about school. Because teachers and administrators are better positioned than students to impose their perspective, aesthetic caring comes to shape and sustain a subtractive logic. That is, the demand that students embrace their teachers' view of caring is tantamount to requiring their active participation in a process of cultural and linguistic eradication (Bartolomé 1994) since the curriculum they are asked to value and support is one that dismisses or derogates their language, culture, and community. (See chapter 5 for an elaboration of the culturally subtractive elements of schooling.) Rather than building on students' cultural, linguistic, and community-based knowledge, schools like Seguín typically subtract these resources. Psychic and emotional withdrawal from schooling are symptomatic of students' rejection of subtractive schooling and a curriculum they perceive as uninteresting, irrelevant, and test-driven.

Immigrant youth resemble their disaffected, U.S.-born counterparts when they, too, become "uncaring" after having acculturated and become "Americanized" too rapidly. However, because the "uncaring" student prototype is overwhelmingly U.S.-born, they are the primary focus here. With their experiences of psychic and emotional withdrawal within the regular track, these teenagers demand with their voices and bodies, even more strongly than do their immigrant peers, a more humane vision of schooling. Since their critique of the aesthetic-caring status quo is sometimes lodged in acts of resistance—not to education, but to schooling—school officials typically misinterpret the meaning of these challenges.

A look at the consequences for youth when their teachers do

or do not initiate relationships reveals how a sense of connectedness can have a direct impact on success at school. After a closing
discussion of the limitations of both aesthetic and authentic caring as currently conceptualized in the literature, a peek at Seguín's
Social Studies Department provides insights into the relation
between caring and pedagogy. The chapter concludes with an
account of Seguín's highly successful band teacher. This teacher's
embodiment of authentic caring, including his apprehension of
Seguín students' cultural world and structural position, demonstrates the enormous benefits that accrue when schooling is transformed into education—or more appropriately, *educación*.

TEACHER CARING

The view that students do not care about school stems from several sources, including social and cultural distance in student-
adult relationships and the school culture itself. Most of the
school's staff neither live nor participate in their students' predominantly Mexican community. The non-Latino teachers who
constitute the majority (81 percent) are doubtful and even defensive about the suggestion that more Latino teachers would make
a difference in school climate. Seguín's high attrition rate—particularly among the newer staff (see chapter 2)—further exacerbates
social distance and increases the difficulty of developing an
explicit ethic of caring.

Some schools have consciously articulated an ethic of authentic caring (e.g., see Danin's [1994] ethnography of one such
school), but no such effort has ever been deliberately undertaken
at Seguín. Except for a minority of teachers for whom aesthetic
and authentic caring are not mutually exclusive, a more general
pattern of aesthetic caring prevails among those who teach the
"middle majority" of regular-track youth.

In my many conversations with teachers, only a few indicated
that they knew many of their students in a personal way, and very
few students said that they thought that their teachers knew them
or that they would be willing to go to their teachers for help with
a personal problem. This is not surprising. Despite perceiving of
themselves as caring, many teachers unconsciously communicate

a different message—to their colleagues as well as to their students. Committed teachers who invest their time in students are chided for their efforts, with the reminder that working hard is not worth the effort "since these kids aren't going anywhere anyway." The subtext is more damning still: Seguín students don't "go anywhere" because they don't, can't, or won't "try."

Teachers sometimes make this view explicit. Consider the case of Mr. Johnson, English teacher and self-proclaimed student advocate. Mr. Johnson is openly critical of the counselors and the administration for their sustained incompetence in handling students' course schedules. No doubt, Mr. Johnson does rescue some students from bureaucratic harm, but his good deeds are nullified by his abrasive and overbearing behavior in the classroom. As the following description of his teaching style shows, this teacher's apparent need to feel and be powerful cuts him off from the very individuals he seems to believe he is helping—or trying to help.

One sunny day in April when I am observing in Mr. Johnson's ninth-grade English classroom, I hear him say to his class—yet somehow I know his comments are for my benefit—in a loud, deep, Southern drawl, "The main problem with these kids is their attitude. They're immature and they challenge authority. Look at them, they're not going anywhere. I can tell you right now, a full quarter of these students will drop out of school come May."

One of the girls sitting right in front of Mr. Johnson smiles awkwardly and rolls her eyes in apparent disgust. Most students simply pretend not to hear him, though a few glance at me and chuckle nervously in embarrassment. The teacher sounds like he is joking but the students do not find him funny.

"See what I mean?" Mr. Johnson says. "They think they can get by in life without having to take orders from anyone."

A student slumped in his chair with his chin and arms on his desk peers up, then lifts his head, responding in a mumble, "Aw, Mr. Johnson, you don't . . . you're just. . . ."

Mr. Johnson interrupts, "Joel, stop thinking, you know it might hurt you, cause you some damage upstairs."

Joel smiles wryly and sinks back into his chair.

As extreme as Mr. Johnson's behavior may seem, teachers at Seguín often engage in such verbal abuse. He communicates—perhaps more vividly than most—a sentiment shared by teachers and other school personnel, namely that Mexican students are immature, unambitious, and defiant of authority, and that teachers have no power to change the situation since it is the students' fault. The school's obvious systemic problems, most evident in its astronomical dropout rate, are brushed aside and the burden of responsibility and the struggle for change is understood as rightfully residing first with the students, their families, and the community. A lack of urgency about the school's academic crisis itself is a sign of dangerously low expectations on the part of Seguín teachers and administrators.

Mr. Johnson articulated this belief that students' academic performance is primarily a matter of individual initiative and motivation when he introduced me to his class. Much to my chagrin, he patronizingly informed his students that I was a "doctor" from Rice University and then added, "Something y'all could be if you just stopped your foolishness and grew up." I could feel myself staring back at the students with the same disappointed and humiliated look that they were giving me.

During this entire interaction, students were passively sitting in their seats instead of working on the *Romeo and Juliet* writing assignment scribbled boldly on the chalkboard. So Mr. Johnson was accurate in one respect: they were challenging his ability to make them learn under abusive conditions. However, Mr. Johnson and other teachers conveniently overlook the fact that they do have sway in the classroom. In this case, for instance, no student showed outright anger, despite the tension in the air. Students were clearly deferring to his authority, thus demonstrating, ironically, the fallacy in the teacher's view. More importantly, they exhibited extraordinary self-control, hardly what one would expect from youth who are inherently "immature" and "defiant." That the students were, in fact, restraining themselves was made dramatically clear to me later when I spoke with Joel outside the classroom. Summing up his feelings toward his English teacher, Joel exploded, "Johnson's full of shit! . . . he's always got an attitude."

The bias most mainstream teachers have toward the majority of Seguín students arises from many sources. Mainly white and middle-class, these adults' more privileged backgrounds inevitably set them up for disappointment in youth whose life cir-

cumstances differ so radically from their own. Students' failure to
meet their teachers' expectations is further complicated by a generational divide. Like most adults, teachers misremember the past
as a golden era; they recall a time when everyone was "honest,"
when old and young alike "worked hard," when school was
"important," and students were "respectful." Some days, the
teachers' lounge could easily be confused with the set of a daytime TV episode, as teachers exchange comments like, "My father
was poor and he worked hard for everything he earned"; "When
I was young, things were different"; "Where I grew up, if you
raised your voice"; and "I never even thought once that I
shouldn't go to class." Without exception, the school's most dedicated teachers avoid the lounge altogether, fearing the disabling
potential of their colleagues' negativity. Contemporary students,
in failing to conform to this misty, mythical image of their historical counterparts, seem deficient, so teachers find it hard to see
them in an appreciative, culture-affirming way.

Moreover, teachers see the differences in culture and language
between themselves and their students from a culturally chauvinistic perspective that permits them to dismiss the possibility of a
more culturally relevant approach in dealing with this population. For instance, teachers and counselors more often lament
their students' linguistic limitations than they do their own. An
affirming stance toward Mexican culture is deemed unnecessary
since, as one teacher on Seguín's Shared Decision-Making (SDM)
Committee explained to me, "the school is already 'all-Mexican.'"

The interrelationship between the tendency to objectify students and the rejection of a nurturing view of education is clear
in everyday classroom experiences at Seguín. An algebra teacher
who appears to have little success in maintaining an orderly
atmosphere in her class perceives rowdiness as evidence that
many youth are not in school to learn. She complained to me one
day, "I'm not here to baby-sit and I'm certainly not their parent. . . . I finally told them, 'Listen, you don't have to be here if
you don't want to be here. No one's forcing you.'" Teachers often
give students the option of remaining in or leaving the classroom.
Typically they justify their actions by saying that they are trying
to inculcate a sense of adult responsibility in these teenage boys

and girls. At issue here is the means by which youth acquire a sense of adult responsibility. When uttered in the absence of authentic caring, such language objectifies students as dispensable, nonessential parts of the school machinery.

Another dismissive expression that has prompted repeated complaints from PTA members involves teachers unilaterally rejecting students who have been assigned to already overcrowded classrooms at the beginning of each semester. As addressed in the previous chapter, chaos always characterizes the first several weeks of each new year. The school's ten to twelve counselors have the demonstrably impossible task of processing over a thousand new entrants, emanating from the feeder middle schools, from other area high schools, and from outside the state or country. If the sheer size of this incoming tide were not enough to ensure the counselors' failure, the additional fact that they do not begin processing *any* students' fall schedules until the week before school opens would settle the matter. With so little time to process so many students, the counselors resort to simply overassigning them to classes. The rationale for this deliberate misscheduling is, predictably, purely bureaucratic: this is the easiest way to get students "into the system" so that they may be counted as enrolled. Interestingly, there is no district policy that states that youth must be enrolled by any particular day.

In a "good" year, counselors "level off" these classes by the third week of school when most students' schedules are finally "fixed"—that is, when students are assigned to the classes they should have been enrolled in from the first day of school. As might be expected, the first few weeks are extremely stressful. Teachers face huge classes composed of a random mix of students, only some of whom belong where they are. Even larger than the actual classes are the rosters of students who are supposedly present in their classrooms. Massively long class rosters, teachers' and students' conflictual relations with counselors, extraordinarily large class sizes despite absent and disappearing bodies, insufficient numbers of desks, books, teaching materials and space, combine with students' displeasure over schooling to make for a state of high tension and intense normlessness.

Regarding counselors, teachers see them as incompetent and overly bureaucratic, while students begin each semester with the sense that "the system," including counselors, exhibits precious little concern for them. In fact, in the fall 1995 semester, several Latino and white teachers grew so disgusted with the counselors that they appropriated a sense of leadership that they did not see operating within the school's administration by usurping the student assignment process from the counselors, superseding the principal's authority. Their actions created even greater havoc. The assignment process turned out not to be as simple as it seemed and relations between teachers and counselors were polarized for awhile. Fortunately, a cadre of Seguín parents and community activists mobilized to make Seguín accountable for the chaos that had developed. With community members participating, working groups formed and by the seventh week of the semester, a modicum of equanimity evolved.[1]

Among the handful of teacher leaders in this revolt, what became apparent was their own sense of authentic caring as markedly contrasting with their view of counselors' penchant for aesthetic caring. Accordingly, one teacher leader said to me, "Yes, things got confused, but we wanted to do what was right for our kids. We're the ones who have to experience the effects of their [counselors'] actions." These teachers' moral authority came from their status as effective classroom teachers as well as from their personal involvement on the school's central committees. Not surprisingly, one was also the social studies teacher who empowered her students with the skills and understandings they needed to carry out the October 1989 protest in a peaceful, nonviolent manner. Hence, despite the confusion their actions created, the constructive dialogue and decisions that resulted would probably not have occurred had matters not indeed grown worse.

Personnel changes in Seguín's administration have made it difficult for principals and assistant principals to make any sustainable progress in improving the efficiency with which the school is run. Nor have they been able to alter the school's culture. Assistant Principal Ana Luera, who by her third year at Seguín had become significantly involved in working toward changing the school's culture, maintains that changing counselors' and teachers' practices is a long process that requires both patience and perseverance. Most importantly, she notes that no change can occur in the absence of mutual respect and trust:

You can't do anything with them [teachers and counselors] your first couple of years because you have to gain their trust. They're just like kids. You have to show you love them. . . . Now, by the third year . . . you don't know *how many* teachers I called in to tell them to show more respect to the students, to not do certain things. Now that I got their trust, I can tell them. Sometimes they deny what they do or they admit it and say that they won't do it again. I respect them and I give them due process. You have to do that. . . . This year, we're going to do some cultural sensitivity training. . . . Students' schedules were also fixed this time at the end of the school year . . . you just can't do anything as a new principal the first couple of years.

Luera reveals the need for teachers to feel cared for. As Noblit (1994) similarly found in his case study of a caring principal in a school, principals can assert their leadership by authentically caring for teachers and also by promoting honest dialogue on how to authentically care for students. The brief tenures of principals is a widespread problem in urban schools throughout the state of Texas. In addition to "burnout," the district loses principals by adhering to an accountability scheme that makes the tenure of a principal's assignment contingent on raising students' test scores on a statewide exam within a three-year time period.[2] One unintended consequence of this "revolving door" approach to posting principals is that it reinforces counselors' and teachers' sense of autonomy and increases their power. In a system where they are the "old hands," they must be continually "won over" by top administrators whose jobs may be hostage to their subordinates' willingness to cooperate.

The intransigence of teacher and counselor culture at Seguín has other consequences besides potentially undermining the efforts of a new principal. Parents, PTA members, and community advocates whose appeals to Seguín staff are routinely dismissed without serious consideration frequently resort to bypassing the school and carrying their concerns directly to the district superintendent or the school board. According to one PTA leader, the highly predictable surplus of students enrolling each semester relative to spaces available is tolerated because school staff know "that the students will drop out anyway by the fifth or sixth week of classes." Enrollments of between 3,000 and 3,400 each semester in a physical facility capable of housing no more than 2,600 students lend credence to this claim. And not surprisingly, the numbers do substantially trim down in a five- to six-week time frame. A small, nearby alternative high school serving approximately 150 students annually—itself a remnant of the 1970 school boycott—rejects an average of 7 students per day who are attempting to re-enroll in school after having "dropped out." Unfortunately, Seguín does not keep records on such students' whereabouts.

Teachers occupy an uncomfortable middle ground. They are both victims of and collaborators with a system that structurally neglects Latino youth. Armed with limited classroom materials and often outdated equipment and resources, and facing large classes overflowing with overage, at-risk, and underachieving youth, teachers frequently opt for efficiency and the "hard line" over a more humanistic approach. The district's emphasis on quantitative measures and "accountability" to evaluate students' commitment to school streamlines some aspects of teaching, but at the same time alienates scores of marginalized students. As the distance between teachers and their students widens, any possibility of an alliance between the two evaporates. Isolated from and unhappy with one another, neither party finds much to call rewarding about a typical day at Seguín High School.

Students who say and act like they do not care about school mystify teachers; the latter profess great difficulty understanding such attitudes. The possibility that an uncaring attitude might be a coping strategy or a simple facade has little currency among Seguín teachers. My interactions and conversations with students, on the other hand, suggest that youth who maintain that they don't care about school may often really mean something else. For example, there are many students like Susana, a young woman with a fragile academic self-concept who takes comfort in the thought that she does not really care about learning in school. She protects herself from the pain of possibly failing to do well by choosing to do poorly. My investigation of Susana's withdrawn attitude (described below) supports, albeit negatively, the caring literature's hypothesized relationship between the teacher's apprehension of the student and the sense of academic competence and mastery that should ensue.

Mrs. Hutchins, a ninth-grade English teacher, asked me to talk to Susana to find out why she refused to answer when called upon in the classroom. I can only guess that Ms. Hutchins enlisted my assistance because she perceived my ethnicity as a possible route into Susana's world. "She always makes faces when I call on her," Mrs. Hutchins said, explaining her request. Then, she offered a theory about the reasons for Susana's behavior. "She doesn't want to be in my class. She may even resent me somehow." Mrs. Hutchins had introduced problem-solving techniques into her teaching, but she said that certain students still seemed beyond reach. When she first started teaching at Seguín, her fellow teachers cautioned her that there were many such students. After two years of teaching, she felt she had to get to the bottom of the problem of mentally absent students.

I was able to approach Susana as she was settling into her desk just before the bell sounded on the following day. I complimented her on the length and beauty of her jet-black, braided hair and told her I was a researcher studying what students think about school. Susana briefly let down her guard. We exchanged a few words about what researchers do and she told me that when she had seen me the day before she couldn't tell whether I was a teacher or a student. She became sufficiently interested in our conversation, enough to upbraid a young man who was trying to get her attention. She told him to "Shut up!" because she was busy right then.

I told her that I noticed many students who did not participate in classroom discussions when teachers asked them to, and I wanted to know what she thought about that. She took a deep breath and said, seriously, "You kinda' have to seem like you don't care because if you say something, and it comes out sounding stupid, then everybody will say you're dumb. And even the teacher will think you're dumb, when they didn't think that before." While Susana may sound unusually protective of her ego, her thinking is quite logical, inverting the relation of authentic caring and academic competence: a dearth of authentic relations with teachers subtracts, or minimizes, opportunities youth have to develop and enjoy a sense of competence and mastery of the curriculum.

My discussion with Susana further revealed that her comportment toward her history teacher was a generalized response to schooling based on several past negative experiences with teachers.

"I've had some bad things happen to me with teachers," she confided.

"Like what?" I asked, just as the bell rang.

"Oh, lots of things," she said, sneering and pulling backwards as if not wanting to elaborate.

Feeling that I was losing her and that our conversation was about to end, I took a chance and asked, "Has anyone ever made you feel like what you said in class was dumb?"

"Oh yeah, but not anymore. Na-ah, not me."

Susana's, withdrawn, defensive posture was most fully revealed in the following statement, which ended our conversation:

> Once this bad science teacher asked me in front of everybody to stop raising my hand so much in class. And all the students laughed at me. I was trying to learn and he was a new teacher . . . hard to understand. I felt so stupid . . . so yeah, that and other things. . . . Teachers say that they want to talk to you, but I notice that they really don't. I used to get mad about it, but now it's like "What's the use?" Not gonna change nuthin'. If I can just make it through the day without no problems. . . . So now if something bad happens, I know that I didn't cause it cuz I'm just here mindin' my business.

Teachers' repeated threats to Susana's academic self-concept have made her lower her expectations about the likelihood of forming productive relationships with teachers. As she was open with me, my guess is that Susana is not yet entirely lost because she hasn't quite given up. Later, when I shared what I had learned about Susana with Mrs. Hutchins, the teacher expressed a mixture of frustration, annoyance, and grief over the thought of having to deal with the consequences of Susana's previous teachers' mistakes and insensitivities.

"As if teaching were not enough to preoccupy myself with," she sighed, and then continued in a more defensive tone, "It's overwhelming to think that this is the level we're dealing at, and frankly, neither was I trained nor am I paid to be a social worker."

"Well, at least you know more of what you're up against in this situation," I offered.

"Yeah, I suspected this would be the case and it's uncomfortable for me to deal with someone who is hard set with the idea that teachers are the enemy."

Clearly, in this case both student and teacher resist a caring relationship. The effects of this mutual resistance are not equally balanced, however. Mrs. Hutchins may have to continue to put up with the distraction of funny faces rather than the positive classroom participation she would like, but Susana's adjustment will be much more costly. As her sense of alienation gets reinforced, her willingness to remain even marginally mentally engaged will steadily erode.

The individual histories that students and teachers bring to their classroom encounters necessarily influence the chances for successful relationship building. Still, in most cases, there is likely to be some room to maneuver—that is, if the situation is approached literally "with care." However unintended, the story of Mrs. Hutchins and Susana captures a teacher in the very process of closing the door to relationship by privileging the technical over the expressive. Notwithstanding her expressed desire to get at the root of Susana's problem, Mrs. Hutchins' rather self-absorbed, emotional response reveals the limitations of her aesthetic framework. In a contradictory fashion, she is angry with Susana's previous teachers' mistakes at the same time that she resists pursuing a possible solution through the alternative route implied within Susana's schooling experiences—that is, a more relational and compassionate pedagogy.

Fine (1991) provides reasons for the technical, aesthetic focus of schools that resonate with this study, in general, and with this teacher's response, in particular. Fine's investigation of dropouts, undertaken in a comprehensive, inner-city school similar to Seguín, leads her to conclude that teachers are committed to an institutional "fetish" that views academics as the exclusive domain of the school. This fetish supports the status quo by preserving the existing boundaries between the ostensibly "public" school and the "private" matters of family and community. Though Susana's problems appear related to the schooling process itself, Mrs. Hutchins observes that she was not trained to be a social worker as an implicit justification for her refusal to pursue Susana's situation any further. Such reasoning is persuasive only if one first accepts as real—and right—the hypothesized public-private dichotomy in the realm of education.

When real-life concerns are thrust into the classroom, many teachers find themselves in uncomfortable and disorienting positions. They may be called on not only to impart their expert knowledge, but also to deal with barriers to students' learning of which they may not be fully aware or trained to recognize. If and when they do become aware of these contingencies, time and skill constraints remain. When teaching effectiveness gets reduced to methodological considerations and when no explicit culture of caring is in place, teachers lose the capacity to respond to their students as whole human beings and schools become uncaring places (Kozol 1991; Bartolomé 1994; Prillaman and Eaker 1994). These are conditions under which teachers and administrators may turn resolutely to face-saving explanations for school-based problems. Rather than address the enormity of the issues before them, they take solace in blanket judgments about ethnicity and underachievement or "deficit" cultures that are allegedly too impoverished to value education.

These kinds of explanations are often embedded in a larger framework that co-identifies underachievement and students' dress, demeanor, and friendship choices. The tendency to place the onus of students' underachievement on the students themselves has been amply observed in other ethnographic research among youth in urban schools (Peshkin 1991; Fine 1991; Orenstein 1994; Yeo 1997; Olsen 1997; McQuillan 1998). Collective problems are regularly cast in individual terms, as if asymmetrical relations of power were irrelevant. Not weighed against individual students' proclivities are the larger structural features of schooling that subtract resources from youth (see chapter 5), preempting a fair rendering of the parameters of low educational mobility. This absence of a self-critical discourse unwittingly promotes condescending views toward students, as the following incident reveals.

On an overcast winter afternoon a counselor named Mr. Ross and I stand guard by a steel exit door. The final afternoon bell has rung and students begin pouring out of the building. A seemingly endless river of brown faces and bodies pressing against each other spews forth out of several narrow exit doors into the school's muddied and rapidly vanishing front lawn. A group of three boys tumble by us, jostling one another and calling each other "*putos*" (whores) and "bitches." I catch a glimpse of the elastic top band of Fruit of the Loom underwear as one boy tries to knock another down. Mr. Ross shakes his head in disapproval as the boys scurry off with mischievous grins on their faces. The counselor turns to me and confesses that he just cannot understand why Latino youth "do not take school seriously":

> I'm just amazed all the time at how much these kids skip and mess around instead of doing their school work. It's different in the black community. It's like you grow up expecting to graduate from high school. It's never a question of whether you're going to go or not. You just go. . . . I try to help these Hispanic kids. I tell them, "Hey, this is the only time anything in your life is going to be free, so take advantage of it." But, you can only lead a horse to water . . . if they don't want to be here, what can you do?

Mr. Ross' analysis fails to consider the disempowering nature of the school's curriculum. Questions of equity persist: entitlement to a "free" public education does not automatically translate into just schooling conditions for all, particularly for poor, minority youth (Kozol 1991). The following section examines how students' self-representations make them vulnerable to school authorities whose caring for students is oftentimes more centered on what they wear than on who they are.

THE "UNCARING STUDENT" PROTOTYPE

U.S.-born, Seguín ninth-graders are especially preoccupied with looking and acting in ways that make them seem cool. Males tend to be more involved than females in countercultural styles, but many females share these same preoccupations. Boys wear tennis shoes, long T-shirts, and baggy pants with crotches that hang anywhere between mid-thigh to the knees. Also popular are *pecheras* (overalls) with the top flap folded over the stomach, dickies, khaki pants, earrings, and, sometimes, tattoos (many of which are self-inflicted) on their hands and arms. Boys, and some girls, may also shave their heads partially or fully. Gold-colored chains, crucifixes, and name pendants often dangle from students' necks. The tastes of these urban teens closely resemble those of Latino Angelino youth (see Patthey-Chavez's [1993] ethnography of a Los Angeles high school).

The mainstream values of the high school and its school-sponsored organizations tend to assure that high achievers and students involved in school activities will be underrepresented in the ranks of the "uncaring-student" prototype. Average- and low-achieving ninth-graders concentrated in the school's regular track, on the other hand, are likely to fit the type. This alignment between student type and student attire leads teachers and administrators to use (consciously and unconsciously) greater amounts of garb as a signal. Although the majority of Seguín students do not belong to gangs, school personnel readily associate certain clothing with gang apparel. Most Seguín parents, by contrast, staunchly maintain that the way their children dress has much more to do with their adolescent need to "fit in" than their proclivity for trouble or their membership in any particular gang.

Though the school disapproves of urban hip-hop styles, and views the more exaggerated manifestations as a "problem" that needs to be "fixed," the school itself cultivates this taste in attire through its Channel 1 television programming—which is accessible in virtually every school space where students congregate.[3] Students huddled around rap exhibitions on TV in the cafeteria or in a homeroom classroom is a familiar sight. Not all youth, of course, prefer rap and hip-hop but the vast majority of U.S.-born youth appreciate it.

It is not hard to pick out Seguín's "hip" urban youth. They strut about campus in a stiff-legged but rhythmic, slightly forward-bouncing fashion and act like they do not care much about anything. This posturing helps mark group boundaries and communicates solidarity. Exaggerated posturing is evident in certain situations, such as before a fight, or when students get into trouble with school authorities, either as a face-saving strategy or to communicate righteous indignation. I witnessed this in a fight that was quickly broken up by the two district security officers on regular duty at the school. The dispute was over a young woman.

One boy's girlfriend was being courted by a male outside of the group. My field notes reveal how the boys' posturing demarcated group boundaries and signaled to others that a fight was about to occur:

> No sooner had I entered the cafeteria than I noticed a student signal to another with an abrupt shake of his head. His friend lunged his head and body backwards as he plowed his hands into his pockets, which hung very low on his hips. His thin frame, erect body, and quick, rigid movements reminded me of those wooden roadrunner toys which simulate drinking when perched at a right-angled tilt. I thought he was reaching for a weapon, but no instrument was drawn or shown. His movements nevertheless grabbed everyone's attention . . . a display of toughness or righteousness for what was about to take place. A third friend then popped onto the scene from out of nowhere. All three approached a smaller guy, who withdrew into a row of students lined up near the nachos food stand about fifteen feet away. A large crowd quickly formed as a couple of punches were thrown, leaving the solitary student on the ground, scrambling to get himself up. Two school cops bustled through the crowd, yelling, "Break it up, boys! Break it up!" The growing crowd started booing and the boys stopped fighting. All four were hauled off in a matter of minutes. A few scrapes and bruises. No one was seriously hurt.

Students who are marginal to the mainstream values of the school overwhelmingly conform to the "uncaring student" prototype. They engage in such deviant behaviors as skipping class and hanging out (lounging in the cafeteria through all three lunch periods is a favorite pastime). Although immigrant youth are typically appalled by the glaring indifference to schooling displayed by U.S.-born youth, whom the immigrant teens view as having become too *americanizados* (or Americanized), a small but noticeable segment within their ranks is seduced into this style of self-representation. Most at risk are youth who have a strong need for acceptance from their acculturated peers. Teachers in the ESL department, in particular, express a great deal of concern for these students who, in the words of one beginning ESL teacher, "wish to assimilate so quickly and so completely that many go too far." This woman is a very caring Anglo, Spanish-speaking teacher with a clear grasp of her students' political reality and a vivid awareness of the strengths they possess as immigrants entering U.S. schools. She tries to drill in her students' heads the idea that *as immigrants* they are uniquely positioned to succeed.

> There's no rush [to assimilate and become American]. *You're* the ones in this school who really and truly possess the capacity to excel. *You're* the ones who have it all. In such a short time, *you* will be bilingual. With your intelligence and your skills, *you*, more than the others, can really make something of your lives.

Except for the handful of wayward immigrant youth, a visit to any of the four assistant principals' offices on any day of the week reveals how homogeneous a group the "uncaring," "trouble-making" students are. Although they tend to be mainly ninth-grade males, girls are increasingly well represented. According to one school police officer, whose opinion is widely shared by the staff, "More and more . . . the girls are no different from the guys." My observations during my many visits to the assistant principals' offices reveal a ratio of one girl processed for every three boys. Despite increasing similarities between males and females with respect to overtly deviant acts, the extreme levels of alienation among many U.S.-born females is still most likely to manifest itself as passivity and quietness in classroom situations. As was manifest in Susana's and even Mr. Johnson's classroom, females deviate less visibly because they respond to the same stimuli within an uncaring environment in a gender-appropriate, and therefore less physically threatening, manner.

The overrepresentation of ninth-graders in this "uncaring student" category is due to three factors. First, many of these students have not yet shed their middle school personae. They are still carrying on with tough, gangster-type attitudes and a clothing style to match. The social pressure to continue in this mode is abetted by the school's high dropout and failure rates, which leave freshmen to make up more than half of the school's total population. Academic failure is so common that in any given year, a full quarter of the students have to repeat the ninth grade for at least a second time. School officials refer to many of these students as "career ninth-graders." Second, because many of the ninth-graders were members of middle school "gangs," loosely defined, they are subjected to intense scrutiny by an aggressive, discipline-focused, "zero-tolerance," administration that tends to approach disciplinary problems in a reactive and punitive fashion. "Withdrawing students for inattendance," for example, is a customary way of handling students like these with high absentee rates. In this environment, even the appearance of gang membership often results in students receiving unwelcome attention from school authorities. A self-fulfilling prophecy develops when youth react negatively against school authorities who breathe heavily on them.

Third, upperclassmen tone down their appearance. Tenth- but especially eleventh- and twelfth-grade students make a point of distinguishing themselves from freshmen by dressing differently. Whereas the upperclassmen may still wear baggy jeans or khakis low around their hips, their pants may be pressed and only somewhat baggy. One student I interviewed reminisced about having been a "punk" himself when he was a freshman. Now that he was a football player and working part-time, he decided that he had to "grow up."

Students' informal discussions of their orientations toward schooling and achievement make their teachers' judgments difficult to endorse. As the stories below reveal, Seguín students' definition of education is markedly different from that of school personnel. To varying degrees, the students advance a view that is in line with the meaning of *educación* and conforms to the ideas of caring theorists like Gilligan (1982) and Noddings (1984). Whereas teachers demand caring about school in the absence of relation, students view caring, or reciprocal relations, as the basis for all learning. Their precondition to caring about school is that they be engaged in a caring relationship with an adult at school.

Laura's encounter with an assistant principal illustrates the trouble youth get into when a school official does not like they way they dress. Laura had come to school that day wearing a long T-shirt emblazoned with the message, "Give Peace a Chance," against a black background streaked with color. She had coupled the shirt with baggy pants that stopped above her ankles, displaying white socks and shiny, black leather combat boots. She exploded when the assistant principal told her that she had to go home and change her clothes. The following excerpt is from the field notes I wrote that day:

> As I sat waiting to speak to the assistant principal, a young woman with white makeup walks in screaming, "What! Are you crazy? What does what I wear have to do with anything? I live alone. I work for my money. And not even my parents tell me what to do or wear. And you're telling me that what I've got on isn't good enough? I don't bother anyone when I go to class. I go to class to learn! School should be about me learning and not about what I wear! This is bullshit!" The assistant principal smiled condescendingly, telling her "Now, now, Laura . . ." and coaxed her into her office where her tirade could not be witnessed by others, including myself. She entered her office, where she continued screaming. She then threw the door open and stomped out of the office all red in the face. Her second outburst, the assistant principal later informs me, landed her with a one-day, on-campus, suspension from school.

I met up with Laura two weeks later at work at a convenience store several blocks from school. She recognized me and immediately divulged that she was still getting "hassled by the school." Although she needed to work in order to support herself, the school counselors were continuing to refuse to enroll her in Cooperative Education, or in the component of the school's Career and Technology Education (CTE) vocational program that enables youth to work for credit off campus for half a day. They based their denials on the fact that Laura had not taken certain prerequisite courses. She was "in violation of the rules."

"So what happens?" Laura asked, rhetorically. "I'm being counted absent every day from three classes to set me up so I'll flunk this semester. They don't even have to say, 'Laura, you're worthless. You should flunk.' All they have to say is, 'We have rules.'"

I recommended that she talk to Ms. Trujillo, Seguín's vocational counselor. I knew that in cases where no other options were available, Ms. Trujillo was willing to use her position as the official CTE counselor on campus to prevent students from dropping out of school by giving them jobs through the Cooperative Education component of CTE. The catch here, for which she and

CTE have drawn fire, is that slipping students in based on their need rather than their academic qualifications weakens the status of the program, which tries to groom and place students into entry-level, corporate-sector jobs. CTE faculty compete against other high schools inside and outside the district for good jobs for their students. Allowing "less-qualified" students to enter the program disrupts the highly selective admissions process, which in turn jeopardizes the corporate relationship, since employers begin questioning the shared understanding of guaranteed student quality.

When I talked to Ms. Trujillo later and asked about Laura, I discovered that the counselor had indeed performed her magic: "Students come first for me and letting a few squeak through the program is a small price to pay if we can keep them from dropping out. We must attend to our students' needs. This young girl has to work to feed, clothe, and support herself."

Laura's conflict with school staff shows the existence of competing definitions of caring. It also makes clear her enormous frustration over being powerless to insert her definition of education into the schooling process. More positively, Laura's story demonstrates the power of a caring counselor who is willing to intervene on a student's behalf, even when that means breaking school rules. The inflexibility of bureaucracies often places caregivers in the problematic position of having to break rules in order to be caring (Fisher and Tronto 1990).

Conflicts between surface and substance are a daily occurrence at Seguín, where great attention is paid to what students wear and it is assumed that style and learning are necessarily connected. In 1994, one of the two parent representatives on the school's Shared Decision-Making Committee suggested that the school require students to wear uniforms as one way to diffuse this conflict. In an ensuing meeting to address the issue, the principal joked, "Their pants are so baggy and lay so far down on the hips that it's no wonder they don't make it to class on time." In this same meeting, a student leader, speaking on behalf of other students, aggressively challenged the recommendation of uniforms, arguing that teenagers' manner of dress is an important aspect of their individuality. In the end, the committee decided to enforce the dress code by outlawing baggy pants for the coming school year. When classes began in the fall, however, the school was so overrun with baggy pants–wearers that enforcement of the new provision of the dress code was impossible. This outcome also revealed the school's lack of connectedness to the parents and community who could have helped inform and educate students about the new dress code.

Another indication of the fragile nature of teacher caring at the high school is apparent in the case of Carla, a tenth-grader. When she changed her style of dress and choice of friends, she quickly became the object of extraordinary scrutiny from her coaches—despite a seemingly close relationship with them.

Carla lives in a one-bedroom house with her sixty-year-old grandmother and her thirteen-year-old brother in an East End area that is also home to many gang members. Abandoned by her mother, who did not want to raise her or her younger brother, Carla has experienced her fair share of suffering. Family life is stressful. She lives under the constant threat of losing her grandmother to a chronic, upper-respiratory illness and her brother to middle-school gangs. The family is on welfare and they barely manage to survive from one month to the next. As Carla speaks, her lower jaw stiffens and her large, brown eyes squint, exposing teeth-gritting strength, the embittering effects of poverty and abandonment, and an intense sense of responsibility for her loved ones. In her own mind, her future is clear. She tells me, with a mixture of determination and confidence, "I plan to get an athletic scholarship and go to college."

Although Carla's background makes her an unlikely candidate for school success, she is well connected to the school, both through her participation in the athletic program and her placement in honors' classes. Her precarious life in the *barrio*, however, places her at great risk. Her relationship to track team members is a key source of continuity and support. The team is a small, tightly knit group that includes the coaching staff as well as the student-athletes. The track coaches treat the girls like family, providing various kinds of help—including money, rides home, and a sympathetic ear when someone wants to talk over a problem. The coaches fear that Carla's recent friendships with "gangster-looking" types at school and her shift toward ganglike attire may jeopardize her dreams of success.

In response to a question I posed about why she dresses as she does, Carla states flatly that she has to be able to "fit in" in her neighborhood. She explains that, far from trying to make a statement, she is doing her best to *not* stand out in her neighborhood. And she sees her friendships quite differently than do her coaches. Carla says that she is merely spending more time with people whom she has known all of her life.

Carla's choices vividly convey the relationship between "fitting in" and survival, a connection that other research has documented among high-achieving, low-income African American youth (Fordham and Ogbu 1986). The irony of Carla's survival strategy is that it only works in one sphere: in her neighborhood, she blends perfectly into the scenery; at school, she calls unwanted attention to herself, even though her clothing actually strike a middle ground. Although her pants are baggy, they are not falling off her body and they are neatly pressed. She does not smoke nor does she display any tattoos. Unfortunately, these compromises seem to be going unnoticed—or unacknowledged—by her coaches.

There is a clear risk in Carla's efforts to negotiate two conflicting identities. If the adults at school view her as separating herself from the academic identity they would prefer that she sustain, Carla may not get the guidance she needs at the point she most needs it. A breakdown in the process of authentic caring could have extremely damaging effects. Carla's coaches care enough about her to notice apparent changes in her clothes and friends, but they fail to go beyond superficial assessments. Instead of empathizing with Carla's need to be an insider in her own community—as the authentic caring model that Noddings (1984) outlines would have the coaches do—they fall prey to aesthetic caring, emphasizing form over content. They interpret the changes they see in Carla as evidence of her failure to reciprocate their caring. They view her as oppositional, when in fact, she continues to care deeply about her future in the very terms they value.

Carla probably should reconsider the decisions she is making about friends and attire, but the "just-say-no" mentality that informs her teachers' judgments is not only unrealistic, but unappealing. Rather than encouraging dialogue and exploration into the complexity of students' lives, it encourages youth like Carla to square off in a defensive posture. Since her trust is not easily secured, a rush to judgment is experienced as heavy-handedness.

In the absence of complete information, teachers must rely on students' self-representations—including changes in their public identities—for signals about their deeper emotional and intellectual states. At the same time, it is important to remember that in some contexts meaning may be severed from representation. What may come across as youthful rebelliousness may be nothing more than youth exploring and finding ways to negotiate their lived experience as ethnic, bicultural human beings (Darder 1991). In an ironic twist of fate, this group's whole-hearted embrace of American urban youth culture—their grandly successful "assimilation"—is what assures their teachers' propensity to negatively label them.

"AMERICANIZED" IMMIGRANT YOUTH

In a schooling context that privileges a North American or English-speaking identity over a Mexican or Spanish-speaking one, there is strong pressure to assimilate subtractively. Because peer models favor the hip-hop attire and comportment that currently characterize urban, dispossessed youth, "American-ness" itself assumes a countercultural connotation. Thus, immigrant youth necessarily emulate a marginal peer group culture when fulfilling their desire to "fit in." The following situations provide some insights that help explain the finding of "accelerated *subtractive* assimilation" among some immigrant youth. These youth share many of the same problems as U.S.-born youth.

Outside Seguín's attendance office in spring 1994, I spoke at length with an immigrant mother whose daughter had not attended classes during any of the previous six-week grading period. Had a family emergency not brought the mother to campus that day, she might never have discovered that her daughter had been "withdrawn for inattendance." Until that day, she thought that her daughter had been attending school daily. The mother had approached an attendance officer to find out which class her daughter was in that period, only to discover that her daughter's name was not listed on any class roster. Because this woman was visibly distressed and the attendance officers were obviously busy with other students and parents, I approached her and offered my assistance.

With her arms wrapped around her waist, Mrs. Treviño doubled over and wept softly as I tried to guide her to the nearby steps in the center of the hall where she could sit down. *"Ha fallecido mi papá y tenemos que irnos a México y vengo a la escuela a descubrir esto?"* she cried. ("My father has died and we have to go to Mexico and I come to school to discover this?") I told her that I was sorry and I suggested that perhaps her daughter could make up the work in summer school. With an incredulous tone in her voice, Mrs. Treviño vented her anger with the school for failing to notify her of her daughter's lack of attendance:

> *Uno deja a sus hijos esperando que las escuelas los esten cuidando y no nos informan que nuestros hijos no han estado asistiendo. O esperan que nos digan nuestros hijos. Cómo nos van a decir ellos si ellos mismos son los que estan quebrando las reglas? Y que si le hubiera pasado algo a mi'jita . . . ? Entonces que?* (One leaves one's children trusting that the schools are taking care of them and they inform us that our children are not attending. Or they expect our children to tell us. How are they going to tell us if they're the ones breaking the rules? And what if something had happened to my daughter . . . ? Then what?)

Mrs. Treviño's daughter rounded the corner carrying textbooks in her arms. She was in the process of withdrawing from school and was returning her books to the registrar's office. I realized that I recognized her from a lunch time discussion during the previous fall semester. I was struck by the incongruity of this young woman being Mrs. Treviño's daughter. She wore extraordinarily baggy khaki pants—which somehow at the same time clung to her narrow hips—and her head was partially shaved in broad strokes around her ears, exposing olive-brown skin. She sported a tiny, golden nose earring. "Yes, I know you. You're Elvia, right? Do you remember me?" I asked. She acknowledged me with a slight nod. I also realized for the first time that she spoke Spanish. In a soft voice with her head lowered, the daughter said, *"Amá, tengo que entregar estos libros. Ahorita vuelvo por usted."* ("Mom, I have to turn in these books. I'll come back for you in a minute.") I also noted that she spoke formally to her mother, using the formal pronoun *"usted,"* instead of the more familiar form, *"tú."* Her mother's voice trembled as she told her daughter that now she would have to contend with her father. Looking humiliated, Elvia glanced at me and walked away.

> *Me da verguenza como se mira y como se viste. Verdadera-mente, me da verguenza! Y cómo la puedo llevar a México vestida así? Y con ese aretito? Imagínate? Ni parece Mexicana!* Mrs. Treviño lamented. ("The way she looks and dresses embarrasses me. It really embarrasses me! And how can I take her to Mexico like that? And with that little earring? Can you imagine? She doesn't even look Mexican!")

She then assured me that her daughter did not learn to be this way in their home. The mother added that she had two older sons and an older daughter, none of whom ever caused her any serious problems. *"Pero ésta, la mas chiquita, es fuerte de carácter!"* ("But this one, the youngest one, has a stubborn character!")

The family situation had been very unstable. Mr. Treviño was a migrant laborer who spent part of the year in Michigan harvesting beets and other vegetables. For the previous two years, he had also spent months at a time in Mexico helping take care of his father who was dying slowly from cancer. The family's story gushed out of Mrs. Treviño's mouth as she repeatedly wiped tears from her face. I embraced her and told her not to feel obligated to tell me anything.

"Al contrario, no quiero ser una molestia para usted," she said. ("To the contrary, it is I who does not wish to trouble you.")

"No es ninguna molestia," I assured her. ("It's no trouble whatsoever.")

So she continued, explaining that she worked evenings as a waitress while her older daughter, who held a daytime job, stayed at home with Elvia during the evenings. Elvia continually challenged her sister's authority and also had her friends over on a regular basis. They spent most of their time talking, although the mother also suspected that Elvia was taking drugs. She noted dryly that Elvia always underestimates her ability to detect the smell of marijuana or to recognize when she and her friends are high.

Mrs. Treviño thought that perhaps she had made a mistake by allowing Elvia to have her current set of friends. But she also admitted that her daughter had shown troubling tendencies since middle school. "*Es cuando empezó a vestirse como un Chicano. Siempre ha sido importante para ella ser aceptada por sus amigas y la influyen mucho,*" she mused. ("It's when she began to dress like a Chicano. It has always been important for her to be accepted by her friends.") By the time Elvia entered high school, Mrs. Treviño had decided not to make an issue of her daughter's attire. The haircut and the earring were recent additions. They had appeared this year when Elvia began hanging out with friends who spoke to one another either in English or in "Spanglish," a dialect that uses both languages. She laments that although she speaks to Elvia in Spanish, Elvia responds primarily in English: "*Y si puede hablar el Español pero parece que no le gusta.*" ("And she can speak Spanish but it seems as if she does not like to.") She found it strange that the daughter she had attempted to spare from the kind of hardships the family had endured earlier is the same one that she has now "lost." I asked her to elaborate. How had she "lost" Elvia?

The mother prefaced her explanation by saying that she was convinced that the success she had with her other children (all of whom had graduated from Seguín) was related to their prior schooling in Mexico. She left her children with their grandparents until they completed *primaria* (grade school). She remarked that leaving the children in Mexico while she and her husband lived and worked in Houston had been very hard—but it was impossible with her youngest. Then Mrs. Treviño sighed. Smiling faintly, she confessed with rueful affection, "*Me la traje conmigo. Yo no pude dejar a mi bebita, mi Elvita.*" ("I brought her with me. I could not leave my little baby, my Elvita.")

A few moments later, Elvia returned. I asked her if everything was okay. "Yeah, I just checked out of school," she replied, her eyes glistening, as if she might burst into tears at any moment.

"Don't worry, Mom," she said, "I'll make it up. I'll take summer school. I promise." With a look of disappointment on her face, her mother shook her head and rolled her eyes in disbelief. When her mother stepped away to use the restroom, I was able to talk to Elvia alone.

AV. It's pretty bad, huh?

ET. Yeah, I can't stand it. . . . I wish she was mad at me instead.

AV. So what's the problem? Why haven't you been going to classes?

ET. I just don't like school and I used to like it. I just can't get into my classes this year. They're all so boring and no one seems to care if I show up. And then they talk down to you when you do show up.

AV. What do you mean?

ET. It's like all of our teachers have given up and they don't want to teach us no more. In one class, I had a sub [substitute teacher] for all the time I was there, for four weeks! And he can't teach us nothing because he don't know math. The dude tried but that wasn't good enough, man! God, it just kills me to give that man even just a little bit of my time! If the *school* doesn't care about my learning, why should *I* care? Answer me that. Just answer me that! A friend of mine dropped out of high school, took her GED, and went on to college. I tell my Mom that's what I want to do, but it's like she don't get it.

AV. So what was your brothers' and sister's experience here at Seguín?

ET. They just took all the crap you get here. It's like, "You're Mexican; take crap." Well, man, I got some pride and self-respect. "Sorry to disappoint you, but *this* Mexican don't take crap." Mexicans who do, embarrass the hell out of me. I just want to tell them, "Lay off the humble trip, man. You some damn *Indio* (Indian) or something?"

Elvia's anger with and alienation from schooling is unmistakable. Her questionable choice in friends combined with insufficient parental monitoring to influence her disaffection from schooling. She was in need of much more concerted attention than an older sister could provide. Whereas certain "shortcuts" or compromises taken within families may be expedient and perhaps unavoidable at the time—especially for poor families struggling to make ends meet—the end result can be disastrous.

Further complicating matters at school was a lack of authentic caring as well as a lack of aesthetic caring in one of her classes that stretched Elvia beyond her limits. Her story made me wonder whether, if she and I traded places, I would be able to tolerate such a bad situation for very long. Elvia's case also brings to the foreground a schooling strategy that is increasingly common among youth in HISD schools: they drop out of high school, secure a General Equivalency Diploma, and enroll in community college.[4]

Elvia's dramatic departure from her siblings' educational experiences is partly evident in her unflattering portrayal of Mexican immigrants. She sees them as spineless individuals, lacking in "pride and self-respect." She further attributes this weakness to cultural factors—that is, to their "Indian-ness." Although expressed off-handedly, Elvia's dismissal of immigrants reveals the complexities of a colonized *mestiza* (Spanish and Indian mixed-blood) undergoing a personal decolonization process. Even as Elvia asserts her Mexican identity in a U.S. context, she negates her indigenous ancestry. "De-Indianization" is a manifestation of the subtractive assimilation processes that operate at a transnational level wherever indigenous communities are viewed with contempt.[5] I never saw Elvia again, but I noted with relief and pleasure that her name was included on the school roster in the attendance office the following year.

Rapid cultural assimilation, marked by a strong orientation either to the peer group or to the culture of the peer group, characterized every immigrant youth I observed who conformed to the "uncaring student" prototype. The contrast in language, clothing, demeanor, and other cultural markers between these young people and their parents is stark. Whatever its source, a need for acceptance by the more Americanized peer group appears to contribute to youths' accelerated effort to assimilate.

In the handful of cases of rapidly culturally assimilated students I observed, the most vulnerable youth within the immigrant generation were those who had been born in Mexico or Latin America but who had lived most of their lives and had been schooled in the United States. These teens, of whom Elvia is a striking example, more closely resemble their U.S.-born peers than their immigrant counterparts and are referred to in the literature as "1.5 generation" youth (Vigil 1997). Still, even the recently arrived are sometimes drawn into accelerated cultural assimilation, as a story told to me by an immigrant mother who was also a custodial worker at the high school, illustrates.

Mrs. Galvez, a single mother with three sons, had been living in the United States for approximately six years. She told me that her oldest son, Ignacio, was her biggest worry. In fact, he was the reason that she had taken a daytime job at Seguín as a custodial worker over a higher-paying evening job at a shipping company. She worked the same hours that her sons attended high school so that she could also be at home with them at night. Notwithstanding his mother's efforts, Ignacio dropped out of school at the beginning of his tenth-grade year *"porque no le gustó"* ("because he didn't like it"). Mrs. Galvez believed that her son's decision was partly a consequence of her divorce from her husband, which had been finalized nine months earlier, during the fall semester when Ignacio dropped out. When his father returned to Mexico shortly after the divorce, Ignacio became withdrawn and depressed.

Mrs. Galvez was currently trying to get her son to return home; he was living with a young white woman whom he had met at a rock concert. He had moved in with this woman after he and Mrs. Galvez had argued over a one hundred dollar bill that had gone missing from his mother's purse. After Mrs. Galvez had tricked Ignacio into admitting that he had taken the money, she told him that if he wasn't going to attend school, he would have to get a full-time job to help support the family. The argument escalated and then ended abruptly when Ignacio bolted from the house. About one-and-a-half months had passed since the argument. Mrs. Galvez still had not seen her son, but she had spoken to him the day before. *"Creo que ahora quiere regresarse a la casa,"* she told me ("I believe he wants to return home now").

She felt that Ignacio was punishing her for the divorce. From her perspective, the divorce had been a matter of self-respect. Her husband had been unfaithful and had taken several *queridas* (lovers) over the course of their marriage. *"También le gustaba la tomada,"* she added ("He also liked to drink.") Her ex-husband's philandering had made home life stressful. His most recent affair proved to be more than Mrs. Galvez was willing to bear. She ordered him out. Sadly, in ridding herself of an abusive husband, she also rid her children of their father. They lost contact with him after he returned to Mexico. Plaintively, Mrs. Galvez summed up the situation: *"Ni una sola llamada. Ésto es lo que mas ha afectado a mis hijos, especialmente al mayor.*" ("Not even a single call. This is what has most affected my sons, especially the oldest.") Ignacio may have been angry with his father for not keeping in touch with the family, "*Pero también lo extraña mucho,*" Mrs. Galvez observed. ("But he also misses [his father] a lot.")

She was not completely sure why of all her children it was her oldest son who seemed the most affected by the father's absence, but she thought that it probably had something to do with the fact that they were very close when Ignacio was just a child, before the extramarital affairs began. Not having any relatives living nearby may have been another contributing factor.

I asked her to elaborate on her son's changes. She said that he had undergone a fairly rapid transformation. "*No lo podía creer!*" ("I couldn't believe it!") she exclaimed. Several months prior to the divorce, but when his parents were already separated, Ignacio stopped wearing belts and began wearing baggy pants and black T-shirts adorned with what looked to Mrs. Galvez like diabolical designs and messages. He began listening to heavy metal music for hours, stretched out on his bed, with his tape recorder headset on. He would come out of his bedroom long enough for a quiet dinner and then retreat to his room once again.

After he dropped out of Seguín, Ignacio cultivated the habit of sleeping through the day and staying up through the night. This schedule left his mother uncertain about exactly what he was up to. Though he had taken money from her, she suspected that he was getting money from somewhere besides her purse, because he could afford to attend concerts. He told her that he earned money doing odd jobs as a day laborer; she could never confirm this because she was always at work. Several tattoos appeared on his upper arms and he had his head partially shaved. Ignacio had transformed his bedroom wall into a giant mural, filled with pictures that he tore out of rock music and car magazines. What most worried his mother was that, except for the girlfriend, Ignacio did not seem to have any friends, "*Y rehusa hablar conmigo*" ("And he refuses to talk to me").

I suggested the possibility of either individual or family counseling. Mrs. Galvez said that she had already gotten a referral for her son to see a professional counselor from Communities in

Schools (CIS), but Ignacio had failed to show up for his scheduled appointment. That Ignacio had requested the appointment himself suggested that he knew he was in need of help. Mrs. Galvez commented on how hard it is to raise children in this society. In Spanish, she said, "There's so much confusion. In trying to be someone else, Ignacio forgot who he was." She wished that the school could help her son, and others like him, with the kind of counseling they need to make wiser decisions. As a high school custodial worker, she sees how many youth are tempted to go off in the wrong direction. Her conversation with her son earlier that day had left her hopeful.

"*Espero que regrese pronto a la casa. Creo que ya se le ha acabado el dinero,*" she confided. ("I expect him to return home soon. I think he ran out of money.")

"*Sería bueno,*" I agree. ("That would be good.")

Growing nervous about the time we had spent talking, Mrs. Galvez shook my hand, and then quickly made her way to the nearby teachers' lounge, clutching her dust-mop.

Both Elvia and Ignacio express a need to belong or to "fit in" to the peer group of the dominant culture. The more worrisome of the two teenagers is the solitary and despondent Ignacio who recognizes that he has a serious problem and needs help, but can't quite make it happen. Since schooling factors distinguished Elvia from her siblings, I made a point of inquiring further about Ignacio's schooling experiences the next time I ran into Mrs. Galvez.

Mrs. Galvez said that Ignacio had been a diligent student in Mexico but that the *primaria* (elementary school) he had attended through the fifth grade had not been particularly good. Ignacio had attended a rural school near the family's home in the countryside outside of San Luis Potosí, Mexico. Low teacher salaries and poor working conditions, especially very large class sizes, resulted in a high attrition rate among the school's students and staff. The lack of staff had resulted in the school being closed for half a year when Ignacio was to have entered the first grade. Though she had not given it much thought because Ignacio never talked about school, Mrs. Galvez said that Ignacio's prior learning experiences in Mexico may have contributed to his apparent unhappiness with school in the United States.

Ignacio serves as an important reminder that not all immigrant youth are able to translate their schooling experiences in Mexico into a positive schooling experience in the United States, as the following chapter finds, is generally the case. Schools in the homeland must also have been accessible and able to provide youth with continuous learning experiences. In the absence of such a foundation, immigrant youth are at great risk of dropping out of school. If, in addition, they strive for rapid cultural assimilation, the result may be acute maladjustment. In their rush to claim a new identity, these young people become marginal not only with respect to the academic mainstream, but also in relation to their family's social identity. This dynamic is clear in both students' cases; their mothers agonize over the "loss" of their children. In each case, what had been lost was the child's Mexican cultural identity.

Though revealing the importance of prior schooling experiences, the preceding discussion also highlights the interplay between subtractive cultural assimilation and student disaffection. With her wish for a school-based "cultural therapy," Ignacio's mother conveys her recognition of the destabilizing consequences of rapid cultural change, as well as her belief in schools' potential for playing a productive role in helping youth negotiate their emergent cultural identities. Her son's psychological well-being could have been better protected had the school mediated a discussion of the potential pitfalls that exist in the dominant culture, as well as the dangers attendant upon the attempt to assimilate very quickly.

From a critical perspective on biculturalism (Darder 1991, 1995), students' "choices" in identity, however constrained, are optimally premised on an affirmation of the new identity that effectively expands one's cultural and linguistic repertoire. "Choices" based on a disaffirmation of self—that is, one's original identity—is hardly a choice at all since this set of options pits one culture against the other. Expressed differently, the two cases reveal the alienating consequences of schools' failure to be additive, by confirming the language, history, and experiences of the cultural "other." If some immigrant youth are susceptible to the messages that demean their worth, how much more vulnerable are U.S.-born youth—whose Mexican identities are often less firm—to such messages? The following section examines some of the ways in which students resist these messages.

"NOT CARING" AS STUDENT RESISTANCE

What looks to teachers and administrators like opposition and lack of caring, feels to students like powerlessness and alienation. Some students' clear perception of the weakness of their position politicizes them into deliberately conveying an uncaring attitude as a form of resistance not to education, but to the irrelevant, uncaring, and controlling aspects of schooling (Callahan 1962; LeCompte and Dworkin 1991). Take Frank, for example.

Frank is an unusually reflective ninth-grader. As a C-student, he achieves far below his potential. One of Frank's teachers, Mr. Murray, tells him that if he would only apply himself more, he could prepare himself well for college. Instead, Frank exerts himself only when a classroom assignment happens to interest him. Mr. Murray, who correctly noted and followed up on Frank's interest in science, has become the boy's mentor and sounding board. Whereas Mr. Murray sees Frank as he truly is—as a "thinker"—his other teachers generally perceive him as passive and indifferent. In a very thoughtful, intense discussion with me, Frank explained his approach to schooling:

> FRANK. I don't get with the program because then it's doing what *they* [teachers] want for my life. I see *Mexicanos* who follow the program so they can go to college, get rich, move out of the *barrio*, and never return to give back to their *gente* [people]. Is that what this is all about? If I get with the program, I'm saying that's what it's all about and that teachers are right when they're not. Except for Mr. Murray, I don't care what teachers think because then they can control me.
>
> AV. Does Mr. Murray control you?
>
> FRANK (*smiling*). He does make me think about college but I still ask myself for what. I could go to college if I wished, but for what?

For Frank, not caring constitutes resistance to teachers, school, and a curriculum that he views as meaningless because it is not helping him to become a "better" person, that is, a socially minded individual who cares about his community. Moreover, teachers' definition of caring—which involves a commitment to a predetermined set of ideas—is equivalent to cultural genocide. Success in school means consenting to the school's project of cultural disparagement and de-identification. Frank is not unwilling to become a productive member of society; he is simply at odds with a definition of productivity that is divorced from the social and economic interests of the broader Mexican community. With his indifference, Frank deliberately challenges schooling's implicit demand that he derogate his culture and community.

Frank's critique of schooling approximates that of Tisa, another astute U.S.-born, female student that I came across in the course of my group interviews ("Friends from the 'Hood" group). When I asked Tisa whether a college education was necessary in order to have a nice house and car, and to live in a nice neighborhood, she provided the following response:

> You can make good money dealing drugs, but all the dealers— even if they drive great cars—they still spend their lives in the 'hood. Not to knock the 'hood at all. . . . If only us *raza* [the Mexican American people] could find a way to have all three, money . . . *clean* money, education, and the 'hood.

In a very diplomatic way, she took issue with the way I framed the question. Rather than setting up two mutually compatible options of being successful and remaining in one's home community, Tisa interpreted my question in either/or terms that in her mind unfairly juxtaposed success to living in the 'hood. That I myself failed to anticipate its potentially subtractive logic—at least according to one legitimate interpretation—caused me to reflect on the power of the dominant narrative of mobility in U.S.-society—an "out-of-the-*barrio*" motif, as it were (Chavez 1991; but also see Suro 1998).[6] These findings bring to mind the ethos that Ladson-Billings (1994) identifies as central to culturally relevant pedagogy for African American youth. Specifically, effective teachers of African American children see their role as one of "giving back to the community."

Returning to Frank, his relationship with Mr. Murray inspires hope. His teacher reminds him that he does really care about education. Because his other teachers do not distinguish between schooling and education, they are unlikely to notice and nurture Frank's interests the way Mr. Murray has.

I asked Frank if he ever expresses his very thoughtful and important opinions in class. He says no, explaining that he's sure that he'd never get any "backup" from other students.

"Mexicans are too damned polite, taking whatever it is the teacher tells them. It's like you say something and it's like you never said anything when no one says, 'Yeah, Frank, what you said was right.'"

"Why don't Mexicans speak up?" I question.

"Because they're afraid of what the teacher will say, or they think other students will laugh at them, or maybe it's like no one ever does, so what's the use?" Aggravated, Frank asserts, "It doesn't matter to speak up anyway. For what? What's the point? So I never open my mouth."

As critical as Frank is about the subtractive nature of the curriculum, his relationship with Mr. Murray illustrates that at least in the short term, there is a possibility of salvaging disaffected youth through a caring relationship. Mr. Murray demonstrates genuine interest in Frank as a person. Most of the time the two spend talking, they focus on topics of interest to Frank; sometimes these include science, sometimes not. The mainstream curriculum is thus demonstrably accessible through a route responsive to students' definition of caring, that is, *caring as relation*.

A senior male, Rodrigo's approach is an even clearer example of how some students use "not caring" as a strategy of resistance. Though capable of excelling in honors' classes, he chooses to remain in the regular curriculum to which he had automatically been assigned after transferring to Seguín from a magnet school in another area of the city. Besides being an avid reader, Rodrigo has been writing poetry and prose for much of his young life. Wellsprings of inner strength emanate, in great part, from his role in his family's protracted struggle with his mother's long-standing comatose condition. "The last time I saw my mother was in kindergarten," he reminisces, referring to the last time he saw her as a whole, healthy person. After seeing Rodrigo off to school one day, she went to the hospital for a routine hysterectomy. During the operation, human error resulted in oxygen loss to her brain, causing extensive brain damage. Despite a decent monetary settlement and the passage of more than a decade, neither Rodrigo's father nor his two older half-sisters and half-brother have fully recovered from this catastrophe.

Rodrigo's breadth of knowledge of Chicana and Chicano literature easily rivals that of any college graduate specializing in this field. Not only does he have detailed knowledge of poetry and fiction, poets and authors, he also knows which publishers are the most progressive on questions of multiculturalism. He has an expansive portfolio of written works, parts of which he takes to high schools and community gatherings where he has been invited to read. Gifts of books from publishers, professors, and other donors stand on shelves alongside those he purchases, filling a large space that he refers to as his "library" in his backyard garage.

Rodrigo laces his conversation with lines of poetry from various works, including his own. A memorable verse from one of his poems, titled "Woman," brought tears to my eyes as it flowed sweetly from his mouth: "I have touched Mexican women, but not as much as they have touched me." Personal tragedy, coupled with his literary expeditions, have made of Rodrigo the feminist he is today.

When he and I first met, Rodrigo was involved in preparations to teach a multicultural literature class after school to at least ten fellow students who had expressed interest. Although he secured the principal's permission to teach the class, in the end, Rodrigo's plans came to nothing. The principal was unable to come up with the funds needed to cover the cost of the text Rodrigo wanted to use. The process of preparing the class was an education in itself. According to Rodrigo, when he came into contact with teachers at the high school who had not met him before, they wondered where this remarkable young man had come from. Some wondered, as well, whether he might be half white because of the lightness of his complexion. Rodrigo was insulted by the implication that a dark-skinned Mexican could not be either as gifted or as accomplished as he. One of the aims of his course was to combat just that kind of stereotyping, as well as other negative images teachers held toward his fellow students in the regular curriculum track:

> They have this image of kids, that we are just messed up in the head. That's not really true because many students here—I think their intellectual ability is just too high for them to be in regular classes, but they don't enter honors classes. There are people out there who just think that we are into sex and drugs. That's not true. I can't say that I'm just one exception because

there are many exceptions. At this school, there are many students, but some teachers at this school . . . I'll start saying this
because it's true. Certain teachers say, "No, let's not read this.
This is too hard for these kids. No, let's not read John Keats.
No, Shakespeare's Hamlet. Let's show the movie or let's not
learn about Excalibur. Let's not read it, but let's watch the
film." That's something that I see, always some other kind of
source that they turn to that is some kind of a secondary source,
something that is not on level, but a little bit more basic.

Rodrigo's decision to remain in the regular track at Seguín
was influenced by his disappointment with the magnet program
at the high school in which he had been enrolled before transferring to Seguín. "There they paid more attention to the grades
rather than to your thinking ability," he said. One result of this
narrow focus, Rodrigo observed, was that although "kids have
good arguments . . . they have absolutely no argument skills.
The only argument they have is probably to curse. Say the F-
word and that's it." He added that if it were not for his commitment to self-education, he would never have realized how
wrong-headedly schools approach their mandate to educate. He
further speculated that it was his independent-mindedness that
made school tolerable and kept him from dropping out. He
blamed widespread academic failure on the administration and
teachers, not on the students. Schooling was thus an obstacle to
Rodrigo's education and his devaluation of scholastic achievement represented his silent rebellion against uninspiring curricula, misplaced priorities, and teachers' lowered expectations.
Health was the class he valued the most at Seguín. In a pragmatic tone, he remarked, "Health is important to keep your
body maintained."

Rejected from Rice University and the University of Houston
because his high school grades and SAT scores were low, Rodrigo
enrolled as an undergraduate student at Kenyon College, a prestigious liberal arts college in the Midwest. He found out about the
college from an information brochure he plucked out of the
wastebasket in a Seguín counselor's office. The school looked
beyond the "objective" data of grades and raw scores and admitted Rodrigo on the basis of his vast and creative intellect. The earlier rejections still rankle, however:

U of H told me that I needed to apply through special admissions. I told them, "No! Look at my portfolio. This is who I am and what I can do. If I didn't do well in school, it's because I didn't care about school. It wasn't challenging. Accept me for who I am, not for some number or letter on a piece of paper."

Rodrigo's words and experiences summarize students' experiences, generally, of profound alienation from, and hostility toward, uncaring bureaucracies. Universities' and colleges' insistence on evidence of student conformity to the high school curriculum, regardless of whether that curriculum is challenging and supportive or degrading and meaningless, closes off an important avenue of advancement for many potentially productive youth. There is little reason to bother aspiring to higher education if the price of admission must be prepaid in yearly installments of humiliation and alienation. Making schools and schooling affirmative, truly educational experiences for all students requires implementing changes that reach deep into the structure of the educational system. Using daily life at Seguín as a guide, the first and arguably the most important step is to introduce a culture of authentic caring that incorporates all members of the school community as valued and respected partners in education. The next section explores some of the positive effects that emerge when teachers and teachers, as well as teachers and students truly connect with one another.

CARING AND PEDAGOGY

The art of initiating a relationship is well expressed through the words of one of Seguín's most beloved social studies teachers, Ms. Aranda. In my interview with her, she conveys her philosophy of teaching as caring:

> Kids have to know the line so that they know not to cross it and so they know that they've crossed it. Whenever students are acting up, I take them out of the classroom and ask them, "What have I done that would cause you to act that way?" This question always disarms them because usually they can't imagine that me, a teacher, would suggest that I had done something wrong. And then after they say either yes, that I was the prob-

lem because they thought I was picking on them in class or no. I ask them what it is that's causing them to act in the way that they do? I always try to work things out with them individually. Sometimes, kids have certain problems that make me work out a personal arrangement with them. Like if they work a lot at night, I may tell them that they don't need to take a test but that they could be evaluated by pursuing another kind of project. What's important is that they need to know that I am fair, that I will listen to them, that they can come to me and talk and deal with a problem.

The need for a culturally sensitive curriculum is not lost on Ms. Aranda who works at structuring her classes so that all students feel included:

ESL kids are the most shy and they benefit a lot from group activities. I provide opportunities for them by giving them the chance to bring something of interest from their country for show and tell. This gets them talking. I also provide opportunities for them by allowing them to work on assignments bilingual—like a bilingual newspaper. Or I allow them to write a story about an event that goes on along the border. So the paper might deal with Piedras Negras or something like that.

Since Ms. Aranda is also the chair of the Social Studies Department, her leadership is key. Their collectivist, team-building approach makes it one of the stronger academic departments on campus. Consider further Ms. Aranda's winning strategy:

Collaborative planning with teachers is essential. Teachers need to share with other teachers, exchange information and ideas, and they need to feel supported for their efforts. Teachers who have less time don't necessarily have to be creative. They just have to be able to copy. So we meet a lot, which is something that other teachers don't do. And so while it might seem like an extra demand that's placed on them, it gets passed off as support because we all happen to get along.

The productive power of healthy professional relationships rings clear in Ms. Aranda's account. She exemplifies the desirable qualities Assistant Principal Ana Luera is attempting to develop in other teachers. Interestingly, one advantageous factor mentioned by faculty inside and outside the Social Studies Department is that they are at greater liberty to provide an enriching curriculum because they are far less responsible for raising students' test scores than their counterparts in mathematics and English. Since no comparable social studies' test exists, these teachers are not reduced to the curricular imperative that they "teach to the test."

Though I did not have the opportunity to examine in greater depth the extent to which all other social studies departmental members embody Ms. Aranda's near-perfect mix between aesthetic and authentic caring, one thing is certain. Through her leadership, she helps create space and opportunity for her faculty to advance beyond the aesthetic, or technical, toward a more authentic pedagogy. Ms. Aranda is thus helping build a framework for institutionalized caring. At least one other faculty member I came to know in her department responds on cue.

Ms. Novak, a youngish African-American teacher, is an exceptionally caring and giving individual who openly expresses her love for her students: "I just love the ninth-graders. I think they're so funny! I don't know why other teachers don't like them. I only like the ninth grade! They make me laugh all the time." The following representative comments expressed by students I came across of both Ms. Aranda and Ms. Novak reveal the power of their double-barreled caring:

> Ms. Novak is the best teacher I ever had. The way she laughs at us makes us happy, you know, like she *really* likes us. I learn easier that way. (Third-generation, ninth-grade female student)

> What makes Ms. Novak a great teacher is that she's organized and laid-back at the same time. Everything looked too pretty, too stiff when I first walked in her room. But now I see that she's just doing everything she can to make sure that we learn and that we're happy about learning, too. Even when I'm sick, I still come to school to be in her class because she makes you feel nice, you know, like you're wanted or something. (Second-generation, ninth-grade male student)

> Ms. Aranda is the best teacher I ever had. I never got bored in her class. And I learned so much. I came to respect her even more after she helped out this friend. She wanted to drop out of school and missed a lot of homework and tests. Other teachers

flunked her but Ms. Aranda helped her catch up. If something like that came up with me, I know I could go to her with it. (Second-generation, ninth-grade female student)

Like I like the way Ms. Aranda is nice to the ESL students. It's like they just got here and they need special help. They got to do some stuff [assignments] in Spanish and we all learned. It's nice to see your language be part of your learning. It's like, wow! That's me, my culture, my language. . . . She's *gente* [good people]! (Third-generation, ninth-grade male student)

Some of the most compelling evidence that students do care about education despite their rejection of schooling is found among the great number of students who skip most classes chronically, but who regularly attend one class that is meaningful to them. Terry is a good example of this group. Although his overall attendance is erratic, he never misses his mechanics class. Auto mechanics, taught by Mr. Lundgren, is the only class where he feels he really learns something. Mr. Lundgren confirms that he sees many boys like Terry. He tells me that these boys find most of their classes irrelevant and thus consider them unimportant: "Mechanics is more closely connected to their sense of the future than their academic classes." Mr. Lundgren is certain that were it not for the CTE vocational courses, many more students would find school meaningless and drop out. His sentiments are shared unanimously by Seguín's other CTE teachers.

My extensive observations of the CTE program lead me to conclude that the acquisition of work skills is compatible with the acquisition of both academic knowledge and an aspiration for postsecondary education. Most CTE teachers make a point of positively reinforcing the academic curriculum. They feel misunderstood by their colleagues in mainstream academic fields, who tend to dismiss the CTE program on the mistaken grounds that it is insufficiently intellectually rigorous. Several CTE teachers told me that they suspected that part of the reason for the disdainful treatment they often receive from other teachers and administrators was simple envy: CTE staff earn higher salaries, teach smaller classes, and have final say over which students may enroll in the higher-level courses they teach.

Mr. Lundgren provides a good model of a positive interface

between the academic curriculum and the CTE program. He pays close attention to his students' writing. When he assigns a descriptive paper on internal combustion, for example, he knows that the majority will find the subject interesting and thus he expects—and requires—that his students produce well-written papers. In addition, after he grades the papers, he gives every student a chance to rewrite the assignment if they want to try for a higher grade. Because Mr. Lundgren provides a detailed evaluation on each paper he hands back, most students take advantage of the opportunity to rewrite. Few settle for a poor grade on a written assignment.

In some cases, Mr. Lundgren gives his Spanish-dominant students the opportunity to do the assignment in Spanish. He mentioned a female student whose poor English-language skills would have made the paper assignment overwhelming. "She struggles a little bit but she does read a little bit in English." For the most part, language is not a barrier for Mr. Lundgren, partly because he understands some Spanish, but also because he makes use of other students in his class. "The ones who don't understand [English], I know who they are and they're sitting next to a friend of theirs who translates to them and tells them what I expect," he says. While I found his capacity and willingness to reach out to students extraordinary, Mr. Lundgren could not have been more unassuming about his approach: "My goal is to get them to write and what language they write in makes no difference to me."

Mr. Lundgren regularly counsels students, advising all—and convincing a few—that to be good mechanics, they need math and that to be able to run their own auto shops, they need to be able to read and write well. Mr. Lundgren indicated to me that what Terry (and others like him) needs is someone to care enough to take the time to help him see the connections between what he learns in school and what he wants to do with his life.

The virtues of a standardized curriculum that middle-class youth take for granted are difficult for the Terrys of the world to appreciate. Terry's behavior is his critique of schooling, namely, that it is meaningless, unrewarding, and irrelevant to his life. Terry did change his behavior the following semester largely because of Mr. Lundgren's advice, encouragement, and gentle prodding. Whereas Terry skipped continuously before, he now religiously attends all of his classes. He now desires to work toward the goal of owning his own auto mechanics shop someday. Like the scores of youth who skip every single class except the one where a caring teacher may be found, Terry's renewed interest in school is directly attributable to Mr. Lundgren's connectedness to him.

Though I never pursued the issue, Mr. Lundgren made me contemplate the effects of an inclusive pedagogy that respects all youth regardless of their linguistic abilities. While the immigrant youth he mentioned directly benefited, it is easy to imagine that his capacity to work with youths' differences have contributed to the authority he commands in the classroom. Since relationships with teachers like Mr. Lundgren are often either short-lived or nonexistent, however, Seguín would do well to heed Noddings' (1992) call for continuity (in place, people, and curriculum). Such continuity permits the development of trusting relationships and preempts students from turning exclusively to peers and strategies for academic survival that often increase their marginalization.

WHEN TEACHERS DO NOT INITIATE RELATION

Students' desire for reciprocal relationships with adults at school is tempered by their experience, which teaches them not to expect such relationships. As Noddings (1984) has noted, students' weak power position relative to school personnel makes it incumbent that the adults be the initiators of social relationships. Mark, an academically average ninth-grade student, explains why he is content to achieve far below his potential:

> MARK. It's cool to look like you don't care 'bout nuthin' 'cause then you're bad. Maybe some students act that way to get at the teachers, I don't know. I do it just to be cool, I guess, though I don't really think about it.
>
> AV. But underneath, you really care about school, huh?
>
> MARK (pausing). Yeah, I guess so.
>
> AV. You had to think about that.
>
> MARK. I know like school is good for me, but there's lots of things I don't like about it.

AV. Like what?

MARK. I don't know, I can't explain.

AV. Like your classes?

MARK. The teachers . . . they're not bad. It's just that they're not good.

Further discussion elicited the basis for Mark's assessment. He had attended a Catholic private school during the eighth grade because his parents were concerned about his declining grades and the rowdy set of boys he had befriended. He told me that he had accepted his parents' decision because he was not learning much in his middle school anyway.

With each addition to his story, Mark's thin layers of aloofness and defensiveness dissolved, exposing an impish personality. I began to anticipate a "punch line." He said that he had really enjoyed his one-year stay at the school, and he would have continued, except that his parents could not afford the tuition after his father had lost his job as the manager of a small business. Mark recalled how the interest that one of the nuns, Sister Mary Agnes, took in him helped him to discover that he had an instinctive talent for world geography.

"I can name you the capital of almost any country in the world," he boasted.

"What's the capital of Ireland?" I quizzed.

"Dublin."

"Zaire?"

"Kinshasa."

"Honduras?"

"Tegucigalpa."

"Excellent!" I exclaimed, simultaneously realizing that it was this unusual talent for geography that was his punch line.

"I don't know why, it just comes to me," he said, snapping his fingers as the ends of his lips turned downward, with pride. "I know all the states and capitals in the U.S. and Mexico, too." The pleasure apparent in his now-radiant face contrasted sharply with the studied nonchalance he had displayed at the beginning of our conversation.

"She took me just like I was, you know, like I don't want to be pushed to do things, like I need time to think about it," he continued, explaining his relationship with Sister Mary Agnes. Most importantly, she let him use her computer with the world atlas software on it.

"I liked it so much! It'd be just me 'n her after school sometimes," he reminisced.

Stimulated by his year with Sister Mary Agnes, Mark has become an avid map collector. During his family's summer trip to and from Mexico, he applied his newly developed talent by assuming primary responsibility for navigating. To encourage his interest, Mark's parents promised to buy him a world atlas for his next birthday.

He regretted losing touch with his former teacher, paying her homage with his description: She was *"really, really* cool," with all her students. "No one here is like the Sister," he added, softly. "She liked you no matter how you were or how you looked." I asked Mark whether he had a map for his life. He said that he would like to do something connected with maps or travel.

"The Sister said that I could be a plane pilot and I liked that," he said, smiling.

"So you'll need to go to college first," I suggested.

"Yeah, she talked to me about that, too."

I hoped that Mark would really do as I asked when we parted—keep reaching for the sky.

Sister Mary Agnes' capacity to accept her students unconditionally had a profound impact on Mark's life. This aura of acceptance lured him into her sphere; but it was the nun's quick apprehension that Mark needed a chance to work alone and at his own pace that brought out the very best in him. Mark learned much more than world geography from Sister Mary Agnes. Her authentically caring attitude set him free to discover some important things about himself. Not only was he an unusually talented geographer, he was also a special person, capable and worthy of the friendship of the *"really, really* cool" Sister Mary Agnes.

It remains to be seen whether Mark will experience any similarly affirming relationships during his years at Seguín. The thinness of his aloofness and the strength of his newfound talent provide some hope that another perceptive teacher will continue where Sister Mary Agnes left off. Until this happens, Mark's peer group will be his most prominent source of school-based connectedness.

However understandable, even justifiable, students' "uncaring" attitudes can make them not merely vulnerable, but virtually invisible, as Mark's and now Ronny's case demonstrates. I met Ronny, a tall, heavy-set, wannabe gangster with a short-cropped crew cut, during a visit I made to his ninth-grade English class. He denies being in a gang, but his two best friends are known to be involved in gang activity. Ronny has been a good reader since elementary school, but he fails to complete half of his homework assignments because they bore him. At home, he reads mystery novels. At school, he shares the stories' plotlines with his friends, who think he's smart.

The English teacher tells me that Ronny never speaks a word in class, though he attends daily. Holding stacks of papers to grade, the teacher sighs, "He just sits there in the corner, and I figure I'll leave him alone if he leaves me alone." Ronny's tough appearance makes him seem unapproachable, even to other students; his teachers never call on him. Ronny prefers the status quo. When I see him later, during his lunch hour, we converse and he is surprisingly friendly. I ask him why he even goes to class if he doesn't participate. He said that he had always "gotten by" with just going to class.

"For all my teachers, it has always been enough—and it's funny how they never, never call on me."

"Maybe because you look scary," I think to myself. "But you're a smart guy," I insist, "why don't you give school greater importance?"

"Well, my friends think I'm smart, but I'm not so sure."

"Don't you like to learn?" I ask.

"It's not that I don't want to learn, it's *what* I learn that matters. Maybe I'm lazy, but teachers could also make school more fun. And besides, I'm doing what I have to do to not flunk and I never do flunk."

"Since you know how to pass and beat the system, why don't you think about going to college?" I ask him.

"I don't think I could do it. My cousin went. He even had a scholarship and he dropped out after the first semester . . . said it was too hard. He graduated from here, too, and he's smarter than me so I don't think I could handle it."

I spent a few more minutes trying to get him to reconsider his decision about college. He told me that he had not really decided against college. He simply did not know enough about it to make an informed decision. I was the first person who had ever talked to him seriously about this possibility.

Ronny's teachers are well positioned to advise him about college but his demeanor and his attire reduce the chances that such a discussion might ever take place. Students like Ronny, those who are subdued and do not cause trouble, are among the easiest to overlook, regardless of their potential. Of further significance is Ronny's disconnectedness from his English class, despite his continued interest in reading. Because schools fail to create environments that nurture the kinds of meaningful experiences that would allow learning to follow naturally, important opportunities for growth are missed (McNeil 1988; Smith 1995). As schooling is currently structured at Seguín, alienation and tension between students and school personnel is ongoing and unavoidable. This corrosive daily atmosphere negates the possibility of creating the collective contexts that facilitate the transmission of knowledge, skills, and resources.

CONTRIBUTIONS AND LIMITATIONS OF THE CARING AND EDUCATION LITERATURE

The literature on caring is properly premised on the notion that individuals need to be recognized and addressed as whole beings. All people share a basic need to be understood, appreciated, and respected. Among many acculturated, U.S.-born, Mexican American youth at Seguín, however, these basic needs go unmet during the hours at which they are in school. These students' culturally assimilated status only exacerbates the problems inherent in an institutional relationship that defines them as in need of continuing socialization (DeVillar 1994).

My findings show that American urban youth culture, filtered through a Mexican American ethnic minority experience, is at odds with adults' tastes and preferences in dress and self-representation. This generational divide combines with a subtractive schooling experience to heighten students' sense of disconnectedness from school and also to remind them of their lack of power.

Rodrigo conveys teens' sense of powerlessness at school in his observation that "Kids have good arguments, but they have absolutely no argument skills." Unable to articulate their frustration and alienation effectively, and inexperienced with even the idea of collective action, most regular-track students settle for individual-level resistance. They engage in random acts of rebellion, posture and pose, mentally absent themselves, physically absent themselves, or attend and participate in only those classes that interest them. The few students who *are* adept articulators, like Rodrigo, condemn schooling, not education.

The maladaptive consequences of subtractive schooling are magnified among immigrant youth who try to acculturate very rapidly. The suggestion by one parent that the school should help youth sort out their cultural issues as they undergo change is echoed by Spindler and Spindler (1994), who contend that schools should engage explicitly in cultural therapy. They suggest that culturally appropriate training might allow teachers to help students better understand themselves and thus make it possible for youth to learn "with less rancor and resistance." (p. xiv)

By examining misunderstandings of caring, a fundamental source of students' alienation and resistance becomes apparent. Schools like Seguín not only fail to validate their students' culture, they also subtract resources from them, first by impeding the development of authentic caring; and secondly, by obliging youth to participate in a non-neutral, power-draining type of aesthetic caring. To make schools truly caring institutions for members of historically oppressed subordinate groups like Mexican Americans, authentic caring, as currently described in the literature, is necessary but not sufficient. Students' cultural world and their structural position must also be fully apprehended, with school-based adults deliberately bringing issues of race, difference, and power into central focus. This approach necessitates abandoning the notion of a color-blind curriculum and a neutral assimilation process. The practice of individualizing collective problems must also be relinquished. A more profound and involved understanding of the socioeconomic, linguistic, sociocultural, and structural barriers that obstruct the mobility of Mexican youth needs to inform all caring relationships (Delgado-Gaitan and Trueba 1991; Phelan et al. 1993;

Stanton-Salazar 1996). Authentic caring cannot exist unless it is imbued with and motivated by such political clarity (Bartolomé 1994).

The finding that students oppose schooling rather than education expands current explanations for oppositional or reactive subcultures that characterize many urban, U.S.-born youth in inner-city schools. Rather than signifying an anti-achievement ethos, oppositional elements constitute a response to a Eurocentric, middle-class "culture of power" (see Delpit 1994, for a similar argument with respect to African American underachievement). This culture individualizes the problem of underachievement through its adherence to a power-neutral or power-blind conception of the world (Frankenberg 1993; Twine 1995; McIntyre 1997). So deeply rooted and poorly apprehended is this culture of power that a 50–75 percent dropout rate at Seguín is systematically rationalized—year after year—as an individual-level problem. Such explanations preserve current institutional arrangements and asymmetries of power.

Noddings (1992) rightly argues that the current crisis of meaning, direction, and purpose among youth in public schools derives from a poor ordering of priorities. The current emphases on achievement and on standard academic subjects may lead youth to conclude that adults do not care for them. Noddings further acknowledges that her call for a re-ordering of priorities to promote dedication to full human growth necessarily means that not all youth be given exactly the same kind of education. Indeed, as the logic of authentic caring dictates, a complete apprehension of the "other" means that the material, physical, psychological, and spiritual needs of youth will guide the educational process.

One final story, that of Mr. Sosa, Seguín's band director from 1991–1994, illustrates how authentic caring can be infused with political clarity, and thus serves as a fitting conclusion to this chapter. To meet the particular needs of his students, Mr. Sosa dissolves the conventional boundary that exists between "public" school and "private" home and community matters. Rather than construing a collective matter (poor nutrition) as an individual problem, Mr. Sosa adjusted his pedagogy in a humane and culturally sensitive way to meet all of his students' needs. The marching band's successes are a testimony to the effectiveness of meaningful relationships in promoting competence and mastery of worldly tasks.

LOVE IS ONE *TAQUITO* AWAY

In a late-morning visit with Mr. Sosa in early fall 1992, he told me that when he first arrived at Seguín (two years earlier), the students did not respect him. They were unmanageable. He said that they "just didn't know," meaning that they had to learn what his expectations were. He explained to me that in order for this kind of learning to take place, he first had to earn his students' respect and confidence. He emphasized that this happened "slowly." He recalled a series of three football games during which three different girls fainted while participating in the marching band's half-time show.

> At the football stadium where the football players play, there is a lot of dust in the air. It just comes up and it happens that the kids start breathing it. So, there are kids that are malnourished. They don't eat any breakfast, lunch, and then they don't have supper. Then they go to participate. They are weak already, and that dust doesn't help any.
>
> These students who fainted were taken by EMS [Emergency Medical Service] for treatment at the hospital and hospitalized. . . . Some kids are still being billed for that. . . . These kids don't have insurance. They take them to the hospital, and they're administered treatment, and the parents don't have any money to pay. Yet, if they don't have any money, they are not going to be administered. Some that are administered are billed without the parents having any money. So, I try to get insurance for them, but it's only accidental insurance through the school. It's cheap, but I can't find any insurance that will take care of their hospital stay.

He pointed to a large, bright-blue, vinyl bag that he brings to school every day. It is packed with bean- and meat-filled, flour tortilla tacos wrapped in foil. He gives this food to his students. "At first, I would come to school with a little bag. Now, I bring this one because I can feed many more students with it. I used to begin handing them out during the lunch hour. Now I begin earlier than that. They come here to eat breakfast," he says, with a smile.

I remark that he must spend a lot of time preparing these meals. Nodding his head, he responds, "I spend one-and-a-half to two hours every night making these. He then pulls out a *taquito* (small taco) and offers it to me. I'm dying to taste Mr. Sosa's *taquitos* and so I accept his hospitality. He gives me one of his prized bean-and-meat versions, which I savor slowly as we talk. Mr. Sosa tells me how his gift of food helped create a strong bond between him and his students:

> I usually finish by ten-thirty or eleven. A big part of the trust that I have been able to build has been because of this. At first, they were overly defensive with me. If you tell them something they don't like, they are ready to hit back. Now, I can go ahead and tell them to do things which they don't understand, but they will do them anyway. That's what I'm up to with them, but it has taken almost two years.

"So feeding your students has really made a difference in your relationship with them?" I probe.

"It all happened by accident," he responds. You see, the food thing, I don't bring it just to win them over. It was because they don't eat. They don't have any money. They don't even have breakfast . . . don't have money for dinner. And then we practice 'til five or six after school. So, consequently their physical endurance is spent. I really got after the kids, to try to get them to eat something. I then would do my part by bringing them food, and then I would have them talk in here while they are eating. I would give them advice. Some kids come in and sit down and talk to me about personal things. Just last week, I pulled a kid out of jail. This changed everything around for me because when I first came in and tried to tell them things that are not exactly the way they've been told by other students and by other teachers, they resented me.

"So, to reach these kids, what is your advice to other teachers?" I ask him.

Characteristically, he answers my question by telling me another story:

When I first got here in 1990, this is what actually happened. I came and was interviewed by the principal. The principal was outside and he called some of the band students that were there. They were practicing there by themselves because they didn't have a band director. He had left. So, he called the kids around to where we both were and he introduced me as their possible new teacher. So, one of the girls put her arms around me. *Me abrazó.* [She hugged me.] And she assumed that I was going to be their teacher and director. She told me in front of everybody, "Sir, just one thing. Don't lie to us." So, it kind of hit me. These kids want the truth. They want sincerity. For the teacher, it's one thing to say you care and it's another to show it. You can show your sincerity, your honesty, when you talk to them or you can demonstrate that you are sincere and that you care.

Recently, some kid told me when I offered him some food, he said, "I don't take handouts." So, I told the boy, "This is not a handout. It took a lot of love. It took not only my own money, but my own time." I'll spend an hour or two making, preparing this food, plus buying the materials I need every day. So, it's not a matter of being a handout. It's a matter of love. They are like my children to me. It's not a handout. It's like giving something without expecting something in return. I don't expect something in return.

To complete the story, Mr. Sosa led his band to the city championship title for three consecutive years. They also competed well at the state level and the band had the privilege of participating in the "16th of September" parade in Mexico City for two consecutive years. Mr. Sosa's story, the example he set as a caring human being, would be moving under any circumstances at any high school. At Seguín, where the importance of personal worth is often overlooked, where the links between academic achievement, cultural integrity, and mutual respect are so fragile, and where helpfulness and hopefulness are often in short supply, Mr. Sosa reminds us that a different, more affirming and positive world may be only a *taquito* away—that is, if it is one made with sincerity and love.

CHAPTER 4

Everyday Experiences in the Lives of Immigrant and U.S.-Born Youth

If schools are to become truly caring institutions for U.S.-Mexican youth, they must begin with a more complete understanding of both the social and academic milieu confronting Mexican immigrant and Mexican American youth. An authentically caring pedagogy considers the strengths that youth bring with them to school alongside the subtractive social- and school-related forces that disrupt what would otherwise be a more natural development of those strengths were schools more additive in vision. Beginning with an ethnographic observation, this chapter considers the strengths that immigrant youth, in particular, bring with them to school and sets the stage for the following chapter's exclusive concern with the ways in which schooling subtracts resources from youth. In both chapters, data from group interviews come into play (see appendix for an elaboration of research methodology).

On September 25, 1992, I joined Maricela, an outgoing, first-generation student, as she entered her second-period classroom. I was interested in finding out more about her volunteer work as a school math tutor. Once a week, she tutors classmates after school. She also belongs to an informal "study group" with other immigrant girls who enjoy discussing and researching career opportunities. Maricela hopes to become a public accountant and plans to attend a university either in the United States or Mexico. Students peel off their backpacks and make their way toward their seats; the bell has already rung. As I edge my way into the room, I encounter a U.S.-born, third-generation, ninth-grade female. Later, I learn her name is Adriana. An underachiever, she failed ninth grade the previous year and is now repeating several courses. Adriana also failed a grade during elementary school, so she is older than many other students at her level. She doubts that she will graduate from high school. Nevertheless, she plans to attend a community college to get training "in something having to do with medicine." She indicates that the best part about school is being able to spend time with her friends and plan the next weekend out.

Talking aloud to no one in particular, Adriana announces that she hates school. I ask her why she doesn't simply get into school, study, and try her best?

"I don't do the school thing because nobody else does, so why should I?"

"Nobody?" I thought. In light of my purpose that morning, her words took me aback.

In a quiet voice to avoid any potential embarrassment, I suggest to Adriana, "Maricela works hard at school."

Adriana whispers back, "I wouldn't know about that. Anyway, she's one of them."

"What do you mean?" I ask.

"They talk to each other in Spanish and all. They think they're better than us Chicanos. Can you believe? And she's from Mexico! Mexico sucks! I'd rather be American than Mexican any day."

I ask her if she has ever been to Mexico.

"No, and I don't wanna go."

"Why not?" I probe.

"It's dirty and poor over there. I haven't been but I just know. It's them who come here not us who go there. So why should I go?"

While this chance encounter with Maricela and Adriana alerted me to the social divisions that exist among youth—the main subject of chapter 5—it also helped focus my attention on how the dramatically disparate peer group realities among immigrant and U.S.-born youth are related to the presence or absence of social capital. By social capital, I mean the social ties that connect students to each other, as well as the levels of resources (such as academic skills and knowledge) that characterize their friendship groups. This chapter examines the relationship between social capital and schooling orientations among all-immigrant, all-U.S.-born, and "generationally mixed" friendship groups comprised of both immigrant and non-immigrant youth. Quantitative analyses focusing on gender (see chapter 1) further reveal that females are higher achievers across all generations. And, in gender-mixed groups, they play a central role as purveyors of social capital.

I attribute the existence of aggressively school-oriented students like Maricela to their possession of greater social capital, which is in turn demonstrably linked to their prior schooling experiences in Mexico. Immigrants invoke these prior experiences through their comparative or dual frame of reference, which not only motivates their achievement but also mitigates their critique of U.S. schooling. Mexican immigrants' dual frame leads them to evaluate their circumstances in the United States through the lens of their prior schooling and living experiences in Mexico (Ogbu 1991; Suárez-Orozco 1991). Their positive assessment manifests itself as an esprit de corps that undergirds both their higher achievement and their pro-school ethos. This orientation squares with findings from another study wherein youth living in Mexico and Mexican immigrant youth in the United States exhibit greater self-motivation to achieve in an atmosphere of social interdependence in comparison to their U.S.-born counterparts (Suárez-Orozco and Suárez-Orozco 1995).

In contrast, I attribute Adriana's lack of a well-defined and effective achievement orientation to a paucity of social capital. With some exceptions, discussed below, academic achievement is not an overriding concern among U.S.-born youth such as Adriana. In general, U.S.-born youth are best described as "socially de-capitalized" (see Putnam 1993, 1995).[1]

This chapter emphasizes the role of generational differences in the experience of schooling. Here, I expand on discussions of caring presented in previous chapters by drawing on interviews I conducted with specific groups of Seguín freshmen and sophomores (see appendix for a discussion of methodology). Factors that emerged as important in the analyses—students' dual frame of reference, academic competence, social capital, and the centrality of females in academic-related endeavors—are examined in the context of discussions I had with students about school.

My conversations with three immigrant groups (recently arrived "Urban Youth from Monterrey," long-term-resident "English-Speaking Immigrants," and recently arrived "Pre-Literate Youth") help illustrate the range of sentiments concerning schooling (see table A.1).[2] These interviews highlight the importance of the students' dual frame of reference and their relatively high levels (compared to both mixed-generation and U.S.-born friendship groups) of social capital. I examine the intersection of social capital with gender, on the one hand, and juxtapose it to the concept of *empeño* (or diligence) as an emic explicator of immigrant achievement, on the other.

I then turn to mixed-generation and U.S.-born groups to investigate the role of social capital among these students. I conclude the chapter with insights I gained from discussions with a U.S.-born youth group with uncharacteristically high levels of social capital. These students' experiences help illuminate the everyday ways in which friendship groups generate social capital, and how that capital, in turn, positively shapes individual and group perceptions of, and experiences with, schooling.

THE EXPERIENCE OF SCHOOLING FOR MEXICAN IMMIGRANT YOUTH

Urban Youth from Monterrey

This friendship group, comprising five males and three females, met regularly in the center of the cafeteria during fall 1992. All members of the group are from the urban industrial center of Monterrey, Nuevo León. Two of the males, Joaquín and Cuahtemoc, have dashing, genteel personas that make them seem older than they are. All members of the group are well dressed; several wear jeans, leather belts, and cowboy hats. Two of the girls, Evi and Mona, wear tight, showy blouses, jeans, and cowboy boots; the third, Amalia, wears a long skirt and high-top, leather boots. All of these students have a clean-cut "northern Mexican look," which includes a forthright, confident demeanor. They approach each other and their space in the cafeteria as a group absorbed in itself, laughing and commanding attention as their trays hit the Formica-topped tables.

I first guess Joaquín and Cuahtemoc to be the core members of this group, but I soon discover that Amalia is key. Noting my pregnant state (see appendix), Amalia orders Joaquín and

Cuahtemoc to make room for me. Embarrassed for not thinking of this on their own, they quickly reposition their food trays, with one boy saying "*Desde luego*" ("Of course") in a low voice. After some small talk about my pregnancy and the book I am writing, I learn that Joaquín and Beto are related and that the rest have friends and relatives in Mexico in common. According to Amalia, these interconnections are what explain the group's closeness. After a lengthy conversation with these students, however, I realize that her explanation is only partly true. Her modesty prevents her from disclosing that both she and her family actively promote solidarity and cohesion among this group of students.

I ask them to talk to me about their schooling experiences both in Mexico and in the United States. Joaquín says that he believes schooling in Mexico, especially beyond the *primaria* (or elementary) level, is better. He notes that Mexico does not have the problems with drugs or gangs that exist in U.S. schools. With his friends nodding their heads in agreement, Joaquín asserts that schools in Mexico are more serious places. "*Allá en México, es un privilegio poder asistir a la secundaria.*" ("In Mexico, it's a privilege to be able to attend middle and high school.")

Cuahtemoc recalls that when he lived in Monterrey, he was enrolled in a *colegio de bachilleres*, a specialty secondary school with an advanced curriculum designed to prepare students for a university education. What he most appreciated about his old school was its strong emphasis on science education. Cuahtemoc explains that before moving to the United States two years ago, he was close to attaining a *bachillerato* diploma, which would have secured his entry into a prestigious institution of higher education in Mexico. A reversal in his family's economic circumstances forced him to abandon this plan. When Cuahtemoc pauses, I ask the rest of the group if economic reasons help explain why they are now living in the United States. As expected, economic hardship in Mexico is another common denominator.

When Amalia asks Cuahtemoc how he felt about having to change his career plans, Cuahtemoc quips in response, "*El que adelante no ve, atrás se queda.*" ("He who is not forward looking stays behind.") Elaborating, he says with much maturity that even if one doesn't always get exactly what one wishes or desires in life, looking forward and anticipating the future is always a good thing. This is a key lesson he has learned from his family's experience with bankruptcy. After their small grocery store business failed, he and his family had no choice but to move to the United States in order to secure decent jobs. As Cuahtemoc sees it, to grow up in Mexico is to live with an ongoing sense of life's precariousness, "much more so than here," he says in Spanish.

While everyone else listens, Amalia describes her parents, who were teachers in Mexico. They, too, decided to move to the United States for economic reasons, following a lengthy teachers' strike in a suburb of Monterrey. Because teachers' salaries have not kept up with the rising cost of living, Amalia explains, her parents regularly held two or three jobs between them, in addition to their primary jobs as teachers.

I ask Amalia how she sees her future. She explains that she hasn't yet decided whether to stay in the United States or return to Mexico. If she remains in the United States, she would consider pursuing the teaching profession; Mexico's grossly inadequate teacher salaries preclude her from considering being a teacher there.

Joaquín's cousin, Beto, observes, cynically, that all Mexicans say that they want to return home to Mexico. Conveying a kernel of wisdom to the group, Beto remarks, "*Tenemos que mantener los pies sobre la tierra*," meaning that they should all keep their feet on the ground and be realistic about the possibility that they might never return to Mexico. Continuing with her train of thought, Amalia sighs deeply in agreement and expresses her view that teachers in the United States are less committed to their students than they are in Mexico.

"Not my teachers," counters Beto, in Spanish, indicating that he likes all his teachers.

Unconvinced, Amalia continues. She notes that Mexico has a yearly celebration, *Día de la Profesora* (Teacher's Day), that rivals Mother's Day in magnitude and importance. Everyone brings gifts for their teachers. As teachers of the fifth- and sixth-grade levels at a *primaria* in one of Monterrey's impoverished fringes, her parents, Amalia says, dedicated their lives to teaching the children of the poor and made great sacrifices for their students. Sometimes this meant that her own family, which includes two more girls, would do without so that both parents could help meet their students' needs. Amalia comments that there were never any extra pairs of shoes or clothes laying around at her house, because these always went to their students' families. Acknowledging that her family's economic situation in Mexico was stressful, Amalia also points out that it never compared to "*la miseria*" ("the misery") that others cope with on a daily basis. Then, she turns, with obvious pride, to the subject of her parents' accomplishments as teachers.

On Teacher's Day, her family was always honored by the children and the families in the school community. Her parents had taught at the same *primaria* for ten years, and they were well known. As teachers, they promoted the idea that the classroom was a family and that all had a responsibility for others' well-being. In a demonstration of great respect and *cariño* (affection), the community traditionally honored her parents with a grand feast, games, and generous gifts for the whole family.

It is a great shame, Amalia says in her most serious voice, that her parents no longer teach. Her mother cleans hotel rooms and her father works as a cook in a restaurant that caters to "*bolíos*" ("whites"). As her father speaks English fairly well, he wants to be a waiter (in order to make more money). However, it seems unlikely that he will achieve this goal, since only whites wait on tables at the restaurant where he works. The cooks, on the other hand, are all Mexican and mostly immigrant. Amalia makes it clear that she is very proud of the fact that her parents were excellent teachers who had a productive relationship with their school community. (Again, out of modesty, she fails to note her parents' present contributions to youth. I elaborate on these later in this chapter.) Contradicting her earlier statement, she concludes that despite her love of teaching, she probably would not become a teacher in the United States because students are too "*chiflados*" ("spoiled") and do not appreciate their teachers.

I ask Amalia to clarify where she thinks the fundamental problem lies—with less committed teachers or with spoiled students. In response, she reiterates her feeling that students in the United States are spoiled, but she maintains that teachers are also responsible because they do not teach youth about the country and culture they come from. In Amalia's opinion, if "Chicanos" knew their origins and history, they would not only cherish their educational opportunities, they would also get angry at poverty. Clearly, Amalia has fully embraced her parents' unimpeachable ethic of social responsibility as a core belief and guiding principle.

Nodding his head in tacit agreement, Joaquín comments that he thought that Amalia was going to argue that teachers in the United States are less committed to their students than teachers in Mexico. He mentions an elementary school teacher in Mexico who reprimanded his mother for keeping him away from school too often. This teacher befriended his mother, who was experiencing serious marital problems at the time. The teacher's concern and guidance made a tremendous difference in their lives.

Cuahtemoc adds that in the *secundaria* he attended, teachers were less focused on rules than they are in the United States. He remembers teachers encouraging all of the students to speak up and to speak clearly—even in the English classes he took. He thinks that things are very different at Seguín. "*Aquí, nos tienen sentados en las sillas, calladitos, todos humillados*" ("Here, they have us sitting in our chairs, quiet, all of us subdued.") Cuahtemoc also recalls that most teachers in Mexico urge their students to work together in groups, while in the United States, teachers often think you're cheating if you work together. He recounts experiences that he, Evi, and Mona have had. They all have the same ESL teacher (but each at a different time during the day). Because they study together, they often get the same or similar grades. When their teacher found out they were all friends, he asked Mona jokingly just how "*acercada*" (or "close") she was to Cuahtemoc and Evi. An otherwise quiet Mona breaks in to say that she did not appreciate the tone of her teacher's voice. "*Que no podemos estudiar juntos?*" ("Can't we study together?")[3]

At this point, Joaquín remembers how his middle school science courses consisted of group projects that were always connected to real-world issues. He describes a class project in which the students studied micro-organisms in the city's water supply. His class initiated a letter-writing campaign against city water officials because of weak water-treatment standards. In another class project, one on science and ethics, his class visited several *maquilas* (factories) along the U.S.-Mexican border in order to study the effects of industrial waste in the Rio Grande. These lessons, Joaquín maintains, made him realize the importance of both chemical engineering and political science. "One must be able to analyze waste and deal with the multinational corporations," he noted, in Spanish. I ask Joaquín if he intends to pursue these fields at a university level. He replies that he does, but fears that he will never be able to afford the cost of tuition for non-U.S. residents. Nevertheless, he plans to begin saving his earnings from odd jobs for college.

Beto, the "realist" in the group, brings the discussion back to the subject of teachers. In his opinion, both teachers and students are responsible for the current situation at Seguín. Then, almost as if interrupting himself, he adds that any comparison to Mexico is unfair because it is another country, with a distinct history. "Expecting better or different treatment in U.S. schools is an unreasonable position to assume because none of us are from here," he insists, in Spanish.

This comment seems to stifle critical discussion, leaving Beto free to impart his view. He describes the middle school he attended in Monterrey as really run down. He recalls how the windows in the building, once broken were never fixed, how the toilets never worked, and how, with few books and no computers, the training was poor. Second-guessing himself, he remarks, *"Pero si aprendimos todos a leer"* ("But we all did learn to read").

Cuahtemoc intensifies Beto's critique by telling a story about a corrupt school administrator who stole school monies. He adds that the Secretaría de Educación Pública (SEP) (Mexico's Ministry of Public Education) never kept its promise to repair his school's cracked walls and leaky roof.[4] Whenever it rained, teachers had to place plastic buckets all over their rooms to catch the dripping water. Cuahtemoc mentions that he had heard that a roof in a nearby school had caved in from the weight of the rain. All during the rainy season, when he went to school, he was afraid that the roof might fall down on top of him. One good thing about U.S. schools, he observes, is that officials do not neglect building repairs like they do in Mexico. Interestingly, Cuahtemoc's dual frame of reference enables him to overlook the neglected condition of Seguín's cracked walls, leaky ceilings, and faulty heating system. Amalia, recalling the hardship that the teachers' strike caused her family, offers, *"Sí, hay que estar agradecido . . ."* ("Yes, one ought to be thankful . . .").

Suárez-Orozco (1991) and Ogbu (1991) maintain that a comparative or dual frame of reference leads immigrant youth to evaluate their situation in the U.S. positively. Ogbu (1991) argues that immigrants in the United States not only regard their public schooling as "far superior," they also believe that they are treated better than they would have been treated in their schools back home. While a dual frame certainly heightens immigrants' sensibilities toward differences in schooling across national borders, the categorical statements of "far superior" schooling and better treatment in the United States merit closer examination.

Discussions I held with Seguín's immigrant students suggest the possibility that Mexican public schools, at least in the urban centers, do a better job than U.S. inner-city schools when it comes to educating Mexican youth. This study cannot provide a conclusive assessment, but the reasons that students provide for negative schooling experiences in Mexico are instructive. They point more to contextual elements impinging on the school, such as teachers' strikes, corruption, inefficiency, limited resources, large class sizes, and family financial issues, than to the teachers, the curriculum, or the quality of teaching. This assessment of better schools prevails despite proverbial class sizes of thirty or more students in crowded *primaria* classrooms, as reported on December 17, 1995 by the *Houston Chronicle* in a special report on Mexican schools titled, "Twilight's Children." At best, this is a provisional hypothesis, however, since comparing Mexican to U.S. schools is probably like comparing apples to oranges.

Anecdotal evidence suggests that "public" schools in Mexico are "selective." Stories abound of the specter of swift and permanent expulsion of children who pose threats to classroom order. Though draconian-sounding, less patience toward unruly children may exist in countries like Mexico that are strapped for resources. After all, the Mexican government only subsidizes education through the sixth grade. Students must afterwards pay for their own books and tuition. Thus, while it may be possible to conclude that Mexican schools are "better" in some ways and not others, selective factors may constitute a primary reason. One cannot help but wonder, however, whether even the most restless of spirits are more easily tamed in an environment where schooling provides the only hint of possible mobility out of a situation of grinding poverty.

More research needs to be conducted to determine the kinds of skills, resources, and assumptions about schooling that immigrant youth from both urban and rural schools bring with them to the United States. One question is whether students generally experience more opportunities for individual expression in Mexican classrooms, and whether at the same *primaria* level, they acquire more academic skills and competence in comparison to their U.S.-born peers as Macías' (1990) classroom study in the state of Jalisco suggests. Macías (1990) further posits that Mexico's challenging national curriculum at the *primaria* level helps students learn the curriculum because it provides for greater uniformity in the instructional process across the land.

Though not necessarily applicable to all Mexican immigrant youth, analyses of students' evaluative comments that I came across about the relationships that they enjoyed with their teachers in Mexico were overwhelmingly positive. Even at the *secundaria* level, strong interpersonal relations with teachers were frequently mentioned. Despite differences between the two nations' educational systems, the extent to which authentic caring mediates achievement and positive schooling orientations in both countries is worth investigating. My guess is that wherever culturally relevant structures of caring exist, such as that exemplified in Seguín's Social Studies Department (chapter 3), youth will prosper.

However provisional from a researcher's perspective, immigrant youth's dual frame of reference leads them to "hypothesize" that schools in Mexico are "better"—at least in certain ways. Their commentary invites a nuanced interpretation of the concept of the dual frame. Amalia, in particular, believes that immigrants' dual frame can and should be accessible to U.S.-born youth. She envisions the positive and creative potential of a curriculum centered around Mexico and things Mexican. She implicitly leverages a critique against Seguín's curriculum as subtractive—that is, as one that denies youth the opportunity to learn about their Mexican heritage. She believes that if others possessed her knowledge and awareness of conditions in Mexico, they would not only cherish their present educational opportunities, they would also "get angry at poverty" and become agents of change. She thus politicizes the question of a dual frame by suggesting its potential applicability to all youth at Seguín. To Amalia's critique, I would only add that immigrants could equally benefit from a more profound understanding of Mexican American or Chicano ethnicity—especially their resistance not to education, but to *schooling*.

Hurtado and colleagues' (1994) analysis of identity from the 1979 National Chicano Survey illustrates the oppositional or resistive elements among adult Chicanos or Mexican Americans. Their identities are not only more differentiated than their Mexican immigrant counterparts, but how they self-identify signifies their adaptation to U.S. society.[5] Hurtado and colleagues find that Chicanos have evolved through their historical experience of subordination a "political *raza*" (Mexican American people) identity that combines the following seven identifiers: "*pocho*," "Indian," "brown," "Spanish speaker," "Chicano," "*raza*," and "*mestizo*" (both Spanish and Indian). As articulated by political leaders throughout the Chicano Movement, Chicanos have not only invested derogatory and stereotypic categories with value, turning them on their heads, they have also affirmed that which they have been denied—that is, their *Mexicanidad* (or Mexican-ness).

Thus, while Chicanos and Chicanas could clearly benefit from a more complete understanding of either their Mexican origins or the experiences of their Mexican peers, Hurtado and colleagues' findings suggest that Mexican immigrants' inclination to preserve their culture is mirrored and finds expression in that segment within the U.S.-born population that has dealt most positively with the most devalued and problematic labels imposed upon them.

Though I failed to come across any single U.S.-born youth with as much analytical clarity as Amalia, enough to explicitly articulate a parallel notion of the importance of a "Chicana/o frame of reference," I nevertheless demonstrate its salience in the next two chapters. Chapter 6, in particular, interprets students' acts of resistance through this interpretive lens. Greater cross-generational communication between immigrants and non-immigrants would most likely reveal the existence of overlapping histories and shared political interests—at least among these broad segments within the larger Mexican population.

Returning to Amalia, the politics of the dual frame itself make her critique—that U.S.-born Mexicans should know more about

Mexico—difficult to sustain. Beto conveys the shared understanding that Mexican immigrants are in no position to criticize the U.S. public school system. Instead, they should be *agradecidos* or "grateful" for the opportunity to attend secondary schools in the United States. They would not likely be able to do so in Mexico, given general economic hardship and the tuition expenses levied at the secondary level. Immigrant youth thus are locked into a logic of self-censorship by virtue of having access to free, universal schooling in the United States. This logic further thwarts the possibility of empathizing with their U.S.-born counterparts. Their comparative frame thus works to simultaneously motivate their achievement while muting their criticism. Whenever immigrant students are called upon to compare schooling experiences, these contradictory dynamics are sure to surface. This is certainly true in the friendship group I turn to next.

English-Speaking Immigrants

When I saw this foursome in the cafeteria in January 1993, I felt drawn to them because I had exchanged words with the two female members of the group earlier that morning in the school library. I classified all four freshmen friends of two females and two males as relatively long-term-resident immigrants, because of their extensive familiarity with U.S.-society derived from their frequent and lengthy visits as children to parents and relatives living in the United States. They collectively boast a fairly fluent command of the English language. One of the males, Lázaro, eventually explains to me the group's instrumental motivation to speak mostly English. "We can speak Spanish any time," Lázaro points out, "and we have to speak it at home. So we try to only speak English while in school, so that later we can get good jobs." I also later discover that one of the four, Fito, had taken English classes in Mexico at the secondary level. Furthermore, as young children, all knew they would eventually live in the United States.

All four students attended the same middle school located in the East End (a Seguín feeder school) and live in the same neighborhood. All come from very protective and authoritarian families. As all four students share similar courses, they see each other often and study together regularly. Good fortune also assigned them the same lunch period. Finally, because their parents all know each other—a parental precondition for their children's choice of friends—group members are able to spend the necessary time together to sustain a warm, platonic friendship.

Fito is fidgety, and he likes to joke around. In a playful tone, feigning ultramasculinity, he tells me that it is his and Lázaro's job to protect their "little sisters." When Ana María responds to this announcement by jabbing her elbow into his side, Fito doubles over with laughter. Linda concurs with Fito's comment, asserting that "the ninth grade is a 'scary' year because there are too many students and so many of them skip and there's a lot of fights at school. It's crowded and I don't feel safe. I tell my parents that we friends protect each other and they're glad about that."

Continuing the discussion with Ana María and Linda that I had begun earlier in the day, I ask them why they like to read. (I had already established that one of their favorite pastimes is to pour over back issues of *Seventeen* magazine.) Each answers with her own story. Ana María says that what she really liked about school in Mexico was that she got to read *Don Quixote de la Mancha* and other great literature. "We don't read much here," she observes. She recalls that in Mexico, her entire sixth-grade class performed a play about Don Quixote before hundreds of parents and relatives. Her teachers used the novel to emphasize the importance of imagination and dreams. The Don Quixote project also involved a written assignment. The students were asked to write poems about their own "impossible dream." Ana María wrote that she would somehow become "somebody" in the United States. Then she would return with her family to Mexico to help improve others' lives through social work.

"Do you still want to do that?" I query.

"Yes," Ana María affirms, "my poem is taped to my mirror in my bedroom. I read it every day."

Ana María credits her interest in social work to her teachers in Mexico. In her school, all the teachers were not only in contact with most of the students' parents, they also visited students' homes on certain days, after school let out. Each student could expect one to two visits annually from teachers. (The high rate of teacher turnover in Ana María's school in Tamaulipas' capital city of Ciudad Victoria was a serious problem, however.)

To Ana María's parents' great pleasure, all visits to their home entailed positive reports on their daughter's progress. It was on one of these home visits by a teacher that Ana María learned about social work as a career option. A former social worker herself, the teacher imparted her experience helping indigents who came to *el seguro social* (the social security office). The teacher had enjoyed social work but had decided to teach because the work hours were better.

Linda chimes in, saying that she, too, got to read *Don Quixote* and that she had the privilege of reading it to her parents, who are poorly educated and do not read very well. After asking me how to say "*fuera de onda*" in English, she describes her sixth-grade teacher as an "eccentric" individual himself. Smiling and dropping her hand at the wrist, she suggests that he may have been gay. Lázaro sneers at this and shakes his head in disapproval. Disregarding him, Linda continues.

Her quixotic teacher was obsessed with science-fiction literature and he began every class period by recounting an episode either from an Isaac Asimov or a Ray Bradbury novel. He was so expressive that he virtually acted out the parts. He shared all of his cherished novels with his students as a way of encouraging them to read. Linda says that she managed to get through a couple. More than any other experience, she feels that being in this teacher's class taught her the value of reading. Her eyes glazing over with emotion, Linda summarizes her teacher's impact on her: "He would have been someone else without his novels. Reading changed him. It made him the teacher we all loved." By imparting his magical world of sci-fi drama, Linda's "*fuera-de-onda*" teacher helped forge in her an enduring love of learning.

I quiz Linda about her other teachers in Mexico. She remembers one "*bruja*" ("witch") in the third grade; otherwise, she loved all the teachers in her school. She believes that the classes were sometimes "too hard" and that the students did not always know what they were reading, but the teachers were always patient with them. Linda describes how her teachers often allowed her to "translate" the material to the other students in the class. She notes that "sometimes, a kid can explain better than a grown-up."

I ask her to elaborate on how her teachers in Mexico compare to her teachers at Seguín. She replies that since she didn't go to elementary school in the United States, it is difficult for her to tell whether teachers are better there or here. But, she comments, she knows that several of her cousins schooled here failed at least one grade, while she has never repeated a class level. "And," she adds, "I'm the only one of all my cousins who likes to read." Given Linda's parents' low level of education, her early schooling experiences indeed seem to have been pivotal in nurturing her interest in reading.

Lázaro and Fito similarly enjoyed positive schooling experiences in Mexico, though Fito confesses that he was so "hyperactive" as a child that he often made life difficult for himself and his teachers. Because his father was a migrant worker in the United States, Fito lacked a father-figure growing up. Consequently, the school principal always placed him in classrooms with male teachers who disciplined him. Fito notes that the "*nalgadas*" (spankings) settled him down by the time he enrolled in middle school. I ask him if his mother approved of the "*nalgadas*." "Oh, yes!" he responds, "It was her idea."

During a discussion with Fito several days later, I learn that at least two of his school teachers were related to some of his relatives on his mother's side of the family. While this fact helps explain their personal interest in him, Fito assures me that in the small *pueblo* (town) in which he lived, the teachers would have done the same for any child. Further, he explains that because of the existence of many kin on both sides of the U.S.-Mexican border, his father was constantly informed about Fito's well-being, and vice versa. Fito's family's interconnectedness appears to have translated into an informal system of accountability, so his needs could not be simply ignored or dismissed.[6]

Lázaro pursues Linda's suggestion that schools are better in Mexico, commenting that he used to be especially good at math.

"I used to be much smarter," he states.

"What do you mean?" I reply, taken aback.

Misunderstanding, Ana María interrupts, "Probably that you read much less now than you used to. I'm sure I would be reading more than I do now if I were in a school in Mexico."

Ignoring Ana María, Lázaro continues, remarking that he has been trying to understand this loss of competence. He tells me that he shared his concern with his math teacher, but the teacher told him that he was just lazy. "It's not that," Lázaro insists, "I know it's not." He wishes that he still had his old schoolbooks to consult. He remembers being able to calculate "much harder" math problems. He says that his teachers in Mexico were very good.

"And here, either I'm dumb or my math teachers are terrible."

"You dumb, Lázaro," Linda interjects, laughing.

Making fun of Lázaro, Fito shifts the tone of the conversation, waving his arms wildly and exclaiming, "You're unworthy! You're unworthy!" His silly posturing elicits our spontaneous laughter.

Getting the group back on track, I ask them to explain Lazaro's comment about schools being better in Mexico. Fito argues that they really can't say whether this is true or not since they can only know about their own experiences.

"Well, like Linda, you have cousins here," I press.

In an analytical tone, Linda asserts that from what she knows about her cousins, there probably is a difference in the quality of schooling. "What you learn is what's better, though, not where you learn." Linda describes how, in Mexico, their desks were falling apart and the students themselves had to clean their classrooms because the school could not afford janitors. Since the toilets never worked, Linda recalls that she always waited to use the bathroom at home. "I don't know," she says hesitantly, groping for an explanation, "we still loved school so much that we never missed a day!"

Linda then complains that Seguín teachers hardly know their students. "I don't expect them to visit me, just to know me a little bit. They're always too busy, or if you're like me and like to read, they leave you alone even more." She also grumbles about how her ESL-transition teacher yells at the students for speaking Spanish. Mimicking him, with her mouth twisted, she yells, "English! English! You're in America! Go back to Mexico!" "Then," she adds in disgust, "he doesn't teach us nothing." Switching from English to Spanish, she notes, "*De donde vengo yo, se les dicen a esas personas, 'mal-educados.'*" ("Where I come from, we call people like him 'poorly educated.'") Linda switches into Spanish here in order to convey the cultural meaning of the term *mal-educado*, a variant of *educación*. Despite his college degree, her teacher is far from being "educated" in the Mexican sense—that is, he is far from acting in a caring, respectful, and well-mannered way.

Shaking her head in disapproval, Ana María agrees that this teacher is "bad news," but she feels "really bothered" to hear anyone criticizing the school.

Looking at Linda, she says, "You try to be a teacher in this school. There's just too many kids and the teachers are frustrated."

"I know that the teachers are frustrated," Linda concedes, "but for even one teacher not to teach us, that's not right. In Mexico, teachers get paid way less than I would make here sweeping the floor. To be a teacher in Mexico, you have to love teaching."

She points out that one of her mother's friends held down two additional part-time jobs just so that she could be a teacher. "There's no teachers like that here."

Linda looks angry and the rest look troubled. Compromising, Ana María reverts into Spanish, "*Que esperamos? Somos Mexicanos!*" ("What do we expect? We're Mexican!") Turning to Lázaro and Fito, I ask them why they are so quiet.

"Just thinking," Lázaro answers, slowly.

"What?" I prompt.

"I guess I don't expect special treatment. I just know that if you try your hardest in school, teachers like you—except maybe for Linda's teacher. Even in Mexico, if you have *empeño* (diligence), your teachers like you better."

Linda gets the last word. "I would love my students even if they didn't have *empeño*. It would be my job to get them to have *empeño*. Like what Fito's teachers did for him."

Linda's implicit endorsement of an authentically caring approach to schooling converges with Amalia's characterization of more committed teachers in Mexican schools. Also converging are Beto's statement that any comparisons to Mexico are unfair and Ana María's unyielding position against criticizing the school, even if such a stance means dismissing Linda's feelings toward her abusive teacher. Perhaps because Ana María's attitude seems nearly as callous as Linda's teacher's, the group lets Linda have the last word.

Linda's report on her cousins schooled in the United States is also suggestive. It is highly unlikely that her cousins ever read *Don Quixote* or the novels of Isaac Asimov or Ray Bradbury during middle school, or even during high school. In contrast, even with wide variation in implementation, Mexico's rigorous and demanding national primary curriculum virtually ensures that by the fifth or sixth year of school, students will be able to read complex literary texts (many of which are international in scope) and to perform advanced (by U.S. standards), ninth-grade-level mathematics (Macías 1990; Martin 1994).

In terms of classroom climate, a walk down Seguín's halls almost any time during the day would confirm the truth of Cuahtemoc's observation that students are characteristically *"humillados"* or subdued. Macías (1990) suggests that classrooms in Mexico are typically "noisy" by U.S. standards because teachers value and nurture in their students an ability to communicate and express themselves with confidence. This emphasis on self-expression may have originated in an earlier time period, when teachers attempted to develop the voices of the peasantry in order to prepare them for an industrializing economy. Nevertheless, a proclivity for dialogue and interaction continues to characterize much schooling in Mexico today (Macías 1990). With these qualities of caring relations, high expectations inscribed in the national curriculum, and expressive classroom environments as their experiential backdrop, immigrants' critique of U.S. schooling makes good sense.

Before specifically addressing the question of differences in levels of social capital—the final piece in the larger puzzle of immigrant achievement and U.S.-born underachievement, a counterexample of unsuccessful immigrant youth is useful. The next group of students constitutes an "at-risk" segment of the immigrant population, and they serve as an important reminder that U.S. schools select out the more "difficult" immigrant students by not servicing their needs. This group's account also enables further consideration of the question of *empeño*.

Pre-Literate Youth

In early November 1992, an Anglo math teacher mentioned to me that two Spanish-speaking, preliterate students had been misas-

signed to her ninth-grade class. She was in the process of negotiating with counselors and the school principal to relocate them to
a more appropriate classroom. Since Seguín's curriculum had no
provisions for preliterate youth at the time, the teacher advocated
placing these students in ESL courses, where at least they could
communicate with a Spanish-speaking teacher.

I meet her students, Carolina and Lupita, and we schedule a
lunchtime interview. At the cafeteria, Estéban, a friend of both
girls, joins us. The three agree to be interviewed as long as I
promise not to tape-record the conversation. To allay their discomfort (and perhaps distrust), I explain my research at length,
put away my tape recorder, and take only short notes. I suspect
that these students' fearfulness reflects either their immigrant
(possibly undocumented) status or their awareness of the stigma
attached to "preliterates," a term the teachers use in a whisper,
with eyebrows raised and an incredulous tone in their voices.

After passing through the sandwich line in the cafeteria, we
make our way to the cafeteria tables outside, where there is less
noise. On the way out, Lupita mentions that they are all considering dropping out of school before the end of the academic year.

"School is too hard. We're always behind in our work and we
don't get enough help," Carolina says, in Spanish. Accommodat-
ing her books on a corner table, she continues, still in Spanish,
"None of us went to school for very long in Mexico."

Estéban comments that besides P.E., the only class he likes is
art, because there he does not feel too "*avergonzado*" ("embarrassed") for not being able to read well.

By now we are all seated and I am groping for an appropriate
response. Perhaps paternalistically, I suggest to Estéban that he
should not feel *avergonzado* but instead consider this an opportunity to learn. Defensively, Carolina reinforces Estéban's view,
noting that their teachers spend more time feeling sorry for
them—or wondering why and how they ended up in their
classes—than they do teaching them anything.

Lupita elaborates, telling me that at the beginning of the
school year, her Anglo math teacher had complained to the principal—out loud and in front of all her classmates—that she did
not belong in the class. Lupita found this experience extremely
humiliating. She is not, she states, so "*pendeja*" ("stupid") not to

understand what her teacher was saying. When I saw Lupita's math teacher the following semester, I asked her if she recalled having embarrassed Lupita. No, she said she hadn't any recollection of that. Shrugging off Lupita's memory, the teacher offered, apparently meaning it to be a cutting observation, the following bit of tortured logic: "When they can't even write their names, makes you wonder why they even come to school at all."

Lupita tells me that six weeks passed before she was removed from the class; in the meantime, her teacher made no effort to teach her anything. So, Lupita's entire first six weeks of school were a miserable waste of time, "*A mi me tenían ahí como pendeja, como sorda y muda en esa clase*" ("They had me in there like an idiot, like a deaf mute in that class"). Along with Carolina, who also had been misassigned, she was eventually placed in an ESL class with a sympathetic and knowledgeable Spanish-speaking teacher. This female faculty member, who was skilled at working with students at varying levels of oral, reading, and writing fluency, left Seguín the following semester. Her departure may have contributed to both girls' decision to drop out of school before the year's end.

Estéban interjects his view that none of them had entered Seguín expecting special treatment. It is the unexpected and uncalled-for mistreatment that has been so difficult to bear. For a second time, he states that he is made to feel *avergonzado* for not being able to read well in either English or Spanish. He also notes that getting help is a problem because it means calling attention to himself. The students in some of his classes treat him differently once they discover that he cannot read. "*Como si tuvieramos una enfermedad*" ("Like if we had a disease"). He ends up asking his friends, Carolina and Lupita, for help.

These students' profound academic needs stem from their parents' very low levels of education, combined with their own low and uneven schooling experiences in Mexico. Carolina's school, located in a rural area outside of San Miguel in Guanajuato, burned down before she ever got a chance to attend. Despite promises from government officials, the school was never rebuilt. Carolina's mother tried to compensate by imparting to her five children, albeit with her second-grade education, some of the rudiments of literacy.

Eventually, Carolina attended a *primaria* in a distant community for about a year. Then her father's pickup truck started having mechanical problems. Carolina acknowledges that she felt embarrassed about attending school with younger children, but she says that she appreciated the attention and care she received from her teachers. Although her father's truck was eventually repaired, she never returned to school. Carolina assumes this was because she shared in the responsibility of tending the sheep and goats on the family's *rancho* (ranch). In late summer 1992, the family's dire economic circumstances forced them to move to the United States. With only one year of formal schooling, Carolina courageously enrolled at Seguín.

In a solemn tone, Estéban recounts several tragic childhood experiences, including his mother's untimely death while giving birth to him, leaving his father with the responsibility of raising three young sons. With two older brothers at work on the farm, a brief window of educational opportunity opened for Estéban. As a six year-old, he traveled to a *primaria* in a *pueblo* (town) thirty miles from his home, catching a ride each way with an uncle who commuted for business purposes.

Because of the high cost of manual labor, Esteban's family had to maximize its earning power in order to save their property. This strategy soon included making use of the extra set of hands Estéban could provide. Consequently, after his second-grade year, which incidentally, he had failed, his father decided to take him out of school. The family's woes nevertheless multiplied. Despite years of hard work growing feed for cattle, economic crises forced his father to sell their farm. The new owner became Estéban's father's *patrón* (boss). This proved to be more than the father could bear. He and his sons left for the United States. They pursued work in Houston because Estéban's father had a cousin living here who had said that jobs were plentiful.

As he and Carolina talk, I notice the redness of their skin and the early signs of facial wrinkles wrought by sheer overexposure to the sun. Estéban's voice sounds scratchy and he rarely establishes eye contact with me, perhaps because of the sadness of his account. He peels scabs—apparently the result of a skin condition—from his knuckles while he speaks. Lupita seems similarly rugged. Her occasional, broad smile reveals several black holes where there should have been teeth. Enduring lives of economic and emotional hardship has aged each of these students far beyond their years.

Lupita explains that for two years, the school that she attended was only open two or three days a week. Its chronic underfunding meant that it had to rely on itinerant teachers who made the rounds among several rural schools in the area. Despite her lack of *secundaria* schooling, Lupita, too, had enrolled at Seguín, hoping to learn enough English to get a job as a receptionist in an office somewhere.

At this point, I ask Carolina and Estéban why they remain in school. Like Lupita, they are instrumentally oriented: each wants to learn how to speak, read, and write in English and in Spanish. Whereas Carolina expresses a desire to someday own a house-cleaning business, Estéban imagines that he would most likely continue helping his father, who works for a local landscaping firm. He mentions that his father's extensive knowledge of plants and farming makes him an especially valuable employee—but his Anglo boss, who always makes use of Estéban's father's suggestions, never rewards him financially for his expertise. Revealing his working class consciousness, Estéban observes, cynically, "*No importa que sea gringo, es otro patrón*" ("It doesn't matter that he's a *gringo*. He's another boss").

Estéban tells me that what motivates him to stay in school is the possibility that he could better his life. He especially wants to avoid the kinds of abusive work relationships his father has had to cope with. With a clenched fist, he divulges another source of his inner strength and perseverance: "*No me quejo mucho porque yo se que ahorita están las cosas durísimas en Mexico. Este entendimiento me da mucha fuerza. Tengo que seguir dándole la lucha*" ("I do not complain too much because I know how right now times are very difficult in Mexico. This understanding gives me a lot of strength. I must keep on struggling").

Despite having attended the eighth grade in a Houston middle school, Estéban complains that he was not well prepared for high school. There he floundered because he was assigned far too many classes that were inappropriate for his needs. He eventually moved to the ESL track where he took ESL courses for most of the day. Although he learned more in ESL than he would have if he had remained in the regular track, his ESL classes emphasized speaking English over reading or writing the language. Now he is failing his non-ESL classes, since these require facility in reading and writing English.

I ask Estéban to clarify what he was doing in the regular curriculum. He replies that he had been misassigned, a mistake he attributes to his middle school having failed to provide Seguín with correct information about him. Hoping to be assigned to more appropriate classes, he spent the first two months of the academic year waiting to speak to a counselor, instead of going to lunch. When he finally got an opportunity to explain his situation to a counselor, he insisted on being tested for ESL because, he reasoned, the test would surely reveal his language limitations. His request was denied. The counselor he had waited so long to see told him that testing was out of the question—but she also told him that she wasn't the ESL coordinator. In scratchy, accented English, Estéban repeats her words, "Not my job description." Feeling humiliated, he never returned to the counseling office. Estéban wonders, rhetorically, how the counselor could deny him testing if she wasn't the ESL coordinator. I agree with his reasoning; the counselor's decision was neither logical nor consistent.

I tried to help Estéban by introducing him to a Community in Schools (CIS) counselor whose job description includes troubleshooting on students' behalf. However, because of institutionalized definitions of turf—with CIS having no formal jurisdiction over the counseling process—their capacity to provide the kind of assistance he most needed was nil. No schedule change resulted. Whereas others would have given up, Estéban's creative ingenuity kicked in. In a February encounter with Estéban, I learned that after Christmas break, he negotiated his grades with his teachers in every subject. In several classes, his teachers allowed him to take oral rather than written exams. In one class, instead of writing essays, the teacher gave him permission to copy paragraphs from the textbook for a grade. Though it embarrassed him, he also negotiated in several classes to have a fellow student read aloud text-based assignments in a back corner of the room so that he would not get behind on material that he was unable to read himself.

Estéban confessed that this strategy had its limits—especially with his mathematics textbook, which he could never understand, even after several readings of the same material. Texts in science and literature were also challenging but somehow less difficult to understand. Another recurring problem was that few students would commit to reading aloud for more than a few days at a time. Even with a renegotiated system of evaluation, Estéban continued to receive mostly poor or failing grades. Amazingly, for awhile longer, he kept trying, perhaps sustained by his purely instrumental desire to achieve oral and written fluency in English.

Despite Estéban's inventiveness and *empeño*, the cards were stacked against him, just as they were for Carolina and Lupita. School records show that all three had dropped out by the middle of the spring semester. They survived as long as they did by clinging to each other and by leveraging assistance from understanding teachers and fellow students whenever possible. Clearly, these youths' lack of human capital layered over the stigma of being preliterate establishes fertile ground for social decapitalization. Under more favorable circumstances, "clinging to each other" and "leveraging assistance" could be first steps in developing social capital. These youth, however, possess nothing obvious to "trade" in order to sustain social capital. This is especially obvious with Estéban, who needs others' skills with little to offer in return, causing him to feel humiliated all the time.

Because, until the fall of 1993, there were no actual classrooms for preliterates, their social decapitalization rested squarely with the structure of the curriculum. Even the more sympathetic teachers had little leeway in this context. Without such supports, achieving even limited, instrumental goals become unrealizable.

Such students have little chance of ever passing the Texas Assessment of Academic Skills (TAAS) exam—the state's standardized examination required for graduation—or of earning all of the required credits for graduation. However, their perseverance in a frequently hostile environment that is decidedly ill-suited to and demonstrably uninterested in their needs is remarkable. It bears witness to the strength of their desire for and commitment to learning. Learning—not TAAS or graduation credits—was what mattered most to them. It was not, unfortunately, what mattered most to the school.

In sum, although *empeño* is a necessary and important quality, it does not in itself guarantee academic success. If students like

Estéban, Carolina, and Lupita, who possess abundant amounts of *empeño*, face tremendous odds in their efforts to achieve an education, how much poorer are the chances for success among the many U.S.-born youth who possess little or no *empeño* and who participate in peer groups that lack a well-defined and effective achievement orientation. Seguín classrooms are filled with students who are described by their parents and friends as "*desganados*" (or lacking in will), the antithesis of *empeño*. Unlike so many immigrant youth who enjoy a pro-school orientation, they lack *ganas* (will) and are "tuned out" of school (LeCompte and Dworkin 1991). A key cause of this apathy is the difference in levels of social capital that characterize each group.

IMMIGRANT YOUTH AND THE QUESTION OF *EMPEÑO*

During the discussion I had with the English-Speaking Immigrants group, Lázaro suggested that *empeño* is an individual attribute that places many immigrant youth in a favorable light with their teachers, who regard them as "model students." Just as Matute-Bianchi (1991) observed in her study of immigrant youth, these students' compliant, deferential, and polite demeanor is an important factor enabling their achievement.

An individualistic perspective on *empeño*, however, disregards Mexicans' historic socioeconomic position as members of the working class who continue to predominate in the manufacturing and lower-level service sector jobs that prop up Houston's underbelly. That Seguín students' parents exude *empeño* and work with smiles on their faces for minimum and subminimum wages does not mean that they would not work for more money if given the opportunity. Nor does it mean that they share in their own exploitation. Instead, their silence and politeness before exploitative social superiors largely reflects their structurally disempowered position in society. Similarly, the "politeness" and "compliance" of immigrant youth follows logically from their lack of social power. Their "politeness" is perhaps as much about deference as it is about powerlessness or an expression of their belief that they are not "entitled" to openly defy school authority or assert their own vision of schooling.

An individualistic perspective on *empeño* also belies Lázaro's highly supportive peer group reality. He personally benefits from a $1,700.00 computer purchase Linda's family made. The computer sits in Linda's family's living room; friends like Fito and Lázaro take turns using it on weekdays and weekends. In contrast to most of their classmates, who submit handwritten papers, members of this friendship group pride themselves on submitting letter-quality printed work. Because of their shared quest for fluency in all aspects of the English language, all especially appreciate the spelling and thesaurus functions on the computer's word processing program. They all firmly believe that their grades have improved as a result of using the computer.

In her response to Lázaro, Linda proposes an alternative interpretation of *empeño*. She sees *empeño* (or a lack thereof) as a process about which a teacher must remain conscious when dealing with youth. She invokes the holistic, apprehending-of-the-other interpretation of caring as integral to the instructional agenda. This leads her to suggest that the job of teaching includes caring for students regardless of their levels of *empeño*.

Students will always vary in the extent to which they manifest such qualities as *empeño* and perseverance. Rather than assigning differential worth to students in accordance with their manifest levels of pro-school orientations, teachers' authentic caring accepts and embraces this diversity in disposition unconditionally. Linda's pedagogical insight squares with caring theorists' call for attention to the total person and the withholding of judgment.

Linda's conceptualization of *empeño* as process approximates my critique of the caring literature (see chapter 1). Focusing on the dynamic and reciprocal aspects of *empeño* helps make clear how returns to *empeño* depend on the level of human and social resources youth have or have access to and the extent to which such resources are collectively marshaled to promote their achievement. The most significant way in which immigrant groups differ from U.S.-born youth—as well as from youth in mixed friendship groups—is their marked tendency to combine *empeño* with other resources in a collectivist fashion.

This tendency is especially evident among the members of the Urban Monterrey Youth. Amalia and her family play an extraordinary role in fostering academic achievement within her friendship group. Several afternoons each week, Amalia's parents provide tutorial support in mathematics in their home to her friends and friends of friends. At first, sessions were arranged casually, with a phone call to the family the night before. As students came to know about this opportunity through word-of-mouth, however, Amalia's parents had to establish a more formal procedure. When fifteen students showed up on their doorstep on the afternoons right before examinations, they began meeting with students in scheduled, half-hour increments. As this cut into the family's dinner time, parents of the participating youth—including Cuahtemoc's and Joaquín's—contributed dishes of freshly made *fideo* (vermicelli), *enchiladas*, or *frijoles* (beans) so that the tutoring could proceed uninterrupted. Reciprocity takes other forms, as well. Cuahtemoc and Joaquín, for example, frequently assist Amalia's father on weekends with house repairs of various kinds.

Amalia and her parents are held in very high esteem by the scores of youth they have helped. Associations that have evolved out of these activities have benefited Amalia, as well. When I saw her the following spring semester, Amalia told me that she was working as an apprentice for a fellow student's parents who operate a small income-tax business out of their home. They hired her because they were grateful for Amalia's parents' help; thanks to their tutoring, this family's son had received high grades in geometry. They taught Amalia enough about taxes and tax returns that she now earns a few dollars for every tax form she fills out for fellow immigrant youth who work but lack familiarity with the system.

A similar admixture of *empeño* and social capital is also found among other members of the group. For example, several share the same ESL classes or have the same teachers; those with a stronger command in English, like Cuahtemoc, often assist those with less. Also, Joaquín's science abilities make him the one everyone in the group turns to for help on science homework or take-home examinations. He is highly regarded by his friends as a very knowledgeable and patient person who explains things well. According to Amalia, though, Joaquín is not consistently helpful. "Probably because of his '*machismo*,'" she tells me, in Spanish. "*A los hombres siempre les gusta que les ayudes, pero luego tienes que doblarles el brazo para que te ayuden.*" ("Men always want to be helped but then you have to twist their arms for them to help you.") Judging by what I saw among the females in the friendship groups I interviewed, girls require no arm-twisting. If anything, they give much too freely of their time and skills. They are indisputably the chief purveyors of social capital.

CROSS-GENERATIONAL GENDER AND SOCIAL CAPITAL

Close to half (44 percent) of the groups I interviewed contained both females and males (see Table A.1 in appendix). Gender-mixed groups are also found in each generation (four groups are first-generation, one is mixed-generation, and six are U.S.-born). Across my sample of eleven gender-mixed groups, females exhibit a clear pattern of being the providers of academic-related support, especially to their male friends and boyfriends. This support ranges from giving advice on courses, translating assignments, offering encouragement to stay in school, acting as sounding boards for problems, and providing assistance on written assignments and exams. Moreover, this pattern is evident cross-generationally, probably for reasons that tie into Amalia's observation of gender-role expectations.

Being a purveyor of support in the academic realm appears to be an extension of females' nurturing role. For example, immigrant and U.S.-born females in the two groups described below regularly completed their boyfriends' entire writing assignments for them. I never found any indication of an opposite situation in which a male assumed full responsibility for a female's schoolwork.

I labeled the first group the "Current Events/ESL Students" because they most enjoy reading Spanish-language newspapers and watching Spanish-language television news. Graciela, a sophomore immigrant in the group, regularly completes her boyfriend Armando's homework assignments, forging his handwriting. She explains that she does his homework because the long hours he works at a local meat market leave him little time for schoolwork. "*Lo hago porque él trabaja mucho [despues de la escuela] y no tiene suficiente tiempo.*" ("I do it because he works a lot [after school] and he doesn't have the time.") Graciela does not have a salaried after-school job, but her daily responsibilities at home include housework and taking care of three younger siblings for several hours until her parents return home from work. Given her own time constraints, I cannot help wondering whether what Graciela really means is that Armando's time is more valuable than hers.

I suggest to them that their actions will minimize Armando's learning if he doesn't do the work himself. "*Como quiera aprendo*" ("I still learn"), he counters. They maintain that he simply skips a step by reading over the work Graciela has already done. This arrangement, which evolved over time, began with Graciela translating the homework assignments Armando received in his regular (non-ESL classes) such as math and social studies, which are taught in English. Graciela fears that without her help, her boyfriend might fail.

"But what good is passing if you don't know the material?" I object. With no apparent misgivings, both assure me that Armando is indeed learning. What strikes me as I talk with them is how perfectly able Armando appears. For instance, he demonstrated a thorough and up-to-date understanding of the L.A. riots when I first joined the group for lunch. He mentioned ex-Police Chief Darryl Gates, Peter Ueberroth—the political leader in charge of rebuilding South Central Los Angeles—and the impending trial of the three African American men accused of beating white trucker Reginald Denny during the riot. Despite the many hours he may work at his after-school job, he clearly has time and energy available for watching and listening to news media. Armando's free time is not really free. It occurs at Graciela's expense—and ultimately at his own, as well.

During the initial interview that I conducted with another group (all U.S.-born), the Rappers, I spoke with Norma, a young woman whose concern for her boyfriend's ego and his cultural identity led her to spend more time on his homework than on her own. Admitting that her schoolwork has begun to suffer, Norma justifies her investment in her boyfriend's schoolwork by saying that if she does not help him, "Chach will definitely drop out of school." She confesses that she is "working on both her boyfriend's attitude toward school and his taste in music." Norma explains that none of Chach's teachers like him. He got in trouble with the law just once and it was all downhill after that. "Don't take much to get a bad rep, you know." She claims that "helping Chach helps him to feel good about himself—you know, getting a good grade now and then." After every good grade, Chach takes Norma out for a "really nice evening out on the town." She adds that doing Chach's homework teaches her "a lot." "It just doesn't show in my grades," she remarks, smiling.

Since both Norma and Chach are freshmen, I take the liberty of mentioning that they seem rather young to be dating. Norma replies that now that she's had her *quinceañera*, or her sweet fifteen ceremony, her parents feel that she is old enough to date. I ask her if her parents know how much she helps Chach. She says that she would never tell them, partly because they are not "too excited" about him.

"They think he's *agringado* [too white]," she explains.[7]

"What about the time it takes away from your own work?" I probe.

"I make Bs and some Cs. Not bad if you ask me. As long as I'm not failing, they don't notice anything."

With respect to his taste in music, Norma is critical of Chach's interest in gangsta' rap, which she believes is too violent and "talks too much about 'bitches and hos.'" Norma likes rap music, too, but she feels that Chach's musical taste is too narrow. She says that he needs to listen to more Mexican and *Tejano* (Texas Mexican) music.

"It's like he doesn't know who he is, like he wants to be black. So I always tell him to take me to *Tejano* clubs when we go out. He's starting to get into Selena, *La Mafia*, and Emilio Navaira. I feel kinda' sorry for him."

Out of curiosity, I ask her if her boyfriend's attitude toward school and his taste in music have anything to do with one another.

"I think so. It's like he's angry and the music's angry. He can't understand why I'm not angry."

"Like with what?" I press her.

"You know, with whites and the system gettin' you down. It's a black thing. What I think is if he's more Mexican or *Tejano*, there's more to live for."

"What do you mean?" I query.

Norma either would not or could not explain.

"I don't know . . . but he's Mexican and I'm helping him to know it and feel good about it."

The coaching, prodding quality of Norma's nurturing reminded me of the dynamics between another couple I came across, this one in a gender-mixed (and racially mixed) group. The pair consisted of Melissa, a U.S.-born Mexican, and Scott, her black male friend. Melissa regularly coached Scott on the principles of positive thinking she learned in her youth group at church. She described her contribution to the relationship this way:

> He says I'm his "self-esteem coach," but I do it as a good friend who cares. During lunch we often talk about visualizing and meditation experiences. I'm teaching him what I learned . . . how high school and life is about mind control and those of us who care enough to do something about it, how we're supposed to help *our fellow man* [my italics].

Despite the New Age overtones, what Melissa really seems to be doing is acting out the ancient, one-way, woman-as-helpmate-to-man role.

The young women I spoke with at Seguín seem oblivious to the imbalances in the favors they give to (as opposed to receive from) their male friends. Nor do they seem to view their support either as a chore or as the fulfillment of sexist expectations. Instead, the girls appear to be involved in exchange relationships akin to the "culture of romance" that Holland and Eisenhart (1990) observe in their study of college-going white women (also see Valenzuela 1999). That is, the construction of a female identity in traditional terms invariably translates into compromises women—and in this case, girls—make to secure the love and affection of a male. Like Chach, who takes Norma out for a "really nice evening out on the town," men often respond to such women with personal attention and gifts. Like Norma, whose own achievement suffers as a result, women caught up in a culture of romance scale back their own aspirations to achieve heterosexual love and attention. Perhaps to escape dreary lives as Holland and Eisenhart (1990) suggest, Graciela, Norma, and Melissa derive pleasure from the thought that their interventions are crucial to their male friends' academic success or to their psychological well-being. A culture of romance thus reveals how gender inequality can minimize what would otherwise be a positive collective impact of social capital.

Gender-based support is also evident among the single, mixed-gender group of three males and two females belonging as well to a mixed-generation group. Among these students, who jokingly refer to themselves as the "Achievement Gang," the females play the role of encouraging and overseeing their boyfriends and a third male friend in the group. None of these students actually does very well in school, and as a group, they have only a low level of social capital. They nevertheless see themselves as an "achievement gang" because they combine elements of a pro-school ethos with gangster-like attire.

Betty, a sophomore, regularly checks up on her friends Jerry, a sophomore, and Benny, a freshman, throughout the day. She monitors whether they come to school, show up at their classes, and turn in their assignments on time. Cued by the information I had already gathered from other groups, I ask Betty whether she provides other kinds of assistance, like helping her friends with their homework. In a bantering tone, with Jerry and Benny listening on and laughing, Betty responds, "Man, I'm the one who needs help! And do I get it? No! From these guys? You know we're in bad shape if *I* am helping *them*." She throws some hard punches, but the young men are unfazed.

In a matter-of-fact tone, Jerry states that Betty helps him to not "mess up." This is important because he says he's "very weak" and easily tempted when someone asks him to "skip and go get high." Benny contends that his only weakness is his best friend Jerry. He appreciates Betty's riding hard on Jerry because he knows that "if Jerry's in line, I won't skip." Jerry and Benny argue over which of them is the worst influence, but they both agree that Betty is a positive influence. Jerry mentions that his mother encourages him to hang around with Betty because, in the past, whenever he's gotten into a group with "all guys," he inevitably "take[s] a wrong turn."

"She knows I'm in good hands with Betty," he says, confidently.

"From one woman's arms to another," I mutter to myself.

Jerry's comment about his mother reminds me of a conversation I had with a parent whose son, David, had run into serious trouble with some boys at school who threatened his life. Throughout middle school, this parent had cautioned her son to avoid other children, telling him, "At school, you are to have no friends! After school, you are to come straight home!" In practice, this directive led David to hang out exclusively with girls. This made his mother feel more comfortable, but David told me that having female friends was a mixed blessing, for it made other males extremely jealous. These jealousies followed him into high school and led to death threats. David's reaction was to transfer to another school before the end of his first six weeks.

Jerry's and David's mothers apparently believe that their sons' interests are best served by females who nurture and watch over them. For their part, the young women in the gender-mixed groups seem very comfortable with and uncritical of this role. The only resistance to gender-role expectations that I heard young women at Seguín express was directed at their parents' expectations. I did not collect data on these specific issues, but a general grievance among the female students was that parents, especially fathers, tend to be more strict with and accord fewer privileges to their daughters than to their sons. Interviews with several Community in Schools counselors support this as a common complaint. At least a third of the problems they address daily are complaints from female students about overbearing parents, especially immigrant parents, who are, at least in their daughters' view, excessively strict.

Olsen's (1997) ethnography of immigrant high school youth delves deeply into these issues of strict parental monitoring of females' behavior. When so confined, Olsen finds that schools become liberating places where girls can exercise more fully their quest for individuality and independence. However, when this quest lands them into demanding and exploitative relationships, the sense of independent thought and action in a system of patriarchy is mere illusion. Ironically, it may be girls' lifelong experience with stronger social control mechanisms that results in their ability to provide "safe spaces" for potentially wayward males.

Evidence on gender-mixed friendship groups thus suggests how social capital is informed and possibly thwarted by gender-role behaviors and expectations. Moreover, as Betty explicitly notes, the quality of school-related support that females are able to provide to their male friends is contingent on their own abilities and prior academic training. The more academically adept, like Norma, appear to strike an "even" balance, at least in their own minds, between their investments in their boyfriends and themselves.

To determine whether gender-mixed groups exhibited a stronger orientation toward schooling than same-gender groups, I compared data on group activities between all-male, all-female, and mixed-gender groups within each generational grouping (i.e., immigrant, mixed-generation, and U.S.-born). In the case of immigrants, I found no differences in the level of preoccupation with schooling.

In contrast, to the extent that youth in mixed-generation and U.S.-born groups exhibit a pro-school orientation, it is largely due to the efforts of the females in these groups—that is, to young women like Norma, Melissa, and Betty. With one exception (discussed below), mixed-generation and U.S.-born groups that were either all-male or all-female ignored academics as a collective concern. Homework and reading assignments, for example, typically were taken care of by the individual.

When asked about the kinds of things that they talked about and did as a group, the most common topics students in same-gender groups mentioned were nonacademic and non-school-related. More than their male counterparts, females in U.S.-born and mixed-generation groups seemed engrossed in others' welfare. Talking about personal and familial problems during and after school occupied most of their time together. The few school-related problems that were discussed dealt either with negotiating bureaucratic hurdles—like getting a schedule change or getting advice on how to deal with excessive absences or tardies—or with relationships with students and school personnel.

The most common activities for the all-female groups were gossiping (universally referred to as "*chismeando*"), hanging out together at school, talking on the phone during the evenings, and attending dances on weekends. All-male groups also mentioned hanging out together at school and attending dances on weekends. The boys' list of favorite pastimes, however, also included beer drinking, cruising, playing sports, and "getting over" (i.e., getting away with illicit activities—eluding the law at school and on the streets).

Not only did students in the mixed-generation and U.S.-born groups seem uninterested in their day-to-day academic responsibilities, they had given little or no thought to their futures. Most consistently expressed a desire to attend college someday, but they always couched this goal in nebulous and noncommittal terms. Students in these groups frequently told me that it was "too soon" for them to be thinking about college. "I'm just a freshman." "I'm supposed to have fun right now." "I'll think about that when I become a junior or senior." "I'll worry about that later." Some consciously opted to defer thinking about college until they had passed the TAAS exam required for graduation. "I'll worry about that if it looks like I'll graduate," was a typical response. Since this kind of student commonly fails the TAAS test repeatedly (the exam is offered once a semester), putting off thinking about college until one passes it effectively means never thinking about college.[8] Ironically, 100 percent of the youth I spoke with agreed, when asked, that to have a nice house and a nice car, and to live in a nice neighborhood, required a college education. This understanding, however, seemed to have no direct effect on their actions or their attitudes toward school.[9] Especially revealing were the more depressed responses I got from several youth:

"Miss, I feel very scared about my future. I really don't like to talk about these things." (U.S.-born, freshman female in the "Kickers" group)

"I hope I marry good because I know I'll never make a lot of money." (U.S.-born, freshman female I met in P.E. class in October 1992)

"You gotta be smart to go to college. I wish I had what it takes." (U.S.-born, sophomore male I met in the cafeteria line in February 1993)

These handful of vexed responses aside, posing questions to youth in the mixed-generation and U.S.-born groups at Seguín about their future plans more typically elicited quizzical looks. They were equally perplexed when I raised concerns about how they intended to actually achieve the few hazy goals they did mention. These kind of exchanges made it clear to me that adults had abdicated their responsibilities toward youth. Very few students possessed any understanding of the relationship between the courses they were taking and the jobs or careers they hoped to pursue. Several students immediately changed their minds about wanting to become medical doctors when I informed them that they would need to take many math and science courses. Aimlessness and a poorly defined achievement ethos prevailed among these youth. They had been socialized toward the ideal of someday attending college but insufficiently socialized into an understanding of the tools and knowledge they would need to reach such a goal. Despite possessing a rational understanding of their need for a college degree, college remained an emotionally and experientially remote notion.

That mixed-generation groups differed so little from U.S.-born groups in school orientations is noteworthy and speaks to the interplay of group composition and cultural assimilation that I problematize in the next chapter as an outcome of subtractive schooling. The immigrant youth in these groups were overwhelmingly long-term resident, acculturated youth who had come to the United States at a very young age. Consequently, they spoke either mostly English or "Spanglish." Though immigrant youth in mixed-generation groups spoke predominantly Spanish at home, they felt more comfortable speaking English or "Spanglish" at school with their friends. This comfort derived in part from having grown up in the United States, and thus having attended U.S. schools for virtually all their young lives. This meant that they identified strongly with, and were hard to distinguish from, their U.S.-born peers in terms of their self-representations. Other factors contributing to their preference for English/Spanglish were insecurities about their verbal skills in Spanish, which typically were much less developed than their skills in English, and social pressures to avoid appearing "too Mexican." (Discriminatory attitudes toward immigrant youth are explored more fully in the next chapter.) To underscore the importance of social capital to adolescents' academic achievement, I present below an analysis of an exceptional case of a U.S.-born youth group with a strong, collective orientation toward schooling.[10]

SOCIAL CAPITAL AMONG U.S.-BORN YOUTH

One U.S.-born youth group departed from the norm of noncollectivist orientations toward academic- or school-related matters. I refer to this gender-mixed group of five individuals as "Spanish Speakers" because of their positive orientation toward the Spanish language. They nurtured their Spanish-speaking skills by taking Spanish language courses, participating in the school's Spanish language club, and speaking Spanish among themselves. I met the members of this group in spring 1993, as I waited in a pizza line during the lunch period. They were selling pizza by the slice to fellow students to help raise money for the Spanish Club. After purchasing a slice, I edged into the perimeter of their group to listen in on the conversation they were having about language. In Spanish, a sophomore named Elizabeth chastises her freshman girlfriend Michelle for speaking too much English.

"Por que hablas tanto Inglés? Deberíamos de hablar mas español que inglés! ("Why do you talk in English so much? We should speak more in Spanish than English!")

Michelle takes the criticism well and responds laughingly, in English, "I know, I know. I just start talking in Spanish and then it turns to English!" Using a ridiculing term that immigrants use to refer to acculturated Mexican Americans, she exclaims, "I'm just a *pocha*, dude!"

Jason, a sophomore, reveals how in class, their Spanish teacher is always reminding Michelle to speak Spanish.

Michelle retorts that she wasn't supposed to be in beginning Spanish. *"Yo escogí computers pero me dieron español!"* ("I chose computers but they gave me Spanish!")

They chatter back and forth, with Michelle generating additional excuses for preferring to speak English, while Elizabeth and Jason tell her that they are doing her a favor by helping her practice her Spanish with them. Two other friends, Julie and Edward, stand nearby, listening, as they eat their pizza.

Out of the blue, I ask the group in a playful tone, *"Que pasa con Michelle? Porque no quiere hablar español?"* ("What's happening with Michelle? Why doesn't she want to speak Spanish?")

"Tiene verguenza" ("She's embarrassed"), Jason supplies, softly, surprised by my interjection.

I then explain to the group that I am a researcher and that I found their conversation interesting.

"We just don't wanna lose our Spanish," Elizabeth explains.

They oblige my request to interview them as a group once they have finished selling the remaining pizza. We step out through the nearest exit into a grassy area so that we can sit down and talk.

The formation of this group was institutionally mediated by the fact that all the members belong to the Spanish Club. They joined in the fall semester, but only Elizabeth and Jason have attended regularly. All, however, enjoy spending their lunch time selling pizza. Michelle is the pivotal member of the group. When I ask what kinds of things they do together, Julie responds, only half-jokingly, "Spend time with Michelle's family." Everyone chuckles, but it turns out that they had, indeed, spent the previous two weekends with Michelle's family, attending two family-related dances. The first was a church-related fund-raiser that Michelle's parents had helped organize and the second was a family reunion. Elizabeth tells me that since Michelle's parents are leaders in the same Catholic church her family attends, her parents let her spend time on weekends with them.

Julie concurs, "Yeah, I think that's why my mom lets me go out sometimes, too. They trust and like her parents."

"What about you guys?" I quiz the others, "Do your parents have any rules about going out?"

"*Mi Amá no me dice nada*" ("My mother doesn't say anything"), Jason replies, adding, "I don't have a father."

"*Los míos tampoco*" ("Mine neither"), Edward chimes in.

"We're all good friends because we all like to dance and we're all good dancers," Elizabeth elaborates.

"And speaking Spanish, too, right?" I suggest.

"Well, the Spanish thing just happened," Jason clarifies. "What it is is that we all like school and we would like to graduate from high school being able to talk in two languages because I know we've all lost a lot of our Spanish."

I then begin probing for their reasons for liking school. At first, they offer explanations that make them sound like the "Achievement Gang."

"We all look out for each other," one said.

"If someone's got a problem, we help them solve it."

They also explain that their group is bigger—two other members have different lunch periods. Then Jason provides some additional information that helps me understand their group solidarity. Taking a deep breath, he says:

> My father disappeared this year. He said he was going out to get a pack of cigarettes one night and he never returned. The group came through for me and kept me from dropping out or from hurting myself. I owe them a lot. I knew I had to pull it together, too, because my mom fell apart. I ran away and lived with Michelle's family for awhile but now I'm back home. My mom's still shook up, but it's not as bad now.

Jason's admission gives the group permission to talk.

"We were all scared for Jason," Elizabeth elaborates. "He didn't say how he almost got kicked out of school for losing his cool with a teacher."

"I was in so much trouble last semester," Jason mumbles.

"What happened?" I ask.

"It was this sub [substitute teacher] I had since the beginning of the year," Jason begins. "We were in class for four weeks with him and he didn't teach us nothin'. Here I was upset about my dad and he couldn't get past chapter one in the book. So I exploded with that *gringo* [white man] and asked him who he thought we were, just a bunch of stupid Mexicans? I got up and walked out of his classroom and he warned me never to come back. So I didn't and I failed the class. You know, it's like the school failed me and I had to suffer for it. Does that sound right to you?"

Jason's friends listen to the story quietly, with expressions of despondency.

"We all came together to help Jason," said Michelle, picking up the story. "He lived with us for three months and then everybody would come over to my house to talk to him and spend time together, a lot of the times, studying."

Jason smiles. "Michelle's family's great. There's so many *tíos* and *tías* [aunts and uncles] and a lot of them are like teachers and counselors—you know, people with good jobs and nice families. I'm their adopted son now."

"Did some of that rub off on you?" I wonder aloud.

"Yes, it did," he replies, earnestly. "From talking to her family, the main thing I learned is if you're a poor Mexican, you gotta take *caca* [shit] in this life. But it's so hard . . . like with that sub. I would still say what I said today. I think there is a point where you gotta stand up."

"I guess it's really how you do it that matters," I offer.

"Yes, Miss," Jason agrees. "I would do it different next time."

"We learn from each other's mistakes," Michelle remarks. "I explode with my parents, too, and Jason, Julie or one of us helps the other out."

In contrast to the one-on-one and female-dominant patterns of support that I observed in the other groups, the response to Jason's troubles is collective, expanding beyond the boundaries of his friendship with Michelle. A disproportionate amount of the group's energies are directed toward Jason, but there is no hint of exploitation on his side. In exchange for the kindness of all the parties involved, Jason offers a sincere and respectful self. At least, this is how I interpret his openness and the comments he made about his emotional growth over the previous months.

As the discussion goes on, I gather that Michelle's family has become the hub of the group's social life, mainly because her parents organize social activities for youth in their church. Michelle's mother, it turns out, is a former bilingual education teacher. She has always encouraged Michelle (and now her friends) to develop and maintain fluency in Spanish. She continually tells them that they're all on the path to brighter futures because, in her words, "The future is brown." In addition to Michelle's parents, a couple of her well-educated aunts have also embraced the group, encouraging them to begin thinking about their college careers. Elizabeth and Julie note that they hope to attend the University of Texas, where both of Michelle's aunts went to school. So that these teenagers and others might achieve their dreams, Michelle's parents helped start a scholarship fund at their church. Help from supportive, activist adults, combined with the closeness and cooperation Michelle and her friends have developed among themselves, give this group a sense of momentum and direction rare among freshmen and sophomores at Seguín High School.

Because I wonder how Michelle and her friends view their

school, I ask the group some general questions. The query "How helpful has the school been in helping you pursue your dreams?" results in an animated discussion about whether teachers at Seguín are good or bad. With keen insight, Michelle, characteristically moving back and forth between Spanish and English, offers the following perspective. Note how her criticism zeroes in on basic elements of aesthetic caring:

> How can teachers help us go to college when they can't see that our problems are right here . . . *aquí con la familia o con esta consejera o aquel maestro que no enseña bien o con el director que no maneja bien la escuela o con este horario que no está compuesto? Están ellos tan enfocados en los detalles que se olvidan de nosotros y también de nuestros futuros!* (. . . here with the family or with this counselor or that teacher who doesn't teach or with this schedule that's not fixed. They're so focused on the details that they forget about us and our futures!)

To support her opinion that Seguín teachers are good, Elizabeth argues that Michelle's criticism reflects a larger problem: In general, teachers don't like freshmen students (Michelle is a freshman). As a sophomore, Elizabeth finds that her teachers are mostly nice; some encourage their students to consider going to college.

This encouragement is very important to Elizabeth. "But," she says, "I think it flies over most students' heads."

"Why, do you think?" I press.

"Maybe because they don't have support like we do," she guesses.

Julie chimes in, fist clenched, saying that as a group they are "tight."

Jason is less convinced that matters improve by the sophomore year. He complains bitterly about how counselors mishandled his schedule. Because he had been assigned to—and taken—two courses that he didn't need, and had failed one course, the only way he can graduate with his freshman cohort is to take summer school classes for two consecutive summers. He found out about this dilemma by chance, when he went to see his counselor about another matter.

"Pisses me off! How can I even think about going to college when getting out of high school is such a pain in the ass! What if I wouldn't have gone to see my counselor?"

"At least you got to see him," Julie consoles him, with the same delicate and respectful tone that all the group members use toward Jason.

Concerned, but still confident, Michelle says, "It's been hardest for Jason, but he'll graduate just the same. We're all going to make sure of that. He's already doing better in school than he was."

Jason agrees, "Yeah, my grades are better. I don't know how anybody puts up with me. *Pero éste lugar me da ansias!* ("But this place makes me anxious!") Think about it, it's one thing if *I* fail a course, but it's another if *I* have to pay for *their* mistakes."

I assure him that he doesn't have to convince me. "Don't let go of your group, man!" I advise him.

"Don't worry!" he responds, acknowledging that he knows just how important his friends are to his personal and academic well-being.

Teachers, whether good or bad, seem surprisingly peripheral to this group, given these students' conscious efforts to nurture a pro-school ethos. They never arrive at a consensus about whether the school and its teachers and counselors are mostly "good" or "bad." They do, however, have clear opinions about what qualities define the "best" kind of teacher or counselor. The best teacher or counselor, they tell me, is one who "helps you to be a better person book-wise and social-wise," "looks for ways to help and praise you, even if you think you don't deserve it," "connects with you rather than talking down to you," and "loves Mexicans and the Spanish language that we speak." These definitions embody the essential elements of authentic caring: connection, unconditional love, and a comprehensive apprehending of "the other."

As I had with the immigrant youth, I left this group of students feeling a strong sense of the power of interdependence. Their peer group reality is yet another reminder that adolescents welcome opportunities not only to care and nurture, but to be cared for and nurtured in ways that are sensitive to their present needs as well as to their future goals. As Michelle and Jason suggest, both kinds of sensitivity are essential and they address what it means to be a Mexican in this world.

Michelle's family's involvement in her friends' lives is tremendously important because of the tangible support it provides these youth. Her family not only opened their home to someone in desperate need, they also have redefined the boundaries of their extended family circle to include Jason and all of Michelle's other friends. This social milieu shapes and strengthens the bonds between the friends and reinforces their individual and group commitment to academic achievement. It also insulates them from the many distractions facing their peers in the other mixed-generation and U.S.-born groups. As a result, this group has developed enough confidence to build an academic identity and to recognize the compatibility between that identity and their Mexican, Spanish-speaking selves. The high levels of social capital embedded in their web of relations make it likely that these youth will successfully negotiate their passage into productive adulthood.

CONCLUSION

This chapter opened with a description of my chance encounter with Adriana, a disaffected, U.S.-born youth. The many discussions I held with immigrant, mixed-generation, and U.S.-born students suggest that Adriana's extremely tenuous academic identity emanates from her exposure to "subtractive schooling." These experiences have led her to define her world in terms even narrower than her classroom. Her generalization that no one at Seguín is "into school" reflects not only her own peer group reality, but also her social, cultural, and linguistic alienation from students like Maricela and the other Spanish-speaking, immigrant youth in her midst.

The varied experiences of the students I interviewed at Seguín also make clear that it is neither fair nor accurate to reduce the problem of poor achievement among U.S.-born youth to a lack of *empeño* (diligence). To do so is to individualize a collective problem that includes a paucity of social capital in their friendship groups. The importance of social capital to productive schooling orientations is especially apparent in the peer group world of immigrant youth: In most cases, a pro-school and pro-academic esprit de corps characterizes these groups. Mixed-generation and U.S.-born groups were rarely so oriented. Immigrants' collectivist orientation is enabled by the academic skills many acquired from earlier schooling experiences in Mexico. Thus, in their peer group, human capital based on the level of schooling and cognitive skills attained in Mexico *becomes* social capital. Nurturing a pro-school ethos sets these students apart from their U.S.-born peers who appear to reserve their collectivist ethos for nonacademic ventures. Academics are, for the most part, an individual concern.

A paradoxical finding obtained in the quantitative analysis is that while U.S.-born youth rate Seguín less positively and describe their teachers as less caring than immigrant students, U.S.-born students' achievement is significantly affected by teachers who provide them with help and support.[11] The lack of social capital among U.S.-born youth helps explain this finding. When youth are unavailable to one another as potential models for success or as providers of support, caring teachers become much more salient.

The critique of schooling offered by the immigrant students I focus on in this chapter needs to be reconciled with the quantitative evidence, which points to their significantly more positive schooling experience in comparison to U.S.-born youth (see chapter 1). Both views are compatible once the bidirectionality of the dual frame is considered: it simultaneously undergirds their more positive dispositions toward schooling and their reluctance to criticize their current situation. On balance, combining both of these factors would result in a relatively positive appraisal of school.

The qualitative evidence also sheds light on a key quantitative finding that young women make higher grades and do more homework than their male counterparts in every generation. Consistent with gender-role expectations, girls frequently serve as purveyors of social and academic support, particularly for their male friends and boyfriends. Since girls in the regular track tend to academically outperform their male peers (see chapter 1), the centrality of females with respect to academic-related endeavors is significant.

Finally, if achievement entails a social process whereby orientations toward school are nurtured in familiar contexts, and among those with similar dispositions, and if the curriculum to which youth are subjected is subtractive, then the weakened academic status of U.S.-born youth is best understood as a key consequence of schooling.

CHAPTER 5

Subtractive Schooling and Divisions among Youth

Many social forces contribute to the divisions that exist among youth at Seguín. This chapter focuses on the important role that subtractive schooling plays in deepening these divisions and undermining opportunities for cross-generational relationships.[1] The discussion amplifies current conceptualizations in the literature regarding the process of cultural assimilation (e.g., Vigil 1997) by highlighting the school—or more pointedly, the schooling process—as a powerful, state-sanctioned instrument of cultural de-identification, or de-Mexicanization. The chapter has three main parts. I begin by recounting a classroom experience that reveals how *Mexicanidad* ("Mexican-ness") is not only a negotiated identity but a point of contention. The classroom discussion highlights the existence of divergent forms of consciousness among Mexican youth, on the one hand, and helps illuminate the school's role in perpetuating these divergences, on the other.

The experiences of Mexican youth provide a unique opportunity to extend McCarthy's (1993) analysis of the "politics of difference" to a group whose internal differences are routinely masked by such inclusive terms as "Hispanic," "Latino," or "involuntary minority" (Ogbu's [1991, 1994] term). McCarthy argues that researchers who study subordinate groups in educational settings would more accurately account for observed educational outcomes if they paid greater attention to the "multivocal, multiaccented nature of human subjectivity and the genuinely polysemic nature of minority/majority relations in education and society" (p. 337). He maintains that what separates minorities from each other, as well as from majority whites, are their distinct needs, interests, desires, and identities. These differences inevitably surface in educational settings because groups do not share an identical consciousness.

McCarthy's (1993) injunction to accord greater attention to human subjectivity is especially important in the case of Mexican immigrant youth, whose schooling experiences demonstrate that schools may be simultaneously subjectively additive and objectively subtractive. That is, immigrant youth may acquire useful skills and knowledge but at the cost of losing significant cultural resources, including a rich and positive sense of group identification. Olsen's (1997) ethnographic study in a northern California high school observes this problematic as well. This subjective experience gains added significance when one considers that the history of public schooling for U.S.-Mexicans shows schools to be key sites for both ethnic conflict and the production of minority status (San Miguel 1987, forthcoming; Spring 1997). Moreover, that immigrants become an "ethnic minority" within one or two generations, challenges McCarthy's unexamined assumption that minority status is neatly a priori or exogenous to schooling.

According immigrant subjectivity serious attention requires reframing racial and ethnic differences: they are more than "stock" that individuals possess, manipulate, and bring to bear on institutional life. These differences are dynamically linked to a larger historic process of subtractive cultural assimilation, more commonly known as Americanization (Hernández-Chávez 1988; Bartolomé 1994). So, when we examine the day-to-day school lives of Mexican youth, it is important to recognize that these experiences unfold against a much larger backdrop that is neither neutral nor benign.[2]

In the second section of this chapter, I use documentary data and evidence gathered from participant observation to examine Seguín High's subtractively assimilationist practices. The discussion highlights the institutional impediments to a more additive, culture-affirming vision of schooling and furthers the thesis that schooling subtracts resources from youth. I demonstrate how the structure of both the Spanish language and English as a Second Language (ESL) programs neglect the needs of Spanish-language youth. These programs provide an illusion of inclusion, but the institutional message they convey is that Spanish is a second-rate language and that the goals of bilingualism and biculturalism are neither worthwhile nor expedient (Valdés 1998).

In the last section, I return to the group interview data to investigate attitudinal differences among immigrant, mixed-generation, and U.S.-born friendship groups. This analysis reveals how attitudinal differences in the areas of culture, language, and identity underlie the social cleavages that exist between groups. Mixed-generation youth groups who share in a bilingual and bicultural identity appear to have the most balanced and favorable attitudes toward their immigrant and U.S.-born peers. Their statements contrast markedly from their peers located in immigrant and U.S.-born groups. While immigrants see U.S.-born youth as "too Americanized" and as negligent for succumbing to the corrosive influences of the dominant culture, U.S.-born youth are either hostile or reticent, evading the subject of immigrants. I conclude by suggesting how the capacity of individuals to manipulate their ethnic identity in educational settings is largely mediated by a schooling process aimed at divesting youth of their *Mexicanidad*.

RELATIONSHIPS AND THE "POLITICS OF DIFFERENCE"

The following account of a discussion in a sophomore English class helps concretize the meaning of McCarthy's "politics of difference." The exchange makes clear the contested nature of the relationship between the Spanish language and a Mexican identity. It also shows the students' divergent conceptualizations of the term "Mexican." Finally, the episode described below brings into clearer focus the effects of subtractive schooling on relationships among youth and between youth and adults.

One September morning, I came across a teacher named Mr. Perry from the English Department. He was only temporarily employed at Seguín, "subbing" until the principal could find a permanent replacement. He recognized me as "the person from Rice," and he asked whether I would be willing to be a role model and talk to his students—whom he described as a "lively bunch"—about college. Since he was behind on his grading, he also confessed that he could use the break that my visit would provide. I agreed to talk to the class.

There were about twenty students present, all sophomores. It was a "low-turnout day," according to Mr. Perry. After reviewing his students' homework assignments, he introduced me to the class. I talked for a few minutes, encouraging the students to consider going to college and explaining about college admissions requirements. Then, an immigrant student named Aarón spoke up.

"How well do students have to know English for college?" he asked in a heavy accent, and with a long blade of grass lodged between his teeth.

I told him that being able to read and write English rather than speaking it especially well is what is most important. Aarón said that his counselor had discouraged him from taking Spanish because he already knew it, so he was wondering if he was wasting his time taking Spanish classes. I told him that any class that helps students read and write well, regardless of the language, is good preparation for college.

Aarón's friend, Michael, who was sitting next to him, told the class, smiling, "I'm teaching him English."

"Good, and your friend helps you keep up with your Spanish, too," I suggested.

"Naw, I don't speak Spanish," Michael responded.

Aarón interjected, "He does. He just say he don't."

Turning to Aarón, Michael gave him a sour look. "Just because I speak it *un poquito* ("a little") doesn't mean I speak it."

"He does, Miss. He does. I heard him," Aarón insisted, still with the blade of grass in his mouth.

Aarón then punched Michael's shoulder and Michael responded in kind, missing Aarón, who had dodged the punch by jerking his desk away. The desk tilted dangerously, teetering on a single leg for a split-second until Aarón wrestled it to the ground.

"Stupid!" Michael hissed, stonefaced as his classmates all burst into laughter.

Mr. Perry, who until then had been shuffling through papers on his desk, stopped and peered at the boys. "Okay, guys," he admonished them. "Settle down."

Despite the touchiness of the subject, I decided to pursue the language issue after the class had calmed down.

Empathizing with Michael, I said, "Look, I understand how it can be real hard when people expect you to know Spanish when you don't and especially when you haven't even been encouraged to hold onto it. And I'm writing about these things because this is a Mexican school where what language you speak is a big deal. So help me understand what you go through."

At first, everyone was silent. Then Jamail, the only African American male in the class, spoke up.

"I . . . I think it's hard for the immigrants here who don't know English because everyone expects them to know English," he offered, in a slow, thoughtful way. "In my classes, if no one translates for them, too bad. I couldn't do what they do."

A female student, who was filing her brightly polished red nails said, pointing first to me and then to Jamail, "Okay, so now I'm confused. You're saying some are expected to know Spanish and then you're saying some are expected to know English, two different things?"

Jamail explained, "I am expected to know English only."

Smiling, Aarón muttered loudly under his breath, "*Porque eres Negro.*"("Because you're black.") This was somehow funny to the rest of the class.

"No, seriously," I protested, addressing the young woman with the red nails. "You raised a good question."

An impatient Aarón clarified, "Teachers want Mexicans to know English. Mexicans want Mexicans to know Spanish."

As Michael began to stew in his seat, the closeness of his relationship with Aarón became even more apparent to me.

"Look, we talked about this already, Aarón," he said testily. "I can be Mexican and not know Spanish. I hate anyone to think that just because I am darker than Jamail over there, that I have to speak Spanish."

Again, the other students laughed, including Jamail, whose complexion was lighter than Michael's. Aarón peered toward the corner of the room where another friend and ally, an immigrant male, sat frowning at Michael's comment.

Speaking more assuredly, Aarón declared, "That's not Mexican. You're a Chicano!"

"So I'm a Chicano *and* Mexican," Michael retorted. " So I'm both!"

"Hey, hey, Michael. Chill!" Jamail coaxed. Several students chuckled, but most were listening intently as the discussion became more serious.

Then, from the furthest corner of the room, a young girl named Annalisa began to speak in a high-pitched, nasal tone. At first, her voice trembling, she produced only garbled words. The teacher put down his papers to listen to her. Annalisa paused, stared at the floor, and took a deep breath. Recovering from her false start, she began to describe a recent trip she had taken with her family to visit relatives in Mexico. She spoke of cousins who knew only Spanish and the difficulties she had in communicating with them because of her own lack of fluency. The most poignant statement she made was that her cousins referred to her as a *gringa* (white female) because of her poor command of Spanish.

"And I ain't no *gringa*," she told the class, still looking down at the floor. "They laughed when I said I was Mexican. And they said I lived in *Gringo-landia*."

Her classmates sat in silence until, dragging the consonants in his words, Jamail asked quietly, "Wh-what's th-that?"

"It means '*Gringo*-land' or America—the land where white people live," I explained.

"Ohhhh," he whispered.

Turning to Annalisa, I asked her if she had told her cousins that she felt insulted by their comments. She replied that because she had just met them and because she wanted them to think well of her and her family, she felt that she could not reveal how truly miserable they had made her feel. Instead, she smiled and laughed along with them, pretending that everything was fine.

"I don't like feeling this way," Annalisa continued, summing up her reactions to the trip, "but I feel like I never want to go back to Mexico to see them again."

Jenny, a student wearing three sets of gold hoop earrings of different sizes in her ears, suggested to Annalisa that maybe her cousins were jealous because she lived in the United States and they didn't.

"Maybe," Annalisa conceded, "but that still don't give 'em no right. . . ."

"No, it don't," Jenny agreed, interrupting, "but that's how I deal with it when my *güelito* (grandfather) says not to speak

Spanish if me and my sisters are going to speak it all *pocho*. I just always think he's jealous or something. He lives half a year with us, the other half in Mexico. I think he wishes we were all Mexican . . . Mexican only, 'cause he tells me and my sisters we're '*americanizadas*' ('Americanized'). I guess 'cause we listen to heavy metal and wear black or 'cause I got my ears this way." (Some students laugh.) For real, I heard him say *agringadas* ('whitened' women) about us one time. And that made me mad! Super mad! I'd hit anybody else who told me that! (More laughter.) Maybe I'm not Mexican. Maybe I'm just brown. But I sure ain't *agringada*!

Annalisa nodded slowly and sadly, the edges of her lips turned downward.

Trying to comfort Annalisa, who continued staring at the classroom floor, as if her ability to remain in control depended on her fixed gaze, Mr. Perry spoke up.

"Dear," he began, "I'm sorry they were mean to you, but can you help me understand just a little bit. . . . Uh, you *are* American and, uh, is it the word *gringo* or *gringo-landia* that hurt the most?"

In a frustrated tone, Michael replied for Annalisa. He told the teacher that the issue was not that Annalisa didn't think of herself as American, but that she was being told that she was not Mexican.

"Oh. Uh, you do think of yourself as American, then?" Mr. Perry questioned, failing to appreciate both the importance and the complexity of the identity issues with which the students were struggling.

"Of course," Annalisa replied, despondently.

At this point, all of the students paused. They looked at their teacher, disappointment and disgust apparent on every face. Some students shook their heads in disbelief.

Embarrassed, Mr. Perry apologized. "Okay, I'm sorry. I'm learning, too. . . ."

Ignoring the teacher, Jamail pointed to Aarón and began to verbalize what he had just learned by listening to his classmates. "So you be like her cousin when you tell Michael that he not Mexican. And Annalisa and Michael be mad because their family be Mexican even if they don't speak Spanish."

All heads in the classroom nodded approvingly.

"That's right, man," Michael confirmed, "and that's why I get mad at you, Aarón."

Flicking the blade of grass in the air like a tiny airplane, Aarón announced, "*'Ta 'ueno, 'ta 'ueno, ese* [Okay, okay, man] you Mexican, me Mexican, we all Mexican."

"You can't never be serious, man," Michael complained, rolling his eyes at Aarón's response.

Noticeably proud of his ability to grasp the meaning of the discussion, Jamail instructed Aarón, "So lay off on Michael, dude. Michael be Mexican and that's that."

That comment made Michael crack his second smile that morning. Aarón shrugged his shoulders as he began to collect his things. The bell rang, and the students rushed off to lunch with smiles on their faces, including Annalisa, who also looked relieved.

"The spotlight's tough, but you did good," I told her as she walked past me.

Still silent, she offered me a parting smile.

The relation of language to identity was the heart of the discussion. Aarón sees Spanish fluency and a Mexican identity as inseparable. As Annalisa's story shows, for Mexican Americans, this is a psychically threatening stance. Annalisa has to be Mexican because she knows that she is not white. She, Jenny, and Michael must also rely on their lived experience as "Mexicans" in order to legitimate their claim to a Mexican cultural identity. Within this brand of *Mexicanidad*, the presumed association between the ability to speak Spanish and the possession of a Mexican identity is relaxed. To not relax this presumption is to invite anomie or total normlessness and alienation.[3] Aarón's distance from the U.S.-Mexican experience accounts for his flippant attitude toward his friend Michael.

First-generation immigrants like Aarón have trouble understanding the psychology of marginal, ethnic minority youth who identify as much with the term "Mexican" as they do with other self-identifiers like "Mexican American," and to a lesser extent, "Chicana/o" and "Hispanic."[4] Two factors are responsible for this lack of understanding. First, because many immigrants are preoccupied with acquiring fluency in the dominant language and culture, elaborating a Mexican identity in the United States seems regressive. Second, immigrants like Aarón have trouble seeing beyond their framework of *Mexicanidad* as a national identity, inextricably linked to Mexico. For Michael, Annalisa, and most U.S.-born youth, such a narrow, geographically based definition defies the word's common, everyday use. In their social world, *Mexicanidad* is an ethnic minority experience that has evolved (and continues to evolve) in relation to the dominant culture (Ogbu 1991, 1994).

From what I could tell, Aarón was one of only a few immigrants in the class. He was thus not in an ideal position to insist on what was, in his mind, the "correct" use of the term "Mexican." Consequently, the ethnicized, particularistic definition embraced by his Mexican American classmates prevailed.

Another theme that emerges from the students' exchange is the importance of the ability to speak Spanish and to speak it well. This is an extremely sensitive issue in the U.S. Mexican community. Accordingly, Trueba (1993) asserts,

> Language is one of the most powerful human resources needed to maintain a sense of self-identity and self-fulfillment. Without a full command of one's own language, ethnic identity, the sharing of fundamental cultural values and norms, the social context of interpersonal communication that guides interactional understandings and the feeling of belonging within a group are not possible. (p. 259)

As young adults, Michael and Annalisa are finding themselves held individually responsible for what is, in fact, a pressing collective issue—the "loss" of their language and the experience of marginality that follows from their poor command of Spanish. As the spheres of these teenagers' intimate social relationships widen to include Mexicans from Mexico, their inability to speak Spanish well leaves them vulnerable to derisive labeling and a particularly painful form of teasing. Their very identity as Mexicans is challenged when friends or relatives refer to them dismissively as *"gringa," "agringada," "pocho,"* or *"americanizada."*

Jenny apparently has attained psychic equilibrium in her own experiences with similar forms of humiliation by concluding, at least for the time being, that the problem lies not with her, but with her grandfather, whom she views as being resentful of the fact that he is not an American himself. Jenny deflects the pain of her grandfather's remarks by substituting anger for shame, guilt, or remorse, and she suggests that Annalisa might find a similar approach constructive when dealing with her relatives. Despite their short-term usefulness, however, depression, anger, and defensive cultural posturing are limited and counterproductive responses if the ultimate goal is genuine dialogue and understanding. In the absence of sustained efforts toward cross-generational communication and solidarity, relationships—even intimate, family-based ones—are at risk.

Were youth to experience a politics of shared material or cultural interests, the mirror image of the politics of difference, their relationships would likely improve. They might even redirect their emotions and focus on the role of the school's assimilationist curriculum in promoting the confusion and conflict that surrounds their sense of identity. Such a reorientation would not only embody their collective interests but would also link them to the U.S.-Mexican community's broader historical struggle for equal educational opportunity (San Miguel 1987; Rosales 1996). Mr. Perry's disconnectedness from the most basic elements of the students' social and cultural world, however, indicates how difficult it would likely be to achieve this type of revised, politicized understanding at Seguín.

One reason Mr. Perry's insensitivity seemed especially striking was that it emerged at the very same time as Jamail's understanding of his peers' predicament perceptively deepened. Each time the discussion flagged, it was Jamail who came to the rescue. His questioning and prodding gave the exchange the impetus it needed to eventually assume a life of its own. Although he had no apparent emotional investment in any particular perspective on the relation of language to identity, Jamail quickly picked up on the social cues that signaled the need for a sensitive handling of the situation. He was so adept that he not only lowered his voice at appropriate moments, he also came through at the end with a fitting sanction of Aarón's behavior. In addition to the obvious fact that Jamail was a careful and skillful listener,

I suspect that his experience as a racial minority and as a student in a virtually all-Mexican school contributed to his acute sensitivity to the delicate nature of the discussion. With his use of the Ebonics be-verb, "be Mexican," Jamail further invites a transborder interpretation of *Mexicanidad* as ever-present, embodying past, present, and future. He and Mr. Perry had become privy to a discussion rarely held publicly—much less between immigrant and U.S.-born youth—wherein the cultural "dirty laundry" was exposed.

Unlike Jamail, Mr. Perry did seem to feel that he had a stake in the outcome of the discussion. He had an emotional investment in Annalisa seeing herself as an "American." This personal agenda prevented him from being able to listen to what his students were saying—so much so that he disrupted the logical flow of the conversation (which Michael then brought back into line). The possibility that one could possess a bicultural identity appeared to be a wholly new, and disorienting, idea for him. His comments to me after class about being in the minority at the school led me to conclude that he felt defensive about the references to white people in the discussion. Further revealing his distance from the Mexican community was his numerical rather than political interpretation of the word "minority." The East End Mexican community exerts precious little control over the curriculum and process of schooling. While Mr. Perry should not be held up to a higher standard than regular, full-time faculty at Seguín, his lack of sophistication encapsulates problems endemic among the permanent, mostly non-Latino, faculty.

Mr. Perry's shallow, knee-jerk analysis of *Mexicanidad* was of great concern to me initially, but a conversation that I held with him later showed that he had grown significantly from the experience. He said that he had made the classroom discussion into the basis for a writing assignment that he then reinforced with more discussion. The title of the new assignment was "Being Mexican." He asked each student to write about what she/he thought it meant to be Mexican. Since some students did not identify with that term, preferring instead "Mexican American" or "Chicano," he allowed them to substitute the term that they believed best defined them. (Jamail wrote an essay on being African American.) Mr. Perry said that he had learned that "Mexican" was the most popular term among the students in his classroom, "no matter whether you're immigrant or homegrown."

According to Michael, in a follow-up discussion I had with him, all the students thought the assignment was "cool, especially the discussion part." Given the sensitive nature of the identity issue, Mr. Perry's students' eagerness to write down and continue to talk more or less publicly about their Mexican-ness deserves attention. Their response may signal just how badly youth need to use one another as sounding boards. The experience perhaps brought some closure to some of the healing that our discussion seemed to initiate. That these students are willing to write and talk for and in front of the likes of Mr. Perry, suggests possibilities for even greater openness in classes run by more culturally attuned teachers. Seguín high school classrooms could more regularly provide a positive forum for discussion. In speculating on my role, I feel that my presence helped Mr. Perry build on the interchange. My ethnicity not only helped give legitimacy to students' identity-related concerns, it also helped create a space for pedagogical action. My guess is that in the absence of shared understandings, an assignment on such a highly personal issue would require much more preparation.

Although many youths at Seguín are bicultural and bilingual, verbally proficient in two languages, they still tend to divide along generational lines, divisions which in turn signify differences in their levels of cultural assimilation. This situation is mediated by a host of schooling practices, to which I now turn.

SUBTRACTIVE SCHOOLING

"No Spanish" rules were a ubiquitous feature of U.S.-Mexican schooling through the early 1970s (Rosales 1981; San Miguel 1987). They have been abolished, but Mexican youth continue to be subjected on a daily basis to subtle, negative messages that undermine the worth of their unique culture and history. In sum, the structure of Seguín's curriculum is designed to divest youth of their Mexican identities and to impede the prospects for fully vested bilingualism and biculturalism. The single and only occasionally taught course on Mexican American history aptly reflects the students' marginalized status in the formal curriculum.

On a more personal level, students' cultural identities are systematically derogated and diminished. Stripped of their usual appearance, youth entering Seguín get "disinfected" of their identifications in a way that bears striking resemblance to the prisoners and mental patients in Goffman's essays on asylums and other total institutions (1977). ESL youth, for example, are regarded as "limited English proficient" rather than as "Spanish dominant" or as potentially bilingual.[5] Their fluency in Spanish is construed as a "barrier" that needs to be overcome. Indeed, school personnel frequently insist that once "the language barrier" is finally eliminated, Seguín's dismal achievement record will disappear as well. The belief in English as the ultimate panacea is so strong that it outweighs the hard evidence confronting classroom teachers every day: the overwhelming majority of U.S.-born, monolingual, English-speaking youth in Seguín's regular track do not now, have not in the past, and likely will not in the future prosper academically.

Another routine way in which the everyday flow of school life erodes the importance of cultural identity is through the casual revisions that faculty and staff make in students' first or last names. At every turn, even well-meaning teachers "adapt" their students' names: "Loreto" becomes "Laredo"; "Azucena" is transformed into "Suzy." Because teachers and other school personnel typically lack familiarity with stress rules in Spanish, last names are especially vulnerable to linguistic butchering. Even names that are common throughout the Southwest, like Martinez and Perez, are mispronounced as MART-i-nez and Pe-REZ (instead of Mart-I-nez and PE-rez). Schooling under these conditions can thus be characterized as a mortification of the self in Goffman's terms—that is, as a leaving off and a taking on.

Analyses of three years' accumulation of documents provided by the school reveal a generalized pattern of cultural insensitivity. For instance, the only passage in the 84-page staff handbook that explicitly acknowledges the prevalence of Spanish-speakers among the student body is a single guideline intended only for the teacher whose job it is to discipline students. This sentence, found in the section that discusses the on-campus suspension policy and regulations, reads, "Rules will be posted in the center in English and Spanish." Similar instructions for counselors, teachers, nurses, or librarians do not exist. Not even in the section on homework policy—that encourages teachers to be resourceful and inventive with their assignments—are teachers advised to build on students' cultural backgrounds and experiences.

Another peculiarity of the staff handbook is its failure to mention, let alone quote, the school's purported commitment to multilingual literacy embodied in its mission statement:

> The graduates of Seguín High School will be able to participate, compete, and communicate effectively in an ever-changing multilingual world.[6]

With few students ever graduating, this statement is strikingly disconnected from what actually occurs at Seguín. In a school where English is the privileged medium of instruction in both curricular and extracurricular, faculty-sponsored activities, the sincerity of the commitment to producing multilingual students hardly seems credible.[7] The word, "multilingual," sounds suspiciously ambitious when Seguín has yet to deal effectively with its *bicultural* student body.

The student handbook has never been printed in Spanish. Moreover, despite the school's burgeoning Spanish-dominant population, the handbook makes no mention of the English as a Second Language (ESL) program. Instead, curriculum program information, which informs students about the number of credits required for graduation, is limited to youth who are enrolled in the "Regular" and "Advanced" high school programs (euphemisms for "tracks"). Thus, the type of schooling trajectory to expect or to work toward if one is a Spanish-dominant ESL student is not specified. Nor, at the other end of the spectrum, is any mention made of how to get into the school's honors program. Though all students are instructed to discuss their school plans with their pre-assigned school counselor, most students know that *no* counselor, pre-assigned or otherwise, will actually be available for such a discussion.

Another egregious handbook "oversight" regards the Texas Assessment of Academic Skills (TAAS) test. The handbook informs students that in addition to the minimum required credits for graduation, they must also pass this state-mandated exit exam. What it does not say is that the TAAS test is available only in English. Thus, students are not forewarned that their success or failure on the exam may turn more on their relative fluency in the English language than on their command of academic material. Given that large segments of the student population are not English-dominant, withholding this kind of information can spell last-minute failure for otherwise capable youth.

The subtractive elements in the school's curriculum have not gone unnoticed by all teachers. There are a few persistent faculty—most, but certainly not all of whom are Latino—who have promoted awareness of how the extant curriculum fails to build on students' skills, knowledge, and cultural background. Ms. Martinez, a Spanish language teacher, is especially active in this regard. She has developed a set of sound-bite responses to the many teachers who have questioned her additive philosophy. For instance, to the frequent query about why students in high school need Spanish courses at all, she typically replies, "For the same reasons you take English every year throughout middle and high school."

Through her work on various departmental and administrative committees, Ms. Martinez has focused on bringing about three interrelated policy changes: a separate Spanish Department, greater flexibility in the course assignment process for ESL youth, and improved linguistic assessment of Spanish-speaking youth. These recommendations critique the "blind" bureaucratic processes that obstruct the academic progress of all Mexican youth, but especially of Spanish-dominant students.

Departmental autonomy for Spanish would help avert the curricular mishandling of students that follows directly from conceptualizing Spanish as a "foreign language." The issue is quite simple to Ms. Martinez, who curtly states, "Spanish is foreign to people who don't speak Spanish." Her additive vision of schooling is clear in the following exchange we had in fall 1994:

Ms. MARTINEZ. In an ideal world, this school to me should be a bilingual high school where every student who walks out the door with a diploma . . . should be literate in English and Spanish . . . speak, comprehend, read, and write.

AV. Are there any high schools like that anywhere?

Ms. MARTINEZ. I've never heard of one, but the students in this building have that ability, I think, and nobody is building on that asset.

Her sentiments are shared by a Latina ESL faculty member whom I had interviewed only days earlier. According to this teacher, one consequence of locating Spanish in the Foreign Language Department is that Mexican students are treated as any other immigrant group originating from distant lands, meaning that course offerings do not correspond to their needs. Because organizationally, Spanish is conceived as similar to such "foreign languages" as French and German, the majority of the courses are offered at the beginning and intermediate levels. Very few advanced Spanish-language courses exist. Rather than designing the program with the school's large number of native speakers in mind, Seguín's first- and second-year Spanish curriculum subjects students to material that insults their abilities. Taking beginning Spanish means repeating such elementary phrases as "*Yo me llamo María*" ("My name is *María*"), "*Tú te llamas José*" ("Your name is *José*"). According to both teachers, even students whose linguistic competence is more passive than active—that is, they understand but speak little Spanish—are ill-served by this kind of approach. A passively bilingual individual possesses much greater linguistic knowledge and ability than another individual exposed to the language for their first time. Since almost every student at Seguín is either a native speaker of Spanish or an active or passive bilingual, the school's Spanish program ill-serves all, though not even-handedly.

Many of the language teachers find ways to creatively circumvent the deficiencies of the curriculum. But this always entails working around their bureaucratically assigned textbooks, since these invariably fail to correspond to their students' actual skill levels. Teachers of Spanish-dominant youth must spend their own money on materials if they wish to compensate for the curriculum's deficiencies. Thus, in very concrete ways, schooling subtracts resources from teachers, as well.[8]

Since support for a separate Spanish Department has not been forthcoming, Ms. Martinez and other faculty have requested that counselors exercise greater flexibility in the assignment process to make current offerings more relevant. For example, if students have taken advanced courses in Spanish, say as students in Mexico, they should be able to skip beginning Spanish and perhaps even intermediate-level courses and begin with advanced Spanish. According to existing guidelines, students who are genuinely interested in developing their first-language skills must weather many semesters of elementary-level Spanish before engaging advanced subject matter. This penalty, of course, is highest for students whose levels of educational attainment in Mexico are also high. According to Ms. Martinez, counselors should be able to suspend course-sequencing conventions to match students' actual skill levels. While they have this authority, they never exercise it:

> We express our concerns at the end of each spring semester. The summer comes, and by fall, the counselors continue doing what they've always done. It's like Spanish IA always has to be first, then IB and always in that order.

Ms. Martinez is well aware of the wider significance of her suggestions. Were they implemented, a major shift in the academic program would occur. An upside-down curricular pyramid would result, with far fewer beginning courses and many more advanced-level courses in Spanish. As Ms. Martinez indicates, because of the social distance between school personnel and the student body, it is difficult to persuade decision-makers of the importance of this kind of restructuring. Change would require a leap of faith that has so far not been forthcoming.[9] She attributes counselors' and administrators' obstinacy both to their reluctance to take on the logistical problems that restructuring Spanish classes would entail and to their failure to comprehend the relationship between first- and second-language development:

> One of the major problems is that many of the counselors are not bilingual and don't understand the importance of the first-language development of the students and they send them with good intentions to the classes they think [are best] or wherever there's room. They don't have a choice many times. They just send them wherever there's space for another body. . . . Students are not learning as much as they could when they are in the wrong class.

Even when placement decisions are "rationally" executed, they are typically based on crude measures. One is the school's home language survey, which asks students to report which language is predominant at home; the other measure is test score data from a language test administered before the student entered high school (typically, the test is given in middle school). Because the former index measures speaking ability rather than reading and writing abilities and the latter is frequently outdated, placement errors abound and the ESL program experiences huge fluctuations in size. For instance, between spring 1992 and fall 1993, the ESL program dropped from 600 to a total of 300 youth.

Clearly, with counselors carrying caseloads of 300–plus students each, expediency rules in placement decisions. However, as I discovered when I talked to Ms. Cardenas, who was at the time Seguín's only Spanish-speaking Latina counselor, other factors may play a role as well. Ms. Cardenas' advisees spanned a wide range, including all grade levels, ESL students, and regular track youth. She set her own priorities; that these sometimes resulted in a dismissive attitude toward ESL students and others was simply a hard fact of life. She explained her approach this way:

> What it is, is like everybody else. . . . Everybody wants their . . . their own student and they demand that we stop everybody else for stuff and take care of them and I think that's a problem. That they [ESL teachers] want us to, you know, handle the ESL students like they're number one. I mean, they're their priority. To me, every student is priority. I start with the seniors. To me they're the priorities because they have to . . . hurry up and graduate. And I work from seniors down, and if ESL runs in between there, I work on ESL. To me ESL and regular are exactly the same. I don't treat them [differently] or give anybody any preference. And that's what they [ESL staff] want.

This privileging of the graduating seniors over all others is universally employed by Seguín counselors and dates back at least to the October 1989 walkout (see chapter 2). Because undue curricular mishandling of youth in the privileged rungs of the curriculum contributed to the walkout, counselors either learned or were reminded about which segments of the student body were the most important for them to "protect."

Ms. Cardenas' seemingly merciless stance may be traced directly to her unenviable structural position as the only Mexican American, Spanish-speaking counselor at the school. A classic "token," she found herself constantly in a double-bind. If she failed to conform to the bureaucratic culture and expectations of the counseling department, she would risk being ostracized by her fellow counselors. However, conforming to counselors' practices was certain to make her a pariah in her own community of Mexican teachers, parents, and students. Over time, her "choice" to side with the counselors made her persona non grata at Seguín, especially among several vocal Latina ESL and vocational teachers who complained to the principal that she was dismissive toward their students. Ms. Cardenas lasted only three years in her position before the principal asked her to leave. A formal complaint to the principal from an ESL vocational teacher who felt that her students' needs were unduly neglected—alongside other similar complaints from other faculty—appeared to have influenced the principal's decision.

In a conversation I had with her weeks after her dismissal, Ms. Cardenas made clear how unprepared she had been for what befell her. "I can't believe this happened," she said, still shocked by the turn of events. "I did everything just like I thought I was supposed to." The contradictory aspects of token status were apparent in her account. Her experience suggests that if for no reason other than to mitigate the pressures toward conformity, instituting an ethnically balanced counselors' office would promote a more just working and decision-making environment.

The assessment of Spanish-dominant youth is the third issue that often brings Ms. Martinez into conflict with school counselors. Ms. Martinez maintains that through diagnostic testing, teachers can help students raise their test scores because they can apportion their instructional time to target those areas where students need the most help. Although such testing is supposed to be routine, the chaos that characterizes the beginning of each new school year at Seguín results in a systematic failure to test ESL students. Ms. Martinez concludes that the kinds of changes she has advocated will never come about in the absence of effective school-, district-, and state-level leadership.

Finally, Seguín subtracts resources from youth in ways that

are directly related to how the state of Texas views the purpose and goals of its school-based ESL program. ESL is designed to impart to non-native English-speakers sufficient verbal and written skills to effectuate their transition into an all-English curriculum within a three-year time period. This transitional ideology (see note 2) translates into the organizational practice of segregating Spanish-speaking students from English-speaking ones. Hence, layered over the school's academic tracking system is a "cultural tracking" system. I am not advocating the removal of immigrants' much-needed (though often deficient) school-administered language support systems. I do wish, however, to point out several key consequences of cultural tracking.

By obstructing possibilities for fully vested bilingualism and biculturalism at the individual and collective levels, cultural tracking creates and reinforces divisions among youth. These divisions encourage U.S.-born youth to nurture a false sense of superiority and to equate the ESL program and, by extension, Mexican immigrants and the Spanish language, with second-class status. Cultural tracking thus stigmatizes immigrant youth. These divisions also influence the level of social capital students possess in their peer groups (see chapter 4). Finally, cultural tracking restricts immigrants' achievement potential by limiting the courses offered within the cultural track to those taught in the general academic track: honors-track ESL courses do not exist. "Graduation" out of the ESL track is thus always horizontal into the regular track (see Valdés [1998], Olsen [1997], and Romo and Falbo [1996] for other similar critiques of ESL tracking).

In more specific terms, cultural tracking at Seguín means that Spanish-dominant students take ESL language courses that focus on developing their conversational skills in English. Because these courses focus on oral fluency, there is not enough attention to writing, reading comprehension, or to academic vocabulary (see Olsen 1997, who expresses similar concerns about the ESL curriculum). If these students are lucky, however, they may get placed in ESL content-area courses. Content-area ESL courses cover the same material taught in the regular track curriculum, but the former are taught by ESL-certified teachers skilled at working with Spanish-speaking populations and trained in ESL methodologies like cooperative learning, the use of manipulatives, whole-language learning techniques, and so forth. These courses are referred to as "ESL-Math," "ESL-Science," "ESL-U.S. History," and so on. However, because the "proper" number of content-area ESL courses the school offers is a continually contested issue, such courses are always in short supply.[10]

Moreover, since none of these courses is offered at an honors' level, immigrant youth are denied yet again the opportunity to achieve at an advanced academic level. While academic tracking is itself problematic, in the context of Seguín's tracking system, it is additionally so because cultural, nonacademic criteria block Spanish-dominant students' access to the honors program. However benign in conception and intention, programs that result in cultural tracking curtail youths' achievement potential and foster divisions among them.

DIVISIONS AMONG YOUTH

During the fall 1992 semester, I became aware of differences in the types of students who congregated inside and outside the cafeteria during lunch (see appendix for a discussion of methodology). Over one thousand students eat during each of the school's three lunch sessions. Students convene either in pairs or in groups of various sizes. Group boundaries are well marked; immigrant and U.S.-born youth associate with their respective immigrant and U.S.-born peers. Within the immigrant population, youth tend to subdivide further according to recency of arrival (among the more recently arrived, many students know one another from classes in the school's ESL program).

Although the particular spot that any given group occupies inside or outside the cafeteria tends to shift over time as students move in and out of groups or as good weather encourages more students to eat outdoors, social and linguistic cleavages remain constant. The cleavage between immigrants and U.S.-born youth is remarkable if one considers that, all else equal, a given individual has close to a 50 percent chance of having a friend who is either immigrant or U.S.-born. All is not equal, however. Societal forces, including subtractive schooling, drive a wedge between

these groups. This wedge is evident in the attitudes and perceptions these youth hold regarding one another and in the reasons
that they provide for the divisions that exist among them.

Attitudes among Immigrant Groups

Immigrant youths' responses to questions about why they do not
associate with U.S.-born youth took many different forms across
friendship groups. The most common answers mentioned linguistic and cultural differences, traits that were frequently conveyed
through the evaluative comment, "*son americanizados*" ("they
are Americanized"). Although immigrant females often covet the
more liberal gender attitudes and roles held by Chicanos and
especially Chicanas, for most immigrant youth, "Americanized"
is a pejorative term. As a rather generic label, it is often used to
convey a variety of negative perceptions. For example, the statement "Chicanos are Americanized" unpacks into many separate
observations: "We never saw drugs until we came to the United
States." "We do not have a gang problem in Mexico." "In Mexico, we mostly drink at home. Here, they [Chicanos] go to happy
hour." "We take school more seriously than them [Chicanos]."
"Smoking, doing drugs, getting involved in gangs, and not taking
school seriously is an American phenomenon." "We're more
respectful toward our elders."

U.S.-born youth are thus viewed as negligent for succumbing
to the corrosive influences of the dominant culture. Moreover,
their seeming willingness to squander educational opportunities
appalls many immigrant students. Amalia's description (see chapter 4) of U.S.-born youth as "*chiflados*" ("spoiled") and unap-
preciative of their teachers is a variation on this theme. Finally,
U.S.-born youth are viewed as preferring English over Spanish
and as aloof and distant from Mexico and the Mexican immigrant experience.

Latina Female Friends. I met the three young women who make
up this friendship group on my very first day of participant observation at Seguín in 1992. All three were juniors. Mely and Sylvia,
who are fluently bilingual, were honors students; Teresa was in
the ESL track. As I came to know all three well through work
they did for me at different stages of my research project, I

decided to include them as part of the group interview sample, which, apart from these students, is comprised only of regular-track freshman and sophomore youth. These young women's views provide a valuable reminder that we build our attitudes and perceptions about others from many sources. Mely's, Sylvia's, and Teresa's life experiences help explain the nature of the attitudes they hold toward Chicanos/as.

Mely and Sylvia are long-term, first-generation immigrants. They are also long-term friends who first met in middle school. Both are balanced bilinguals who stress the Latina side of their identity. Both also prefer to associate with other Mexican immi-grants. Mely's family is from Sombreretillo, a rural area in the state of Nuevo León, Mexico; Sylvia is from San Salvador, El Sal-vador. Teresa, a more recent immigrant and friend, arrived in 1990 from Reynosa, a city in Matamoros, Mexico.

Mely and Sylvia are A/B students located in Seguín's separate honors and magnet programs, respectively. Teresa is a B/C student in the ESL program. Her non-ESL classes intimidate her and she resists learning the English language, preferring to speak only in Spanish to her friends. Whereas Mely and Sylvia benefit from the rights and privileges associated with belonging to the privileged rungs of the school's curriculum, Teresa's experience is one of estrangement.

All three young women have persisted in school despite tremendous obstacles. Indeed, according to conventional mea-sures of functional family and household structures, these young women fare poorly. Teresa has two older brothers, but she lives only with her mother. They share a tiny, dilapidated, one-room home. Her father is completely absent; he heads another family. He has never acknowledged either Teresa or her brothers as his children, and he has never met any of them. Sylvia, left behind when her single mother migrated, spent ten of the first twelve years of her life living with her grandmother in El Salvador. Sylvia migrated at age twelve and rejoined her mother, but sustaining this reunion has required much effort on the part of both mother and daughter. Sylvia explains, "When I came to the United States, it was like I had to come and live with someone I didn't know. We both had to get used to each other and it was a big adjustment for us both." Mely has no parent at home; she lives only with an older brother. She carries a beeper in her backpack so that her brother and her two sisters (who live in Houston with their own families) can always reach her, and she religiously returns their calls whenever they dial her beeper number.

These young women's unusually truncated family structures deepen the value of their supportive friendship. Interestingly, despite absentee parents, all three students attribute their persistence in school and their academic success to their families' high hopes for them. Their views shook my assumptions about "dysfunctional families" and led me to consider an alternative interpretation that is perhaps more relevant to this community: a family is not dysfunctional until the hope of all of its members has been drained.

Of the three, Teresa has struggled the hardest to hang on to her dreams. Her progress has been impeded by schooling practices, by her lack of fluency in the English language, by extreme poverty, and by traumatic encounters with Chicanos. For example, she once attempted to join a summer program at Seguín, but when several Mexican American youth openly questioned her participation, she changed her mind. "What is *she* doing here?" they asked one another, in voices meant for her to hear. "We don't want no Mexicans here who can't even speak English," they sniped. Teresa's already fragile self-concept was no match for such robust hostility. She never enrolled in that program, nor has she taken advantage of any of the school's extracurricular activities. Virtually every faculty-sponsored after-school program requires facility with the English language, which she lacks.[11]

Teresa's relationship with Seguín has been rocky from the beginning. When she arrived in the United States in 1990 and enrolled at Seguín, she experienced tremendous culture shock. After a day of classes, she returned home and "stopped out" of school for a year. "All I did was watch Mexican *novelas* (soap operas) all day long, every single day, for about a year," she told me in Spanish.

As Teresa had no means to meet or make friends beyond the individuals in her brothers' and single mother's friendship networks, she became increasingly socially isolated. Although she did not realize it at the time, upon reflection much later, Teresa concluded that her family's move to "*el Norte*" (the North) was so traumatic for her that it had left her severely depressed. By the time I met Teresa, she was attending school regularly and she appeared quite sound in mind and spirit. Trouble continued to haunt her, however.

Over the 1992 Christmas holidays, a Chicano male broke into her home and raped her at knife point as her anguished mother lay frozen in fear in her own bed, only a few feet away. The rapist entered through an insecure window that, like the rest of the small, wood-framed house, was in disrepair. Teresa knew that her assailant was Chicano because his Spanish was fraught with grammatical errors. He was never identified nor apprehended. With the help and nurturance of her mother, brothers, and boyfriend, Teresa was able to regain a measure of emotional stability. Her antipathy toward Chicanos, however, only deepened. In addition to being responsible for the deep emotional scars Teresa bears, Chicanos are, for her, emblematic of the difficulties she has had adjusting to life in the United States. "Anglos have never been a problem to me," she told me in Spanish. "It's the Chicanos who have caused me the greatest grief."

School offered no respite for Teresa. After earning an "A" in life and persisting in school courageously through the end of her twelfth-grade year, she did not graduate. She failed the TAAS test which, according to state law, is required for graduation. Not graduating with her friends was the final blow. Opportunities existed for her to retake the test over the summer, but Teresa decided that she had had her fill of institutional humiliation. Today, she is married to the same young man who was her boyfriend in 1992; they are now parents of a newborn child.

Mely and Sylvia believe that Teresa's problems have simply been too great for her to fully benefit either from school or from the kind of help they tried to give her as friends. Mely, in particular, made it her responsibility to continuously encourage Teresa to finish school. Besides occasionally helping Teresa with her homework, she also helped her study for the TAAS test. Teresa acknowledges that beyond her mother's aspirations for her, it was Mely and Sylvia's friendship that enabled her to persist in school.

To Mely and Sylvia's analysis of Teresa's experiences, I would add that subtractive schooling—manifested in conflictual relations with Chicanos, barriers endemic to the school's ESL program, as well as through the English-only language of the state-mandated test—kept Teresa from achieving her full potential. She was a hard-working student who made not stellar but solidly average grades both in Mexico and in the United States. She earned the right to graduate with her peers. In failing the TAAS exam—and thus not getting a diploma—Teresa is representative of many similar casualties of subtractive schooling. Many other Spanish-dominant Seguín students before her, and many who have followed, also consistently demonstrated academic competence but never graduated because they could not clear the TAAS's double hurdle of English and academics.

My data from this and other groups suggest that immigrants' attitudes toward Chicanos may be linked to how recently the immigrants arrived in the United States: the more recent, the more negative. Teresa and Mely illustrate this divergence. Among the factors mediating such attitudes are direct contact with Chicanos, cultural assimilation changes students undergo, and the self-confidence that comes from achieving fluency in English. That is, as immigrants accommodate to the mores of the school's informal status hierarchy—a pecking order that is based on the privileging of English as both the medium of instruction and the ticket to participation in faculty-sponsored school activities—they achieve a better fit.

An absence of categorically negative attitudes does not, however, mean wholesale acceptance. For instance, Mely has had positive relationships with Chicanos and Chicanas (including me). Nevertheless, she sees us as "different." She, like most other immigrant youth, prefers to associate with people she can relate to more easily, namely, other immigrants. Mely's associational preferences became more apparent to me after Teresa withdrew from her relationship with Mely and Sylvia to spend more time with her boyfriend. This shift in the structure of their group brought Mely and Sylvia even closer together, although by their senior year, a fourth friend, named Cati, had been added to the group. A recent arrival from Mexico, Cati spoke mostly Spanish when I met her. Thus, despite the compositional changes that this group underwent over time, it remained all-immigrant.

Mely offered the following explanation for her preference for immigrant friends:

Chicanos are more Americanized. *Tienen otras costumbres* [They have other customs], more liberal ideas. Sleeping out *de la casa* (from home), smoking. They hardly speak Spanish. For me, both languages have to be involved because it is a part of me. *Siempre se me sale el español* [Spanish always comes out of me] and this isn't true for Chicanos because *no hablan bien el Español* [they don't speak Spanish well]. Chicanos do not see Spanish as part of them. *También, los que estan criados aqui en los Estados Unidos no saben aprovechar tantas oportunidades que existen para superarse en la vida.* [Also, those who are raised here in the United States do not know how to take advantage of so many opportunities that exist to succeed in life.] They take things for granted. *Nosotros somos mas luchadoras, mas trabajadoras y simplemente apreciamos muchisimo por lo que luchamos. Realmente todo nos cuesta más porque todo lo que hacemos lo hacemos con mas dificultades y esfuerzo. Mi impresión de los inmigrantes es de que son personas demasiado sufridas y trabajadas que cuando llegan aqui se exponen a mucho trabajo porque ya estan acostumbradas y vienen con esa imagen de trabajo.* [We are more persevering, harder workers and we simply have a deeper appreciation of what we seek. In actuality, everything costs us more because everything we do, we do with more effort and against greater obstacles. My impression of immigrants is that they are people who suffer greatly and have been thoroughly exploited so that when they come here, they're ready to do a lot of work because they are already accustomed to it. And they come with that idea of work.]

Despite Mely's generally sympathetic views toward Chicanos and Chicanas, that they "do not see Spanish as part of them" precludes any meaningful connection with them, as far as she is concerned. Her views further clearly illustrate why bilingualism does not in itself necessarily bridge the divide that exists between immigrant and U.S.-born youth. Mely's personal history (a tale of sorrow, sacrifice, and suffering, described below) is at once poignant and achingly familiar—to immigrants. Immigrant students' unrelenting work ethic resonate with Hellman's (1994) findings on views toward work among adult Mexicans in Mexico. U.S.-born individuals, on the other hand, who typically have not had comparable experiences themselves, seem perfectly oblivious to this ever-present subtext in the lives of their immigrant peers.

Mely's family is from a small ranching community. As a small child, she moved to the United States with both of her parents and her four siblings (all older than she). Mely's oldest sister, Eva, helped pave the way for Mely's success by doing well in school and by helping Mely with school-related responsibilities, including teaching her how to read. Eva's involvement helped Mely gain placement in the honors track during middle school.

When Mely was in the eighth grade, a fateful family decision changed her life. Because her father feared he would lose his land if he stayed in the United States, he decided to move back to Mexico. This left Mely's mother to try to choose between her children and her husband. Recognizing that, as the youngest child, she was her mother's chief concern, Mely took it upon herself to relieve her mother of her tremendous burden. She obscured her own insecurities with her confident, driven attitude. "Don't worry about me," she told her mother reassuringly, "I'll be fine." Her three older sisters and her older brother vowed to watch over Mely. Though tormented to this day by her decision to leave, Mely's mother joined her husband in Mexico.

Thus, at fourteen, Mely became a virtual orphan, living under her siblings' care in their East End family home. It was not until several months after I had hired Mely to transcribe taped interviews that I learned of her family circumstances. The only time Mely ever grew visibly sentimental with me was during this conversation. I was shocked to discover that except for occasional, and increasingly rare, three-month visits by her mother, no parent had been living in her home for over four years.

"My God, you must miss your Mami and your Papi so much!" I exclaimed.

With eyes watering but with her characteristic coolness, Mely responded slowly as she stared deeply into my eyes. Expressing a great deal of sadness, she said simply, "Yes, I do. I miss them very much."

As we spoke, I realized that Mely drew a deep sense of pride and confidence from the trust her parents placed in her. She said, "*Nos criaron bien*" ("They raised us well") and my parents trusted that I would make the right decisions even if they weren't here with me. I never wanted them to regret their decision."

Eva, who still remains both proud and protective of Mely, says of her sister, "She's seventeen going on thirty."

Mely's criticism of Chicanos as Americanized and as taking opportunity for granted is rooted in her subject position as a hard-working, independent immigrant female with a history of extraordinary familial sacrifices. Mely would probably agree with Amalia, who suggested that immigrants' dual frame can and should be accessible to U.S.-born youth (see chapter 4). Greater knowledge of the sacrifices, and of the exploitation, endured by this segment of society could provide a basis for cross-generational empathy, if not solidarity. This potential is especially evident in the following discussion, which describes the views and opinions of three religious immigrant males.

Religious Immigrant Males. Gregorio, Juan Marco, and Demetrio are all recently arrived sophomore males. The three play musical instruments in their Assembly of God church band each Sunday morning. In our conversation about U.S.-born youth, Gregorio became visceral. He sees Chicanos as giving *all* Mexicans a bad name: "*De por si que no nos quieren. Y luego se salen estos Chicanos con unas pendejadas*" ("As it is, they don't like us. And then these Chicanos act crazy and all!"). When I asked him to whom the "they" referred, he said, "Anglos" or more specifically, an Anglo male teacher he has. Gregorio explained that the frequently buffoonish behavior of several Chicanos in that class embarrasses him intensely.

Neither Juan Marco nor Demetrio agreed that Chicanos' behavior automatically reflected negatively on them as immigrants.

"*Nuestros maestros nos ven como mejores estudiantes [que los Chicanos]*" ("Our teachers see us as better students [than Chicanos]"), Juan Marco said.

Smug in his certainty, a prescient Gregorio countered, "*Somos la misma gente . . . de la misma raiz. Si ahorita no parecemos igualitos, dentro de una generación seremos*" ("We're the same people . . . from the same root. If we do not completely look the same right now, we will within one generation").

Demetrio quickly seconded Gregorio's opinion that Mexicans on both sides of the border are similar: "*Tanto allá como acá, somos gente de la clase trabajadora"* ("There as much as here, we are working-class people").

Demetrio's reference to a shared working-class identity highlights the positive identification with work and manual labor that researchers of adult populations have observed (Hurtado et al. 1994; Hellman 1994). Such language is rarely heard among U.S.-born youth. Although none in this group has any Chicanos for friends at school, this was the only immigrant group that nevertheless stressed the similarities between immigrants and U.S.-born youth. Perhaps tempering their critique of U.S.-born youth are positive experiences with Mexican Americans in their church, including one who plays in their band.

Juan Marco chimed in with a story about his own experience, saying that school authorities treat Chicanos more harshly than immigrants. He said that he often sneaks into the school auditorium to play the piano during his lunch hour. His family does not own a piano. Seizing this (unauthorized) opportunity to practice at school during the day saves him a long trip to his church, the site of the only piano he has legitimate access to. So far, school authorities have apprehended him three times. On all three occasions, after a lengthy wait in the assistant principal's office, he has been given a brief lecture and sent to class.

Inferring support for his own perspective from Juan Marco's remarks, Gregorio flatly stated, "*Como pueblo Mexicano, no nos conviene irnos contra la corriente. Tenemos que ser gente bien educada*" ("As Mexican people, it doesn't pay to go against the current. We have to be better mannered"). Juan Marco and Demetrio nodded in agreement.

Notwithstanding these young men's implicit plea for solidarity, to reduce the problem of discipline to a simple matter of student conformity is to paint a gloss over problems that are collective in nature. Gregorio's assessment that buffoonish behavior ill-serves the individual actors is on target. However, calling on U.S.-born youth to behave "better" will do nothing to alter Seguín's subtractive framework.

U.S.-born youth resist not education but *schooling*. Yet, like school officials, immigrant youth have difficulty discerning this distinction. Rather than seeing their own bodies as the site of agency, critical thinking, and resistance to their lack of connectedness to schooling, students like Gregorio expend their emotional energy on feelings of embarrassment toward peers whom they perceive as childishly defiant and as disgracing the race. In the absence of cross-generational communication, awareness, and understanding, harmful misperceptions are likely to prevail, even among the most well-intentioned youth.

The prognosis for the future is not uniformly bleak, however. Perceptions of gender role differences suggest some promising avenues for cross-generational alliances.

Immigrant Females in Trouble. Whenever the subject of gender role differences between immigrant and U.S.-born females arose during the group interviews, immigrant females voiced their desire for the greater freedom and privileges that they perceive their Americanized female counterparts as enjoying. This longing for increased independence is evident in views expressed by four freshman "Immigrant Girls in Trouble," all of whom wish their parents were less strict. In their recounting of a disastrous night out, Rosario, Consuelo, Belia, and Noemí also depict the gender-role boundaries of their social world. All four are long-term immigrants who are able to speak Spanish and English but who prefer to speak mainly Spanish.

These young women's parents, who had consistently refused to allow them to attend football games, finally relented and gave them permission to go to a game one Friday night. Rosario's parents dropped the four friends off at the football stadium with the understanding that they were to meet at the same location after the game was over, around 9:45 PM. Their other directive was to steer clear of the boys.

A mere half hour into the game, Consuelo developed severe menstrual cramps and insisted on going home. Unfortunately, Rosario's family had no phone, so, to avoid problems, the girls would have to make it back to Rosario's house before her parents left to pick them up at the stadium. Rosario made it her responsibility to find a ride for the group. The only person she could find was a Chicana freshman named Marcia who was in her physical education class. Marcia had come to the game with her boyfriend, Jimmy. Also a Chicano, Jimmy was the owner of an Impala with hydraulic wheels and a member of a lowrider club. At Marcia's request, Jimmy agreed to take Rosario and her friends home during half-time.

It was a good plan—and it might have worked smoothly had Jimmy's car not broken down approximately three miles from Consuelo's and Rosario's homes. While Jimmy tried to fix his car, Marcia walked to a pay phone at a gas station several blocks away. She hoped to reach her brother, a mechanic and the owner of a car big enough to transport the whole group should they have to abandon Jimmy's car. Everyone pooled their nickels, dimes, and quarters to fund Marcia's calls. After leaving several messages with parents, aunts, and uncles, she finally located her brother at his best friend's house. In the meanwhile, Rosario, Belia, and Noemí remained in the back seat of Jimmy's car, trying to console Consuelo, who was in agony. Everyone's anxiety grew as the minutes ticked by. Rosario had only half an hour left in which to get home before her parents set off for the stadium.

By the time Marcia returned with the good news that her brother was on his way, Rosario had decided that she should begin walking home immediately. Marcia insisted that they should wait for her brother since walking through the *barrio* (neighborhood) so late at night could be dangerous. Apparently seeing her parents as even more "dangerous," Rosario was unwilling to wait even a minute longer. She left, promising the group that after she got home, she would ask her parents to return to see whether the car had been fixed, and if it hadn't, to give everyone rides to their homes. Though Consuelo only lived a few houses away from Rosario, she decided to stay in the car. She didn't feel in good enough condition to walk the distance. Feeling responsible for the whole situation, Marcia volunteered Jimmy as an escort for Rosario. Jimmy hesitated, expressing unhappiness over abandoning his vehicle. After Marcia grew very angry and accused him of caring only about his car, Jimmy rushed off to catch up with Rosario.

Just as Rosario's parents were pulling out of their driveway, Rosario and Jimmy popped out of the darkness, catching them by surprise. Rosario's father climbed out of the car, looking enraged. Pointing to the house and looking straight at her, he silently ordered his daughter to get inside. Glaring at Jimmy, who stood frozen in his tracks, Rosario's father reached into the car and turned off the engine. Then he and his wife went into the house. After a heated discussion inside, Rosario's parents left with Jimmy, headed for the site of the disabled car. Marcia's brother arrived after all and hauled the car, along with Marcia and Jimmy, to Jimmy's home while Rosario's parents took Consuelo, Belia, and Noemí to their homes.

Deeming Rosario guilty of showing poor judgment, her father whipped her with a belt. He felt that she should have known better than to accept a ride from a "cholo," even if he was with his girlfriend. When I spoke to the group on the Monday after their wild night out, Rosario said that the welts her father's whipping had left on her buttocks and legs were just beginning to heal. Consuelo, too, ended up in trouble because Rosario's parents told her parents what had happened. They, too, felt that their daughter had been too trusting of this young man. They grounded her for a month. Since Belia and Noemí had arrived home nearly on time, neither mentioned the night's adventures to their parents, and so escaped punishment.

I asked these young women what they had learned from their ordeal. "*Nuestros padres son demasiado estrictos*" ("Our parents are extremely strict"), Consuelo lamented. She said that as far as she was concerned, she and her friends had done nothing wrong. She believed that the extreme reactions of her parents and Rosario's parents were not the result of the evening's actual events, but rather were driven by the adults' fear of lowriders. "*Resultó ser bien amable el Jimmy y como quiera estaba con su novia*" ("Jimmy turned out to be really nice, and he was with his girlfriend anyway"), Rosario pointed out. Despite her Spanish dominance and his "*Español mocho*" ("ungrammatical Spanish"), the two managed to have a nice conversation on their brisk walk to her home.

Rosario went on to observe that Chicanas like Marcia "have it good" because they are allowed to date and to stay out late.

Flushing, she exclaimed, "*Hasta tienen relaciones estas chicanas con sus novios!*" ("These Chicanas even have sex with their boyfriends!")

"*Cómo sabes?*" ("How do you know?") I asked.

She told me that she knows of several young women who either live with their boyfriends' families or whose boyfriends live with them. "Mexican parents don't let their daughters do any-thing," complained Belia in Spanish. Belia says that she's always trying to talk her parents into giving her more freedom, but that they always respond by putting down American society. Mocking her father, she lowered her voice, increased her tempo, and said, "*Yo no soy uno de esos padres modernos!*" ("I'm not one of these modern parents!") Following Belia's cue, Rosario said that she can't stand it when her mother tells her that she's better than these "*Chicanas groseras y vulgares que andan en las calles*" ("indecent and vulgar Chicanas who hang out on the streets"). The rapidity with which they both regurgitated their parents' admonitions revealed just how deeply these understandings are etched in their minds.

Taken aback by these sweeping generalizations, I asked Belia and Rosario whether they thought that their parents were truly afraid of U.S.-born youth.

Rosario answered, "*Si tienen razón ellos. Son ellos los que andan en pandillas. Casi cada noche oyemos el sonido de pisto-las. A veces cuando se oye bien cerca, tenemos que acostarnos en el piso.*" ("They're right. They're the ones who are in gangs. Almost every night we hear the sound of guns. Sometimes when we hear them real close, we have to lay down on the floor.")

Seconding Rosario's claim, Consuelo chimed in, "*Nuestra familia también*" ("Our family, too").

Rosario nevertheless maintained that her parents exaggerate matters since the percentage of "*Chicanos buenos*" ("good Chi-canos") by far exceeds the percentage of "*Chicanos malos*" ("bad Chicanos").

When I asked them what else being Americanized meant to them, speaking English was what came to mind.

Sounding much like Mely, Noemí said, "*Ser Mexicana no es solamente hablar el Español, es querer hablar el Español y los de aqui, muchos no tienen el deseo*" ("To be Mexican is not only to speak Spanish, it's wanting to speak Spanish, and many from here, they have no desire").

"*Pero por algunos, no es que no quieren es que no pueden*" ("But for some, it's not that they do not want to but that they can't"), I suggested.

Noemí clarified that she was referring only to those who can speak Spanish but refuse to do so. "They're like me, bilingual, but they don't like Spanish or something," she said, switching to English.

During a lull in the conversation, I asked the group whether their parents see Chicanas as different from Chicanos.

Belia responded, "*Los ven igual de americanizados pero creo que se sienten mas amenazados con los hombres. No todos, pero muchos. No quieren que nos persigan.*" ("They see them both as Americanized but they feel more threatened by the men. Not all of them, but many. They don't want them to pursue us.")

Consuelo said that she thinks her parents feel more threatened by Chicanas: "*No quieren que tenga amigas chicanas porque entonces tienen miedo de que nos van a poner ideas . . . pero no nos pueden controlar completamente. Yo tengo amigas Chicanas.*" ("They don't want us to have Chicanas as friends because they're afraid that they'll put ideas in our head . . . but they can't control us completely. I have Chicana friends.")

"*Y cómo son sus padres?*" ("And how are their parents?") I asked.

"*No tan estrictos*" ("Not so strict"), she responded.

"*Es posible que sus padres tengan razón ser estrictos?*" ("Could it be possible that your parents are justifiably strict?") I asked the group.

Rosario came through with the boldest response, saying that the best part of American culture is the sexual freedom that many women enjoy. She then qualified this by noting, "*Pero si tiene uno que protejerse. Nos puede pegar la SIDA*" ("But one does have to protect oneself. We can get AIDS").

Explaining to me that the issue of sexual freedom is one that the group discusses all the time, Consuelo helped me put the first part of Rosario's statement in perspective and gain a better understanding of these young women's position:

> *La libertad que queremos no es para tener relaciones, sino para poder expresarnos dentro del amor. Si hay unas chicas americanizadas, Chicanas, y aún algunas Mexicanas que son vulgares y nomas quieren tener relaciones y ya! Pero creemos yo y Rosario que la mayoría quieren expresarse con el amor dentro de una relación con sus novios.* (The freedom we want is not just to have sex, but to be able to express ourselves in a loving

relationship. There are some Americanized girls, Chicanas, and even some Mexican girls, who just want to have sex and that's it! However, Rosario and I believe that the majority want to express themselves with love within a sexual relationship with their boyfriends.)

Rosario nodded as Consuelo spoke. Belia agreed, too, saying that she would probably engage in premarital sex, but only with someone she loved. Noemí, on the other hand, expressed her desire to postpone sex until she gets married. "*Tengo miedo de la SIDA*" ("I'm afraid of AIDS"), she explained.

Although the conversation ended up being about sex, the primary observation these young women made was that the relative freedom enjoyed by their Americanized U.S.-born counterparts should not be considered an objectionable aspect of American culture. These immigrant young women are not alone in their views. The girls in the "Current Events/ESL Students" and the "Career-Minded Girls" groups also associated being Americanized with greater sex role freedom. In her ethnographic study of identity in an integrated school setting, Olsen (1997) similarly observed a strong desire among immigrant females for greater latitude from parents in the areas of sexuality, dating, mate choice, and domestic responsibilities.

Current Events/ESL Students. Americanized girls are perceived as having more independence in other areas besides their relations with boys. Graciela (whose many home-based responsibilities are discussed in chapter 4) described her parents as old fashioned because they will not allow her to take a job outside the home. She says that her sister—who is only a year younger—both does a better job with housework and sibling care and enjoys it more than she does. Graciela hates weekends because they confine her to her home for too many hours. "*Me vuelvo loca*" ("I go crazy"), she said. Graciela's comments suggest that at least for some immigrant females, positive schooling orientations may be partly rooted in their constraining family circumstances. As Olsen (1997) similarly found, school can provide a liberating alternative to an otherwise home-bound lifestyle.

Graciela's parents are extremely critical of a Chicano family who lives nearby. They criticize the parents for what they see as a lax attitude toward child-rearing. The Chicano couple not only allows their daughter, Debbie, to work on weekends but also to sit outside for hours in her boyfriend's car listening to loud Tex-Mex music. Graciela's parents say nothing critical about the neighbors' son, however, who comes and goes as he pleases. In Graciela's view, "*No es justo*" ("It's not fair"). When I asked her if she knew the family, she affirmed that she now did. For awhile, she had simply accepted her parents' views. When she figured out that their remarks were part of a strategy designed to keep her from becoming friends with Debbie, however, she decided to act on her own. She made friends with Debbie. In Spanish, she explained, "I did this not to challenge my parents but because it made sense. We both go to Seguín."

Graciela and Debbie are now on very friendly terms. The relationship is helping Graciela to improve her English since Debbie knows little Spanish. Graciela's parents are also warming up to Debbie—but they tell their daughter to be careful, to guard against getting any "bright ideas" from Debbie, such as working outside the home or dating. When I asked Graciela about her parents' opinion of her boyfriend, Armando, who was listening patiently to our conversation, he volunteered: "*No saben que estamos juntos*" ("They don't know that we're together"). Nor do they know that she does his homework for him (see chapter 4). If her parents ever find out about their relationship, Graciela predicts that they'll blame Debbie for influencing her. "*Pero no es verdad. Me junté con Armando antes de conocer a Debbie*" ("But it's not true. I got together with Armando before I came to know Debbie").

At least some immigrant parents appear to use exaggerated views of Chicano males as menacing and Chicana females as morally loose to help them establish boundaries for their children's behaviors. Graciela's parents' positive reactions to Debbie suggest that opportunities for direct contact with U.S.-born youth could be nevertheless productive. The antipathy toward Chicanos/as that many immigrant parents espouse may not, however, be toward this group per se, but rather toward what these U.S.-born young people often seem to represent: academic failure, gang membership, disaffection from schooling, strange tastes in music and clothes, and so on. These parents have so much invested in their children's well-being that they appear to resist even the slightest hint that their children are poised at the beginning stages of a generational passage into social marginality. A fuller investigation than I have provided would assess the prevalence of particular parenting strategies in the Mexican immigrant community. In the interim, it seems reasonable to posit that Americanization underlies much of the familial strain that occurs between immigrant parents and their children, perhaps especially with their daughters, and notably in the areas of sexuality and gender roles.

Career-Minded Females. I conclude this discussion on immigrants by returning to Maricela, the after-school math tutor first introduced in chapter 4's opening vignette. Maricela is a ninth-grader whose friendship clique consists of three "Career-Minded Females." All are recently arrived from central states in Mexico, including Mexico City (where Maricela's nuclear family still resides). On the day I first met Maricela, she and her friends Octavia and Angelica were working feverishly on a math homework assignment. A third student, Paula, bounced back and forth between the table where she was sitting with her friends and Maricela's table. I spoke first to Octavia and Angelica. The two had just completed their assignments and were opening up their lunch bags, ready to eat.

"*Que hacen?*" ("What are you doing?") I asked.

Octavia responded, "*Estamos haciendo la tarea.*" ("We're doing our homework.")

Pointing to Paula, who had just returned to her seat at her own table, I asked Octavia who she was. Octavia explained that Paula was one of several students Maricela regularly tutored in the after-school math program. Since Paula had failed to show up the previous afternoon, both Octavia and Marciela were taking time from their lunch period to help Paula finish her homework assignment.

Amiable and trusting, Octavia, Angelica, and Maricela answered many of my questions before I had even formally introduced myself. All three had completed *primaria* (elementary school) before leaving Mexico, and then they all had attended Houston middle schools. Of the three, Maricela had made the biggest sacrifice. At the age of eleven, she had left her family behind in Mexico City and emigrated to Houston to live with her Aunt Clementina and attend school in the United States. She is the oldest of four siblings. Her parents, who have a *primaria*-level education, earn a hard living from a fruit stand they own in a *mercado* (market) located near their home in one of Mexico City's many *colonias* (neighborhoods). Since she enjoys math, Maricela plans to become a public accountant and help pull her family out of poverty. On weekends, she works at a Korean-owned, East End grocery store, stocking shelves. She has asked to be a cashier, but those positions are always reserved for family members of the Korean owner. She sends all of her earnings home to Mexico.

Since Maricela seemed so nontraditional, I asked her who influenced her to consider higher education. She said that her Aunt Clementina, who emigrated to the United States when she was just a teenager, has been the most significant influence on her life. Her aunt was sent by her family to live with a distant cousin in Houston after she became pregnant out of wedlock. Though she had a miscarriage, she never returned to Mexico.

Smiling with pride, Maricela said, "*Es mas Chicana mi tía que quien sabe que!*" ("My aunt is a real Chicana!"). She said that though Clementina can speak Spanish like a "*Chilanga*" (a Mexico-City Mexican), she prefers mixing the two languages as she speaks.

"I'm learning how to mix both languages," she confided gleefully in heavily accented English.

"So are you becoming a Chicana?" I asked half-jokingly.

Maricela revealed her tacit association between being Americanized and enjoying greater sex role freedom by blurting out that she had invited a boy to a school dance. She said that she would never have done this in Mexico.

One of her friends, listening to the conversation, commented, with a smile, "*Es muy atrevida*" ("She's very daring").

"So how has your aunt helped you?" I asked, seeking to satisfy my intrigue about her "Chicana-like" aunt.

"*Mi tía es muy buena conmigo. Somos buenas amigas.*" ("My aunt is real nice with me. We're good friends.") It was her aunt's idea that she become a tutor.

"*Mi tía quiere que agarre mas experiencia.*" ("My aunt wants me to accumulate more experience.")

Her aunt tells Marciela that the secret to Anglos' success lies in the freedoms they accord women. In contrast, she sees Mexicans as *"atrasados"* ("backwards"), always wanting to keep their women at home. Maricela says that she always defends Mexico since customs are changing there as well, but her aunt always counters with her view that change there is never fast enough. Since Maricela appeared sufficiently sympathetic to U.S.-born youth, I asked her to elaborate on her relationships with them. She responded from her perspective as a math tutor:

> *Lo que he fijado es que se les hace bien difícil la matématica a los estudiantes Mexico-Americanos. No sé. No entiendo. Yo creo que aquí en los Estados Unidos [los maestros] no enseñan tan bien la matemática. Yo siempre les ofrezco ayuda pero casi no se me arriman. Será por el idioma? Aunque domino el Español, si puedo comunicar en Inglés. No sé. Preguntale a la Paula. Ella es Chicana, no?* (What I have noticed is that math is really hard for the Mexican-American students. I don't know. I don't understand. I think that here in the United States, [teachers] do not teach math very well. I always offer them [the students] help but they hardly seek me out. Perhaps it's the language. Although I mostly speak Spanish, I can communicate in English. I don't know. Ask Paula. She's Chicana, isn't she?]

I was at first struck by Maricela's equating a lack of math aptitude with being Chicano, especially since her clientele are all immigrants. When I asked her to elaborate on this point, Maricela said that she first noticed this trait during middle school, where she had a teacher who always announced the homework and exam grades.

"Aún aquí en Seguín, nosotros, los Hispano-hablantes, siempre sacamos las mejores calificaciones." ("Even here at Seguín, we, the Spanish-speakers, always get the best grades.")

As Maricela spoke, Paula bounced back to our table to ask Maricela whether the answer she had arrived at for a particular algebraic equation was correct. It was. Temporarily corralling Paula by placing a hand on each of her shoulders, Maricela asked her to explain why none of the other Chicanos in their class ever showed up for the after-school tutoring. *"Tú eres la única!"* ("You're the only one!")

Before recounting the rare moment of cross-generational dialogue that Maricela's question inspired, it is important to note that Paula is technically an immigrant, not a Chicana. As a "1.5 generation" individual, Paula's interests and behavior are very similar to those of the U.S.-born students who comprise her friendship group. According to Vigil (1997), 1.5 generation youth are a distinct category. Born in Mexico, they come to the United States as small children and thus experience U.S. schooling for most of their young lives. Typically, they are fluent in Spanish and English. These similarities enable them to forge alliances with many Mexican and U.S.-born youth. Paula belongs to a mixed-generation group I initially referred to as "Social Monolinguals" because they are perceived by others (like the "Career-Minded Females") as students who could speak Spanish but who choose not to. After making two important discoveries about Paula's group in a later interview (discussed below), I realized that "Indigenous Mexican-American Females" would be a more appropriate label.

Knitting her eyebrows, Paula silently concentrated on Maricela's question for several long seconds. Having overheard the tail end of the conversation Maricela and I were having, Paula agreed, "*El idioma si tiene algo que ver. . . .*" ("The language does have something to do with it. . . .") Speaking softly in Spanish, Paula began to explain how getting the help she needed from Maricela was not an easy thing to do at first.

"I thought she would laugh at my Spanish because I just talk street Spanish," Paula said, switching to English. "I think Mexicans from here are afraid to be shown up by Mexicans from over there," she continued. "Though I was born in Mexico, I've been on this side all my life, so all my friends are mostly from here."

Octavia and Angelica drew in closer in order to hear Paula better. Meanwhile, Maricela grew tense and whispered in English, "I never imagined. . . ."

Though I could not tell which part of Paula's statement was hard for Maricela to imagine, Paula shot back an immediate response:

"It's true! I don't understand it. We see y'all come from Mexico. You don't speak the language, your first time here, and you do better than us! How do you think that makes us feel?"

"So how *does* it make you feel?" I asked.

"Bad!" Paula exclaimed. "Like we just can't get it!"

Shaking her head with indignation, Octavia echoed Maricela's earlier observation, saying in Spanish, "If Paula had gone to my school in Mexico, she would understand the material."

Ignoring Octavia, Paula attempted to backtrack. "I'm sorry," she said contritely, "I have a big mouth."

"Why do you say that?" asked Maricela.

"Please, don't get me wrong," Paula continued. "I really do appreciate the help. I'm just jealous."

"*You're* jealous of *me?*" Maricela asked, incredulous.

"All of you, I guess. At the end of your four years here, you're going to have a degree and you're going to have two languages. I'll be real lucky if I have a degree—and my Spanish is the pits! So that makes me jealous."

Sounding like Aarón who had tried to convince his friend Michael that Michael's Spanish was just fine, Maricela responded: "*Mira, ojalá que tomes esto bien. Te podemos seguir ayudandote. Octavia, Angelica, y yo. Y sabes que otra cosa? Tu hablas muy bien el español. Lo que te falta es la práctica y te podemos ayudar con eso también.* ("Look, I hope you take this well. We can keep helping you—Octavia, Angelica, and me. And you know what else? You speak Spanish very well. What you need is practice and we can help you out with that, too.")

Paula accepted Maricela's offer of friendship and support, saying, "*Gracias. Si necesito la ayuda. No me cabe todo esto en la cabeza.*" ("Thanks, I do need the help. It just doesn't stick in my head.") The relation of language and identity to academics became the subtext of this conversation.

Distributing hugs to each of us, Paula then excused herself from the group. As I received her embrace, I asked her how she felt.

"Relieved," she replied, smiling.

"Why 'relieved'?" I questioned.

"You know," she continued, "I don't want to feel bad about anybody. That's just the way I feel even if I am from Mexico. My friends are from here and they feel put off the same way, maybe even more."

"Don't worry," I reassured her, "I think everybody understood you."

Maricela added, "*No te preocupes. De veras!*" ("Don't worry. Really!")

After Paula left, Octavia asked Maricela whether Paula was Mexican or not. Maricela said, "*Aunque nació en Mexico, ella es de aquí. Tú la oyiste. Porque?*" (Though she was born in Mexico, she's from here. You heard her. Why?")

Octavia seemed surprised. She had thought Paula was from the United States. Though no one said anything, I felt that Octavia's confusion stemmed either from her limited comprehension of the English parts of the conversation or from Paula's "We-see-y'all-come-from-Mexico" statement. Maricela helped fill in some of the blanks by informing the group that Paula is the youngest sibling in a large family; only her oldest brother and sister are "*mexicanados*" ("Mexicanized").

"*Hay muchas diferencias entre nosotros*" ("There are many differences between us"), she said.

When I asked Maricela whether Paula's answer to her question about why Mexican American students don't take advantage of tutorial assistance had satisfied her, she replied that it had never occurred to her that she could be threatening to Chicanos, especially since she often felt intimidated herself by them. She then began to ponder her relation to Chicanos. She described how, when she first arrived in the United States, she spoke little English. Initially, survival in and out of school entailed finding Spanish-speaking people who could translate for her at every turn. While some Anglos she met were impatient with her weak English language skills, several encounters she had with Chicanos were more disturbing. She offered the example of a Mexican American waiter in a fast-food restaurant who publicly humiliated her by giving her a mini-English lesson on how to order a meal. Maricela said that in Mexico, it would be unthinkable for a waiter or any other service worker to condescendingly coach a "*gringo*" tourist or resident on the proper way to speak Spanish. If anything, Mexicans cater to "*gringos*" by acquiring English conversational skills.

I asked Octavia and Angelica whether they ever felt intimidated by Chicanos. They answered affirmatively, but then explained that these feelings were limited mainly to the first year after they had arrived in the United States. Angelica said that since in Mexico she had only been exposed to Chicanos through movies, she arrived in the United States feeling ambivalent toward them:

"I thought they were like the blacks . . . into drugs and violence. Some are involved, but not as much as I thought."

Octavia assembled her thoughts and contributed an insightful analysis in Spanish:

> In Mexico, we learn about Chicanos from Hollywood and that's all. So when we come to the United States, we find out that there's more to know than what you see on television. What I see is that Chicanos are Americanized but they're not really part of America. It's one thing to not be part of America if you are an immigrant like us. It's a totally different thing if you're American—your name is "Janet" or "John"—and you're still not part of America.

Sighing deeply, Angelica wondered, "*Que significa esto para nosotras?*" ("What does this mean for us?")

With a sudden intuitive realization, Maricela said, "*Aprende el idioma pero sigue siendo Mexicana.*" ("Learn the language but stay Mexican.")

With Aunt Clementina and Maricela's emerging Chicana consciousness in mind, I suggested that being Chicana or even speaking street Spanish isn't necessarily bad in itself. The real problem, as Paula's situation suggests, is being cut off from Mexicans and not commanding formal Spanish while simultaneously being cut off from white America, as Octavia had noted.

The preceding accounts highlight the presence of a politics of difference that defines the relationship between immigrant and U.S.-born youth. The politics of difference are reinforced by Seguín's transitioning brand of Americanization, as well as from the complex and contradictory power relationships that follow from this process. Though youth like Maricela and her friends possess little social power on the Seguín campus—they are shunned by their English-speaking peers and are often targets of discrimination and prejudice—many nevertheless possess academic power that fellow students like Paula are able to benefit from but also resent intensely. Paula clearly conveys the view that schooling is more beneficial (or additive) for some than for oth-

ers (like herself). She fears not graduating and laments her weak
Spanish. While she does not blame her shortcomings on her immigrant peers, she does convey a sense of frustrated entitlement to
the good life that both education and bilingualism promise.
Herein lies the basis of her resentment or her "jealousy" as she
phrases it. Her openness toward Marciela and the other girls is in
keeping with the attitudes and demeanor I observed among other
members of her mixed-generation friendship group.

Attitudes among Mixed-Generation Groups

Paula's group was the only one I came across whose members
embrace their indigenous identity and past. As the discussion
below shows, cross-generational alliances provide an appropriate
antidote to the feelings of vulnerability, jealousy, and resentment
that inevitably surface in the absence of cross-generational communication, awareness, and understanding. Although, as discussed in the preceding chapter, youth in mixed-generation and
U.S.-born friendship groups are similar in self-representation,
they also differ in several important respects: Whereas youth in
U.S.-born friendship groups sometimes harbor feelings of ani-
mosity and resentment toward immigrants, no comparable feelings exist among youth in mixed-generation groups. Rather than
overt hostility, youth in U.S.-born friendship groups are more typically reticent about the immigrant experience. They convey a
profound, psychic distance from the world that immigrants
inhabit. In contrast, the most sympathetic and empathic statements toward immigrants that I came across were made by youth
in mixed-generation groups, suggesting a relation between group
composition and attitudes toward Mexican nationals.

The concentration of 1.5 generation youth in mixed-generation groups is a moderating influence. These young people for the
most part navigate successfully between their Mexican and Americanized identities. In contrast, cross-generational friendships
between youth in U.S.-born and more recent immigrant youth
groups are rare.

Indigenous Mexican American Females. Paula belongs to a generationally mixed group where she and a student named Miriam,
both sophomores, are immigrants who are best characterized as

1.5 generation youth. Becca, the third female in the group, is U.S.-born from Houston. Though Spanish (or Spanish and English in Becca's case) is spoken in all of their homes, all prefer to speak English only at school. Despite Maricela's offer of friendship, Paula remained close to her original group of friends, whom I later met. During that group interview, I mustered up the courage to ask why these youths did not befriend Maricela and her group. Paula readily grasped the question as intended primarily for her:

> I'm not Mexican. I can't do that, even if that's what would be best for me. Don't get me wrong. I love Maricela. I'm just different from them and I really wish I wasn't. That's just the way it is.

This answer, combined with her earlier remarks to Marciela, constitute the strongest expressions of social alienation that I came across among youth located in mixed-generation groups. Paula's case helps illustrate how dynamic and malleable a Mexican identity can be. It can accommodate, when necessary, to the pressures and demands of subtractive schooling, the peer group, and family identity and circumstances.

Paula attributes her insecurities about speaking Spanish to several factors. First, although she is now taking Spanish, prior to this year she had never had the opportunity to study Spanish as a language or to study other subjects in Spanish. She always knew just enough English to avoid being assigned to a bilingual education program. Secondly, because she is a severe asthmatic, her parents have not been able to maintain close, physical ties to their relatives, who live primarily around the outskirts of Mexico City where the air quality is poor. Acting embarrassed and shrinking into her seat as she spoke, Paula expressed her view that closer ties to Mexico and her extended family would help her feel more confident about her Spanish. She also thinks that her Spanish will improve as she takes more Spanish courses.

I tried to allay her concerns by suggesting to her that improving one's Spanish is a never-ending process and that hers sounded fine to me. Looking frustrated, she responded, "That's just it. It's 'fine.' It's not good. I don't know big words or if I'm saying things the correct way. That's why I don't really like talking it to educated people like Maricela."

Rescuing Paula from her discomfort, Miriam broke in. "It's hard because people think you're a snob if you don't talk to them in Spanish. If I'm going to sound like a fool, I'd rather not say anything."

Rumors abound at Seguín of students who are allegedly able to speak Spanish but do not. That is, they consciously choose to reject their Spanish tongue. Maricela and her friends describe Paula's group as being comprised of such students. My initial label for Paula's group was "Social Monolinguals," revealing my own willingness to accept this campus lore at face value. Now that I have reviewed all of the data I collected across the many different groups I interviewed, I am less convinced that such "social monolinguals" exist at Seguín. Students do not reject a language that they can speak. Instead, they reject a language that, in their estimation, they do not speak *well*. One's self-perception of fluency is obviously highly subjective and is strongly influenced by one's level of fluency in one's dominant tongue. Hence, some students can appear fluent to others in a particular language while simultaneously regarding themselves as embarrassingly inarticulate.

As Paula indicates, fear of ridicule resulting from speaking Spanish incorrectly in public inhibits her expression and minimizes possibilities for cultivating relationships with other Spanish-dominant youth. The desire to avoid even the *possibility* of public humiliation is likely to exceed anxiety over the *actuality* of being misconstrued as "snobs" who reject their Spanish tongue.

The conversation turned in a different direction when I posed this question: "To be Mexican, does one have to speak Spanish?" No one saw this as a prerequisite. Instead, all believed that being a true Mexican means identifying with one's Indian heritage. "Indians are Mexican and many don't speak Spanish," asserted Miriam. The group informed me that Paula's mother—a proud Nahuatl Indian who speaks Spanish, some English, and her indigenous tongue—has had a strong influence on their views. Paula says that she rarely hears Nahuatl spoken at home, however, because her father is "*mestizo*" (both Spanish and Indian) and speaks only Spanish. "I know some words, though," she asserted.

We then enjoyed a brief interchange on Nahuatl words that are common in the Spanish language. Words mentioned included *guajolote* (turkey), *sacate* (grass), *chocolate* (chocolate), and *tacuache* (possum). I then asked them how they identified, how they see themselves.

Miriam said, "I've learned a lot from Paula's mom and how us Mexicans are all Indian, but it's hard for me to say I'm Indian."

"So you're Mexican," I suggested.

Miriam confessed that she found the whole subject confusing. Practically all Mexicans have Indian blood but rarely ever say they're Indian.

Becca said, "Man, it really bugs me whenever Mexicans as dark as me say they're Spanish—like they don't want to be Mexican."

"You mean Indian," Paula corrected.

Becca responded hesitatingly, "I-I guess I mean both . . . Mexican or Indian."

Paula then described the development of her indigenous consciousness. She said that she and her brothers always used to make fun of her mother for wearing *mantos* (Indian head scarfs) and *rebosos* (Indian shawls) because her attire embarrassed them.

"Now I feel bad that we did that. We were like people who tell Mexicans, 'Speak English or go back to Mexico.'"

I asked what accounted for her change in views. She said that she remembers very clearly the day she noticed her mother no longer looked Indian.

"She came to see me at school and she looked like she could be anybody's mother. I realized I missed what made her special—the bright colors, the Indian designs, and the *rebosos*." She said that though she partly blamed herself for her mother's change, her mother's explanation was that her clothes had gotten old. Paula said, "Now she only wears her *rebosos* on Sundays."

This experience made a deep impression on Paula, who now regularly asks her mother about her Indian heritage. After several conversations with Paula's mother about the richness of Aztec civilization and the conquest of the Nahuatl-speaking Aztec Indians, Miriam and Becca also became intrigued with their own Indian heritage. I asked Miriam and Becca how the thought of being Indian affects them. Becca said, "It makes us feel proud, like we're not this low race." Miriam said that she would like to learn more about the shame Mexicans feel toward their Indian-ness. Paula built on Becca's assertion by saying that Mexicans do not want to be Indian "because they see it as a low race." Paula confessed, "Even I got messed up in the head for awhile."

Because of Paula's mother's influence, these young women were unusually conversant about the indigenous aspect of their *Mexicanidad*, uniquely so among the Seguín students I inter-viewed. Paula, Becca, and Miriam all derived a sense of impor-tance from this knowledge. It helped them turn on its head the assumption that one must know Spanish to be Mexican. In their view, one's *Mexicanidad* is grievously narrow if it is bereft of an indigenous perspective. This group helps underscore the com-plexities of *Mexicanidad,* and their comments suggest that a fully relevant and additive curriculum must address the ongoing hemi-spheric project of de-Indianization (Batalla 1996).

Paula understands that she could benefit from a more intimate relationship with Maricela and her friends. However, to the extent that such a shift would minimize opportunities to continue elaborating her indigenous identity, she judges the cost as too high. The loss of the shared cultural understandings that have developed over time among her group of friends would constitute another major sacrifice. Furthermore, in light of her quasi-subor-dinate relationship to Maricela, another psychic cost might be the confidence that she is able to exude with her close friends who, partly because of her mother, accord Paula much status and respect. Perhaps under more additive conditions, a friendship with Maricela would be less threatening. Obstacles that emanate from Mexicans' colonial past amplify the complexity that may compromise at least some cross-generational alliances.

That youth in other generationally mixed groups experienced far less angst about their *Mexicanidad* attests to the supports in their environment which help promote their bicultural and bilin-gual identities. For U.S.-born youth in these groups, such supports include the fluent bilingualism of their 1.5 generation peers who help reinforce their Spanish abilities and their identification with Mexico. Youth in these groups unanimously lament the divisions that exist among them by asserting the benefits of their culture- and language-affirming friendships and the enriching experiences that tend to follow from these liaisons.

The Achievement Gang. In this group (also examined in chapter 4), Jerry, who is third generation, went with Betty, who is 1.5 generation, on a family trip to Mexico over the summer.

"I fell in love with Betty's family," Jerry announced, unabashedly. "Mexicans are much nicer there than they are here."

Betty smiled with pride and said that she didn't know where it came from, but "this guy popped out with Spanish from I don't know where."

"I realized I could just pick it up. Like it's in my brain somewhere—probably where Selena and Emilio Navaira are," he responded laughingly.

While Jerry's affinity to Tex-Mex music with Spanish lyrics may very well have contributed to his competence in Spanish, his closeness to Betty and her family has also placed him in numerous situations where he has had to speak the language.

Cosmetology Females. A rewarding trip to Mexico was similarly highlighted in a conversation I had with a group of young women who share an interest in becoming cosmetologists. An immigrant student named Caridad and two third-generation students named Cynthia and Margie traveled by bus to León, Guanajuato, on a missionary trip with their church group. Since most of the church members who went on the trip were Anglos who didn't speak Spanish, Caridad acted as translator. By sticking close to Caridad throughout the whole trip, the other two girls improved their Spanish 100 percent. Cynthia thought that it was "neat" seeing how much the Anglos were forced to rely on her. I asked Caridad how the experience made her feel. "Important," she said, "but it was a lot of pressure."

I asked the group if they were friends before going on the trip. The two U.S.-born females said that though they had always gone to the same church as Caridad, they only became close friends with her during the trip.

"Why weren't you friends before?" I asked.

Margie explained that they couldn't get to know each other because they attended different church services. "Caridad attends the early morning Spanish service and we always attended the late morning English service."[12]

Ever since the trip, all three have attended the Spanish-speaking service together. Cynthia expounded on the benefits to this change. "It's earlier, we get church over with, and we continue learning Spanish." Margie added that going to this early service has helped her learn to read Spanish since all the songs she sings now are written in Spanish.

When asked to comment on the divisions that exist among youth, these young women again referred to their church experiences. Cynthia said that she had been wanting to make a break from the English-speaking service for a long time because Anglos are always in charge of those services, and the "Mexicans Americans always end up off to themselves." Margie noted that she still felt awkward in the Spanish-speaking service, but having Caridad there to explain things made a big difference. Caridad, too, felt that she had benefited from her friends' interest in the Spanish service. "Without them," she remarked, "I would have dropped out of church already."

When I asked whether they thought that they would have gotten to know each other if it hadn't been for the trip to Mexico, their response was a resounding, "No!" Since Caridad also spoke English and shared much in common with Cynthia and Margie, this case reveals how the institutionalization of language differences—in the form of separate Spanish- and English-speaking services—was the chief barrier to their friendship. The missionary trip "de-tracked" their church experience, helping them to overcome that obstacle.

Two final examples from interviews with mixed-generation youth reveal how an occasionally hostile and insufficiently sympathetic curriculum can challenge these students' efforts to validate both the immigrant and U.S.-Mexican experience.

Borderline Gang Members. In this group of three freshmen males (labeled "borderline gang members" because of pressures they feel to join a gang) only two spoke, as the third listened on. The two complained that Seguín is "down on Mexicans."

"What do you mean?" I probed.

Mariano, the 1.5 generation member of the group, said that they never get the true story of the Alamo in school.

"Or the Battle of San Jacinto," added his friend Stephen.

Stephen then said that when he was in middle school, he went on some "shit field trip" to visit the San Jacinto Memorial where the Mexicans, led by General Santa Ana, lost their final battle against the Anglo Texans.

"Man, how can I be a proud Texan when there's nothing but dead Mexicans or white men killing Mexicans in every single picture?"

"We were massacred, man!" commented Mariano.

Stephen also recalled how weird it had felt to visit the Memorial with groups of "nothing but Mexican kids from other schools there that day." I asked him what his teachers' opinions on the subject were. Stephen said that his teacher sympathized with the Mexicans but also said that the war was just a matter of time because the West had to be opened up. Stephen said that his teacher could not answer his question about why "the West had to be opened up." I asked him whether he had learned any more of this history while at Seguín.

Stephen answered, "No, nothing. Just a little on Cesar Chavez—as if that's going to do it."

"Do what?" I pressed.

"Like, make us proud that we're Mexicans," he smirked.

On the subject of their bilingualism, these young men described Spanish as protecting them "like a shield." Speaking Spanish lets them say anything they want, since most teachers don't know what they are saying.

"Especially when we're talking about them," Stephen joked.

In a more serious tone, Mariano said that he noticed how many teachers seem not to like it when they speak Spanish. He said that he can't understand why teachers don't want to know two languages. In short, these students' sense of disaffection from, and oppositionality toward, Seguín is intertwined with their identity. That is, they claim ownership over that which they have been denied, especially their sense of history and their bilingualism.

Journalism Females. While I was interviewing this group, a 1.5 generation student named Leila stepped in to contribute to the conversation we were already having about the divisions that exist among youth at school as well as in the community. One female journalism student had just shared her dismay over her father's exploitation of an immigrant male he had hired to help him out with home repairs. In the following account, Leila expresses her rage toward Mexican Americans who fail to acknowledge the exploitation of immigrants. The episode recounted here is also important because it illustrates the way in which teachers' attitudes can manufacture both silence and discontent in the classroom.

> One time, I got so upset with my teacher. I think that he didn't like me. And when I get mad I usually use cuss words, and I was just . . . [*gestures, zipping her mouth*]. All of a sudden, out of the blue he says, "Why do they come here if they don't speak the language?" And I knew he was referring to the Mexican race, right? And I said to myself, now somebody's going to stand up and say something. Nobody got up! And I said, okay, I'm just going to sit here and listen to this punk. I was just sitting there and then he says, "If you're going to live in the United States, you gotta speak English." And then some guy, he started talking, and I said, alright, someone's going to say something. All right! And that guy says, "You're right. They just come take our jobs." And he's Mexican! And I turned around and said, "What the hell are you talking about?" And the teacher looked at me like, excuse me? And I go [to the teacher], "What do you mean 'speak the language'? You go to Mexico and you don't speak Spanish. You *gringos* go down there and give Mexicans a hard time but we don't bitch and moan about you not speaking Spanish." I go, "This isn't your country. Half of it was what?— Stolen!"
>
> And then he [the teacher] goes, "You're just totally losing the point." And I go, "And you're totally preaching racism and that's against the law." And he goes, "No, I'm trying to explain to you that y'all give us a hard time." "So, in other words, when you ask for parent involvement my parents give you a hard time because they can't speak English? You're acting like it's a sin for us to know our tongue, and if you ask me, it's better for us to speak two languages than just one. And as far as speaking English alone is concerned, that's stupid because that's half the population and you [white teacher] don't make up the [total] population."
>
> And then I turned around to talk to the guy in back of me and asked him. "As for you, what kind of jobs are they taking

away from you?" And he like laughed at me. And when people laugh at me, that makes me even angrier. And I told him, "You want to dig ditches? Is that the kind of job you're looking for? Did you go apply to dig a ditch and they [immigrants] took it from you? I don't think so!" This guy made me so mad because we're all *indios* [Indians] with our *nopales* [cactuses] on our foreheads. And it makes me so mad! And the students were all against me. And I love it when I have to argue. I love arguing!

The teacher said, "No, you're missing the point. You're missing the point." I told him, "I'm sorry for being disrespectful but you just totally degraded my race. And I don't sit here and degrade yours because I can say a lot of things about you white people, but I don't. My dad always told me something and it makes me laugh—but it's true. When they call you a wetback, you just tell them, I just jumped 50 yards to get here. You jumped 50,000 miles."

Another guy in the class said, "No, Leila, calm down." And I said, "Hey this dude over here talks like they're taking jobs away from us when in reality they're doing it for a glass of water and bread." I told the teacher, "You do what you want to do. You want to send me to the office, you send me right now." Because my dad's a journalist, too, right? And he [her dad] says, "Whatever happens, you tell me." I was begging him to send me. "You do what you have to do, and I'll do what I have to do." And he says, "What do you mean by that?" I said, "You send me to the office and I will tell those people what you just said. And they're not going to believe me, but I'll go to my father and my father's word against yours is a lot stronger 'cause he's a parent and I'm a student of your school. And what you're doing is preaching racism and it's against the law."

And he goes, "Nooo. . . ." I go, "Then what does 'speak the language' mean? I would rather speak Spanish than speak English. And being bilingual is a preference in lots of jobs now and you're making it look like it's stupid. Like it's nothing! Like it's a sin!" Nobody in the class said, "Yeah. . . ." Everyone in the class was totally focused on me. They looked at me like, oh no, she's going to get up, start throwing pentagrams at everyone, start burning the place down. And that guy in the back kept laughing at me. And I would not shut up. I do not shut up until I get the last word. And sure enough I did. "Just send me to the office, Mr. Waters, I'm begging you! Please send me. You're going to see what's going to result out of this. You're going to regret what you just said." And he goes, "No, just calm down. I didn't mean to insult you." "You didn't just insult me. You insulted my mother and their mothers, but they're not standing up for that. When someone calls your mom a bitch, you get into a fight and get suspended. But when they call your race a wetback, you can't do nothing about it? That's stupid if you ask me!"

Leila's 1.5 generation status and her grounded sense of history undergird her confident handling of herself. That is, she can openly empathize with exploited immigrants at the same time that she can use her knowledge of the schooling process, including her perception of parental power, to protect her from her nonconformity.

Leila felt that she could challenge her teacher not only because she knew she could stand on principle, but also because she had "backup" in the form of a father she knew could intervene on her behalf if necessary. Leila's assertion that "they're not going to believe me but I'll go to my father" highlights the political nature of schooling. Youth, because they usually lack either adequate argument skills or sufficient "backup," are predictable losers in one-on-one battles with faculty and administrators. At Seguín, many youth have neither "backup" nor fathers, so remaining silent in situations like the one Leila described is expedient. The lack of support from her classmates clearly upset Leila; however, what sustained her impassioned outburst was her realization that some youth might actually agree with the disparaging perception of immigrants held by the dominant group. Given their exposure to the kind of schooling experiences Leila describes in her account, it is understandable that many U.S.-born students either harbor uninformed opinions or maintain distance toward immigrants.

Attitudes among U.S.-born Groups

In contrast to the immigrant and mixed-generation friendship groups, whose respective attitudes coalesce around certain themes (e.g., the distance of Chicanas and Chicanos from their Mexican cultural heritage and the benefits that follow from a bicultural and bilingual orientation), the attitudes toward immigrants displayed by youth in U.S.-born friendship groups followed no clear thematic pattern. While two groups were very negative and two others were quite positive, the remaining five were reticent or evasive.

Except for a single mention of immigrant males as being more *macho* than Mexican American males, I heard no discussion of gender roles or sexuality to parallel those that had occurred among immigrant youth groups. To the extent that differences were discussed, the subject of immigrants prompted references to differences in language, culture, and socioeconomic class.

Generational analyses show that these groups are disproportionately comprised of third+-generation youth who lack familiarity with Mexico. The majority are also English-dominant, though some reported some degree of fluency in either Spanish or "Spanglish." To capture the fluidity and far-ranging nature of the attitudes of U.S.-born youth, I report here the opposing ends of the attitudinal spectrum. In the conclusion, I consider the equivocal responses of U.S.-born youth groups.

Rio Grande Valley Students and the Kickers. These two groups provided the most caustic remarks toward immigrants that I came across. Though the composition of the first group apparently changed immediately after this interview, it was originally comprised of three males and one female, all sophomores. These students expressed resentment against the presence of immigrants in their classes.

A male student named Arnold observed, "They always slow us down because the teacher always has to take extra time to explain things to them."

His friend Tony complained that the immigrant students in his classes never "say jack."

"Why is that a problem?" I wondered.

"Looking stupid! That's the problem, like they just swam across the river," he sneered.

"Like, 'Duh'!" inserted their friend Annette, whose comment made them all laugh.

Tony added, "They don't dress cool, man."

Trying to get a better idea of what prompted their hostility, I probed further, asking why they felt so strongly about immigrants.

Tony offered this perspective: "In the Valley, you always read in the newspaper about how these people cross the river into people's yards, drink from their water hoses, ask for food . . . disgusting! I figure, if you can't cross right, you shouldn't cross at all."

"So what's crossing right?" I asked.

"Legal," he quipped, "not through somebody's yard."

My response that not all immigrants enter illegally evinced no response.

Looking appalled by what he was hearing, James, the only non-Valley student in the group, said, "They cross because of poverty and hunger."

Continuing with James' more generous outlook, Arnold asserted that immigrants are not responsible for there being "nothing but low-paying jobs in Mexico."

Tony then attempted to explain his sentiments by saying that he knows a lot about immigrants from his father, a labor contractor who hires "*mojados*" ("wetbacks"). "They take a long time to finish certain jobs so that they can make more money."

"So? What's wrong with that?" pressed James, now visibly uncomfortable.

Annette interrupted to tell James, condescendingly, that because he's not from the Valley, he wouldn't understand. She then launched into a lengthy story about how, before moving to Houston, her family had always had Mexican maids working for them. Now they can't afford these maids, because "Now they won't work below a certain amount."

"Like how much?" I questioned.

"Like three dollars an hour to clean your house."

"Would you work for that much?" I asked.

"No, but what I'm saying is that they act like they're special and want minimum wage even if they're not legal."

"And then there's jobs that they won't do—like they're too good," Tony added.

Out of nowhere, a perturbed James broke in, "I don't need to be from the Valley to know that y'all are cold, man."

In a surprisingly cutting tone that caught me off guard, Tony told James that he would think differently if he actually knew more about what he was talking about. Then, with a "Let's-not-talk-about-this-anymore" comment, Tony signaled an end to the conversation.

James left the group abruptly, saying, "Catch y'all later, man!"

After an embarrassingly long pause, Tony whispered, "James doesn't know how it's easier to be *for mojados* when you're not around them much."

With a look of dismay that he directed toward me, Arnold said, "Aw, let's talk about something else."

I told the group that I was sorry about what had happened.

"That's cool, Miss," Arnold told me, reassuringly.

Annette added, "It all means we gotta talk more about these things. And we can't be getting mad, either."

Sounding like a bully again, Tony insisted, "It means we gotta talk about things we know about."

With this comment, the last remnants of our discussion dissolved. I remained both anxious and curious, however, about James' abrupt departure. With the help of the attendance officer, I tracked him down before his fifth-period class.

I explained to James that I had sought him out mainly to apologize for "starting it all with my questions." He too apologized for walking out on the interview.

"I couldn't take another minute of it. Tony's such a hot head!" he exclaimed.

"Will you still be friends with Tony?" I asked.

With anger once again apparent in his voice, James said, "I don't know. As he was saying immigrants this, immigrants that, I said to myself, 'What if he were saying farm worker this, farm worker that?' My parents were farm workers. Don't get me wrong. I agree with them that we have an immigrant problem. I just don't think we should hate them."

"So what's 'the problem'?" I asked.

James said that he often feels like he does not belong at Seguín because he speaks little Spanish. "So, I was born here and I feel like I don't belong," he lamented. "It's not right."

When I suggested to him that many immigrants don't feel like they belong either, his response revealed his ambivalence.

"I know. A lot of them look scared. Maybe they come across people like Tony who scare them. I'm glad I'm not them."

Clearly, these youths' attitudes have been shaped by the conditions of their daily lives. Their ideas and opinions reflect distance (much of what they "know" comes from newspapers and TV) and relations of dominance and subordination (in interactions with maids or laborers).

In contrast to the "Rio Grande Valley" group, whose members were divided in their attitudes regarding immigrants, the "Kickers" displayed remarkable consensus in their negativity. "Kicker" members included two females, Lena and Martha, and one male, Chris, who spoke in a heavy Southern drawl.

"We can dance to any tune, but *Tejano* (Tex-Mex) and C & W (country and western) is what we like best," Lena told me, explaining the bond among the group members.

Although they don't always go with one another, all of the Kickers attend every possible school dance, *quinceañera,* and wedding to take advantage of the opportunities for dancing. Lena fantasizes about forming a *Tejano* or C & W dance club they could belong to at school. Though I anticipated a negative response, I nevertheless asked them whether *ballet folklórico* (traditional Mexican dance) interested them.

"No-o-o," said Chris, wrinkling his nose in disapproval.

Martha dismissed the idea, saying, "That just ain't us."

"Why not?" I pressed.

"We're not Mexican, that's why!" Lena retorted. "This is *Tejano* (Texas Mexican) country."

After defining *Tejano* identity as loyalty to Texas, Chris said that his family has been in the United States since the mid-1800s. "The school does a lot for them and nothing for us. And we've been here for generations," he complained.

"Like what?" I asked.

"Like ESL. And I see how they become teacher's pet because a lot of them like to kiss butt."

Half-jokingly, Martha mused, "Maybe if I go on welfare and take somebody's job, I'll become teacher's pet, too!"

I asked Lena whether she felt the same way.

Her reservations were different. "My problem is with the guys. They're too *macho.*"

"What do you mean?" I asked.

She explained how one immigrant male had kept on pursuing her, even after she told him to "disappear." He had the "nasty habit" of whispering compliments to her in the halls between classes.

"Ooh, gross!" inserted Martha, with a disgusted look on her face.

"So, how did it all turn out?" I questioned Lena.

She said that he had finally stopped after she had embarrassed him publicly by screaming in the hallway between classes, "We don't do that in this country!"

Chris' response to this story was instructive. With a broad smile on his face, he exclaimed, "Can you believe these guys . . . coming after *our* women?"

He not only failed to see the self-contradiction within his patriarchal statement, he also generalized to all Mexican immigrant males. His assessment was left uncontested.

Spanish-Speakers and Mixed-Raced Students. The first group—comprised of three female and two male Spanish-speaking students (discussed in detail in chapter 4)—offered the most positive outlook toward immigrants. None in the "Spanish-speakers" group had a close, intimate relationship with immigrants. What their attitudes suggest is that some contact with immigrants, combined with friendships that affirm each individual's culture and language, can positively orient students toward immigrants, resulting in attitudes very similar to those held by mixed-generation youth.

Contrasting the Spanish-speakers with the "Mixed-Race" group of three females (two Mexican American and one African American) and three males (also two Mexican American and one African American) shows that socioeconomic class background, too, may positively affect youths' attitudes. The Spanish-speakers nurture their Spanish-language skills by taking Spanish-language courses, being in the Spanish Club, and speaking Spanish among themselves. Students in the Mixed-Race group neither speak Spanish nor belong to school-based clubs or organizations. When a discussion I had with this latter group of students touched on the subject of their lack of involvement in school activities, I got a better sense of the impact of their working-class status.

Several of these students mentioned that they did not have enough money to belong to school clubs or organizations. When I pointed out that most school organizations did not require any money, they corrected me by referring to hidden costs. For exam-

ple, Natasha, the group's only African American female, said that
her family discourages her from running track because they cannot afford to buy her a good pair of running shoes each time she
needs to replace her old ones. When I observed that the pair she
had on seemed fine, she added that she is also responsible for the
care of her younger siblings while her mother, who is single, is
away at work. "So it's the money, plus the help she needs," she
elaborated.

Opportunity costs underlay the lack of involvement of the
group's Mexican American males. Both said that their parents
want them to use their time after school to find jobs.

"And do you find them?" I probed.

Roland, responding for himself and his friend, said politely,
"Yes, M'am—mowing lawns, trimming hedges, painting, or
whatever."

Speaking on behalf of her friend Valerie (upon whom she was
leaning as we talked), Natasha said that Valerie sells newspapers
on weekends. A very serious-looking Valerie nodded her confirmation. A student named Artie explained that all their parents
want them to be busy working all the time so they can all help out
their families—and stay out of gangs.

Natasha said that the big lesson she learned from having her
father in prison is that there's not much room in life for mistakes.
"You gotta be smart and stay away from drugs," she said.

"Is that what he's in for?" I asked.

With a pained expression on her face that made me wish I
hadn't asked, Natasha replied simply, "Yes, M'am."

As far as I can recall, during the three years in which I was a
participant-observer at Seguín, these were the only students who
ever referred to me as "M'am," rather than the customary
"Miss." I interpreted this seemingly automatic deference as a sign
of these students' emerging identities as service workers. While I
worried about their conformity to their social status, I also understood that their access to odd jobs was facilitated by such displays
of deference.

A noteworthy similarity between this group and the Spanish-
speakers is their collectivist orientation. In fact, youth in the
mixed-race group referred to one another as "family" because
none had nearby relatives they felt they could count on.

In utter seriousness, Artie told me, "To belong to *our* group, your family's gotta be screwed up."

"It's true! It's true!" several others chimed in.

When I asked them how they had all come to be friends, they said that attending the same schools, having the same lunch period, and living in the same neighborhood helped. All live near the warehouse district, in an area where the East End intersects with a historically African American neighborhood, just south of downtown.

"It's simple." said Natasha. "We know each other. We look out for each other. No one messes with us."

The similarities between the two groups diminish when the focus shifts from collectivism to social capital. The Spanish-speakers group is well connected; they all live in the heart of the East End community and they are closely involved with Michelle's extended family and with her family's church. In contrast, the mixed-race group members have no parents, family, or extended family members who exert a deliberate, positive presence in their lives. Instead, the glue that binds them is their self-conscious awareness of their dysfunctional families, their poverty, and their shared milieu as youngsters growing up in a very rough neighborhood. Unlike their Spanish-speaking counterparts (see chapter 4), they have had little or no access to role models capable of providing them with tangible support for any dreams they might have.

The two groups also differ in the amount of contact they have with immigrants. Belonging to the Spanish Club and taking Spanish courses has given the first group the opportunity to meet and make friends with many immigrant students, though no immigrant is part of their intimate circle. In a follow-up interview I had with just Michelle and Jason, I asked why there were no immigrants in their friendship group. Michelle replied that people from Mexico are different, "though not in a bad way." Explaining further, she continued, "It's like we're Mexican *and* American and we need to be able to talk English *and* Spanish 'cause that's who we are."

I asked Jason whether he agreed with this view. He did.

"It changes things when everything has to be in Spanish because that's not us, who we are."

Michelle stressed, however, that immigrants are important: "They remind us of our culture and language—which would be really bad to lose."

"Yeah, and as hard as I've had it, I admire them because it's more hard for them than us," added Jason.

Struggling to comprehend this evidence of the enormity of Jason's empathy, I said in shock, "Gosh, Jason! You lost your father!"

A thin layer of wetness gleamed in his eyes. Revealing again his self-effacing character, which probably helps win him the love of his many friends, he whispered, "It *has* been just as bad for me, huh?"

The mixed-race group was equally empathic.

"We think we got it bad," Natasha remarked. "These folk come with nothin' and they work for nothin'."

In a similar vein, Artie observed that "people shouldn't be down on them. They're no different from us. They just wanna feed their kids."

Roland said, "I wish I could get to know them, but I don't know Spanish."

"Well," I suggested, "learn it."

"I don't know," he equivocated, "I'm bad with languages."

I asked them why they weren't "down on immigrants" the way so many other students seemed to be.

In an authoritative voice, Earl, the sole African American male in the group said, "America ain't never closed its doors to people who work, so why should we?"

While exposure to, and contact with, the immigrant experience tends to promote positive attitudes and interaction, the mixed-race group reveals the additional potential for common ground that exists among working-class youth. Talking with these students made me wonder why most Mexican youth do not seem to have a sense that they share a class location with immigrants. A number of cross-cutting factors are involved.

The tremendous sense of threat (which gets translated as dislike or rudeness) that U.S.-born youth perceive from immigrants lies first in the very fact that the former have culturally assimilated in a subtractive fashion. They are products of their environment that through television, newspapers, the movies, music, and previous schooling, defines immigrants, especially in border states like Texas, as poor, benighted peasants who should be grateful for the blessings of life in America. Class identity is thus not a good basis for shared interests when social identity is so distinct. Seguín could of course do much to offset this kind of thinking. At worst, Seguín reinforces differences with its subtractive schooling policies and practices.

CONCLUSION

One type of response that I received from U.S.-born youth groups remains to be examined: reticence. I found this silence on the subject of immigrants difficult to understand. These students' attitudes contrast markedly with that of their counterparts in generationally mixed groups, who readily mentioned clear advantages they derived from opportunities to nurture and expand their bilingual and bicultural competencies. The U.S.-born youths' silence lends support to the complaint registered by so many immigrant youth that this group is oblivious to their experiences.

Before accepting that conclusion, I re-analyzed the data, bearing in mind three rival interpretations. First, these students may have perceived my questions as a subtle way of accusing them of being discriminatory toward or prejudiced against immigrants. Second, these group members were truly equalitarian, and thus saw immigrant youth as no different from themselves, as all on an equal plane. Third, and I believe most likely, the subject of immigrants is an extremely sensitive and potentially volatile topic that inhibits open and honest discussion.

Contradicting the first interpretation, students in immigrant and mixed-generation groups never responded evasively to this line of questioning. Their respective tenuous and inclusive statuses precluded the possibility that they would be characterized as either discriminatory or prejudicial. However, supporting this interpretation was the off-handed, casual tones that marked the responses of U.S.-born youth. It wouldn't be the first time that they react differently to the same stimuli. Consider the following examples from the group interviews:

"Immigrants are no different from anybody else. There's good ones and bad ones." "People are people. What's there to talk about?" "I hate people to say some are more Mexican than others. That doesn't get us anywhere. God made us all equal." Even to a direct question I asked one particular group about the divisions that exist among youth generally, two students answered, respectively, "I wouldn't change a thing," and "We leave people alone if they leave us alone."

The most overtly equalitarian statement expressed above—"God made us all equal"—follows an acknowledgment of the politics of difference implicit in the allegation that some people can be "more Mexican" than others. The "we-they" distinction expressed by another student implies the "othering" of Mexican immigrants. The otherwise more neutral statements seem more like attempts to forestall further discussion rather than to promote lofty equalitarian ideals.

Evidence from the most overtly hostile U.S.-born groups suggests that the subject of immigrants is an extremely sensitive and potentially volatile topic. If students have not had the opportunity to discuss their feelings, opinions, and attitudes among themselves, a logical tendency would be to sidestep the issue by minimizing differences and providing curt responses. The complexity of the situation makes it difficult to conclude that youth in U.S.-born youth groups are simply oblivious. Their reticence may instead represent a covert form of the politics of difference that even my questioning could not jostle.

In conclusion, Seguín participates in the politics of difference whenever youth are deprived of the opportunity to openly evaluate and discuss the differences in social identities reflected among them. As discussed in the previous chapter, the development of divergent identities helps sustain the social decapitalization of U.S.-born youth. When immigrant youth become unavailable either as friends or as potential sources of academic support, U.S.-born youth are shut off from the pro-school, achievement-oriented ethos that prevails among so many of them. They also get divorced from the feedback loops that could alter their more ambivalent or antagonistic attitudes toward immigrants. Expressed positively, when one considers the bi-national experience that characterizes immigrant youth and their families, then having them as part of one's intimate network promises opportunities for life-enriching moments or even life-changing growth at such a critical point in young people's lives. Many such opportunities should exist, especially when the forging of meaningful connections is a realizable goal with a community that is nearly as close to its indigenous roots as it is to its immigrant history. However joyful or painful, the lessons learned and the discoveries made at the crossroads exceed by far anything that could be gleaned from a state-adopted text. An authentically caring pedagogy is optimally centered around such understandings.

Immigrant youth lose, too, from these politics of difference. They have little or no opportunity to fully understand or empathize with their U.S.-born counterparts' implicit critique of schooling. Perhaps more than they can imagine, the attitudes and behaviors of U.S.-born youth are governed by culturally shared criteria. With their *educación* model of schooling, they reject not education, but the content of their education and the way it is offered to them. They particularly resist the school's investment in their cultural and linguistic divestment, something that immigrant youth would do well to apprehend. When the organization of schooling deprives youth of historically derived understandings and the interpretive skills with which to assess these intergenerational cross-currents, divisions and misunderstandings can be expected to prevail.

CHAPTER 6

Unity in Resistance to Schooling

The October 1989 walkout at Seguín High School (described in chapter 2) remains one of the largest organized manifestations of East End students' discontent. Since then, however, there have been other, less organized and less monumental expressions of frustration and dissatisfaction with schooling. This chapter examines three such instances. What makes these occasions noteworthy is that the disunity, distance, and divisiveness that characterizes the day-to-day interactions among students is temporarily replaced by a strong sense of a shared Mexican identity. Also significant is that the stereotypic imagery of "politeness" and "passivity" of immigrant and U.S.-born youth becomes an unsustainable proposition.

On the surface, Mexican students' resistance does not appear to be evidence of a working-class consciousness rooted in the experience of wage labor (Willis 1977; Giroux 1983). My portrayal of students' disruptive actions point more strongly to the salience of ethnicity. Specifically, the following accounts build on current theoretical discussions of resistance by describing situations where that which students affirm is precisely that which is denied through the subtractive elements of schooling. The consummate expression of this affirmation is the unity that immigrant and U.S.-born youth can and do achieve in resistance. Their implicit critique of the relations of domination comes through in their actions that upset the normality of difference and a mutual sense of alienation that Seguín ordinarily fosters.

I do not mean to suggest that class location has no bearing on students' acts of resistance, but rather that experience is mediated through commonsense understandings of identities that are made available to youth. Since class-based identities are not extended to Seguín youth or, for that matter, to most youth in U.S. society either through the media, schools, or organizations, class remains

obscure and *works through* the more palatable category of ethnicity (although see Foley [1990], who sees alienated, working-
class Mexican American youth as acting out their class interests
when they repossess the space of the classroom to subvert the
educational process).

One study (Hurtado et al. 1994) suggests that the assimilation
experience for Mexican immigrants involves a subtraction of
their class-based identities and the adoption of an ethnic minority
identity at least by the next generation. Olsen's (1997) ethnography of immigrant youth also underscores how in the context of
students' peer groups, strong pressures to adopt racialized identities exist and inform much of their adaptation to school.

Guiding the analysis is Mehan and colleagues' (1996) cogent
critique of extant ethnographic accounts of resistance in resistance theory: First is the tendency of romanticizing nonconformity. That is, not all misbehaviors are resistive, imbued with
political content. This critique holds especially well at the individual level where students' actions are often ambiguous. For
example, a students' decision to drop out of school or to confront
a teacher may be more guided by a penchant for deviance than by
a politically motivated desire to transform power relations. However when acts occur at the level of the collective, involving much
more than a handful of youth as in Willis' (1977) account, bona
fide resistance seems easier to infer. Unfortunately, resistance theory does not adequately address issues of scale.

Second, De Certeau's (discussed in Mehan et al. 1996)
assumption that guerrilla tactics are the only alternative subordinates have available to challenge the dominant culture negates
Seguín students' embodied knowledge which informs their action.
That is, Seguín youth "know" that there is power in their numbers and that despite the divisions that exist among them, they
possess in common certain cultural resources and even school-
based understandings from which to draw.[1] When this "knowledge" is further imbued with political content, entailing an affirmation of that which has been historically denied, namely,
students' *Mexicanidad*, ethnicity becomes a readily available collective resource through which the status quo can be challenged.

Finally, Mehan and colleagues (1994, 1996) take issue with
the narrow definitions of resistance and opposition that exist in

the literature. Students taking positive courses of action to achieve their goals can be just as resistive as those who self-destruct with their flagrant, insupportable challenges to the system. Their analysis, derived from their own empirical research of positively resistive minority youth, expands the heretofore restricted repertoire of students' actions. Following suit, O'Connor's (1997) case studies of urban, African American adolescents suggest that youth may also respond constructively and express great optimism in the face of oppressive, exclusionary forces in society. To this, I would add that "positive resistance" is a subjective call, depending a great deal on the eyes of the beholder. As has already been suggested, acts of resistance from youth located in the privileged rungs of the curriculum are seen differently by school officials when committed by regular-track youth.

In each instance of resistance reviewed below, I infer a positive interpretation of students' actions. While their actions may not in any ultimate sense transform the power relations that circumscribe their lives, the *content* of their resistance nevertheless reveals a substantive critique that follows the general storyline of caring and subtractive schooling presented herein.

The first scenario highlights the ways in which misunderstandings about the meaning of caring subtract resources from youth. It involves a ninth-grade English class of mostly U.S.-born youth who openly rebel against their beleaguered teacher, Mr. Chilcoate. These ninth-graders reject their teacher's attempts to forge an authentically caring relationship with them. Mr. Chilcoate's perseverance and willingness to listen—even to extreme, personal criticisms—eventually result in success. By inviting dialogue and by directly addressing the sources of his students' discontent, he reestablishes his authority in the classroom. He also decides to move more cautiously (although no less deliberately) toward his goal of achieving a caring relationship with his ninth-graders.

The collective resistance highlighted in the other two situations reveals latent, culturally relevant grievances with schooling. In a school-sponsored *Cinco de Mayo* program, the cultural nationalism of many Mexican American youth surges into the open when some students begin waving Mexican flags during the American national anthem. Although some teachers and administrators are unhappy with the students' behavior, viewing it as disrespectful, no serious repercussions occur. For the students, the flag-waving and cheering provides a brief, public opportunity to overcome hostilities and divisions and acknowledge and celebrate their shared identity as Mexicans. The event gives Seguín youth a rare chance to experience themselves as simultaneously powerful and Mexican.

The last scenario involves a highly charged incident during the school's talent show. When a vice-principal tries to cut short the performance of a heavy metal band because growing numbers of students begin pushing down to the stage to dance, nearly the entire audience responds by chanting *"culero"* (an extremely derogatory term that means "asshole") at the administrator. Although the chant is brief, the atmosphere is explosive. The talent show ends abruptly when campus police and school administrators assert their authority. The students' mingled fear and anger is palpable as they rush from the auditorium. In all three situations, students' justifications for their actions illuminate their overall critique of schooling.

MUTINY IN MR. CHILCOATE'S CLASSROOM

In fall 1994, the school's journalism teacher, Mr. Chilcoate, was asked to teach a couple of freshman English classes. These classes differed from others in the department because Mr. Chilcoate deliberately integrated the standard ninth-grade English curriculum with his own journalistic approaches and interests. Despite his efforts to make the course interesting, he was finding it difficult to adjust both to teaching the regular curriculum and his feisty freshmen students. Mr. Chilcoate's job was made even more difficult by scheduling problems—he first met his students for the first time three weeks into the semester.

One morning in late October, when I encountered him in the hall, Mr. Chilcoate was visibly distressed. He blurted out that he had "blown it" with the students in his first-period class. "I lost my cool when they complained about a writing assignment I gave them," he confessed. The assignment was to write a personal essay. He explained that the students obviously were not yet ready to write about their lives, but that morning he had simply lost his patience with them. He lamented his too-quick decision to discharge one of the more vocal students, a female, from his classroom. This tactic had far larger ramifications than he had either intended or anticipated. The student he sent out of his class was then caught "skipping" by an assistant principal; and the rest of the students, when they found out, were even angrier with him than they had been initially.

Because Mr. Chilcoate and I had developed a respectful, collegial relationship partly as a result of my having spoken about college to students in his classes on other occasions, I felt comfortable asking him if I could help in any way. He responded readily, asking me if I would be willing to talk to his class the following day. I agreed.

After introducing me to his class of approximately twenty students, Mr. Chilcoate left the room. Except for a couple of African American students, the class was comprised of U.S.-born Mexican youth. When I asked the group to form a circle so that we could talk, one male student refused.

"You don't need to talk to me," he said curtly, with an irate expression on his face.

"That's cool. I'll talk to the rest," I responded, agreeably.

Although this student continued facing the front of the room, away from the circle that had formed, he tipped his head back and sideways, toward a female student sitting next to him. Then he began carrying on a separate conversation while I was trying to talk. His action momentarily tested my patience and undermined my confidence that I could make a difference in this tense situation.

I decided to ease matters by fully introducing myself and by asking the students for their permission to tape the conversation, explaining that I planned to make it part of my study. Predictably, the students liked the idea of having their thoughts and feelings appear in a book. In an assortment of soft voices, they expressed their willingness to talk openly about the antagonism that had developed toward Mr. Chilcoate. First, the students described their teacher as coming into class "with an attitude," and then they recounted how he had unfairly ejected the female student. Once these basic points had been made, the following exchange about Mr. Chilcoate took place:

AV. I heard he exploded. He told me. He feels real bad about that.

MALE STUDENT 1. He was screaming at us.

AV. Yeah, he feels real bad about that.

MALE STUDENT 1 (*expressing disbelief*): Aaahhh!

FEMALE STUDENT 1. He doesn't make the class interesting and nobody wants to learn what he's teaching.

MALE STUDENT 1. He doesn't know how to teach.

FEMALE STUDENT 2. If we take out our paper, he's all slow and he tell us to get up! What are we going to "get up" to? [To] listen to what? There's nothing to listen to! He talks like he's real tired. Aaaaah, he talks all slow.

FEMALE STUDENT 1. He wants this to be an English class and all we do is like journalism class. He want us to be writers and we don't wanna be.

AV. But writing is good in all your classes, though. Right?

FEMALE STUDENT 2 (unintelligible). Yeah, but he wants us to write ten minutes straight and he wants us to write about our lives.

MALE STUDENT 1. He's over here making me think of my tenth birthday (*everyone laughs*).

AV. You don't think that is interesting?

FEMALE STUDENT 2. Nothing that he does is interesting.

MALE STUDENT 1. I don't like his office.

AV. So, uh, is there a way, a better way to deal with . . .

MALE STUDENT 3. Bad teachers.

AV. . . . with bad teachers?

FEMALE STUDENT 2. . . . He ain't a bad teacher.

AV. He's not a bad teacher?

MALE STUDENT 1. He just needs to chill out sometime[s].

FEMALE STUDENT 2. He has a nice personality, but what he teaches is not right. I don't like what he teaches.

SEVERAL VOICES. Yeah.

MALE STUDENT 1. He needs to chill out.

FEMALE STUDENT 2. He needs to have a better temper.

AV. So do y'all act up in all your classes?

MALE STUDENT 1. Well . . .

FEMALE STUDENT 2. Noooo!

FEMALE STUDENT 1. Yeah, the ones we don't like (*chuckle*).

AV. You act up in the ones that you don't like?

SEVERAL VOICES. Yeah, the ones we don't like (*chuckle*).

AV. Is that a rule?

MALE STUDENT. *Our* rule.

FEMALE STUDENT 1 (*In a loud voice and obviously not completely understanding what I meant by "Is that a rule?"*). It's not a rule. It's like you've been bored and so you're going to act up and make it funny.

AV. Which classes are boring?

FEMALE STUDENT 2. Reading, math, science . . .

MALE STUDENT 1. All of them! (*much laughter*). All of them except ROTC.

AV. You don't have any classes that are real interesting to you—that you go into and you say, "Man, I enjoyed learning this!"

FEMALE STUDENT 1. Not usually.

MALE STUDENT 1. I got zeros in all of my classes.

AV. You got zeros in all of your classes? Why?

MALE STUDENT 1. I don't do my work.

FEMALE STUDENT 3. Aw, you be sleepin' all the time.

MALE STUDENT 1. Yeah.

AV. Doesn't it scare you a little bit?

MALE STUDENT 1. Why . . . [unintelligible]?

AV. To, uh, you know, to like . . .

FEMALE STUDENT 1. To be in the ninth grade all your life? (*much laughter*)

MALE STUDENT 1. It doesn't matter to me a lot.

AV. Well, a lot of people aren't. . . . You know that 25 percent of the ninth-grade class, a full quarter, was repeating the ninth grade for at least one time? Some were repeating it three and four times. How many years have you been in the ninth grade?

MALE STUDENT 1. Two.

AV. Are you going to get out of the ninth grade?

MALE STUDENT 1. No (*laughter*).

FEMALE STUDENT 1 (*laughing*). Yeah, in two more years!

AV. So you mean it doesn't bother you?

MALE STUDENT 1. I don't know.

AV. You think it will?

(*Male student 1 did not respond.*)

FEMALE STUDENT 3. It gonna bother him when he sees his friends [unintelligible] graduate and they walk across . . . [unintelligible].

The discussion grew increasingly serious and the topic shifted to the school's lack of caring teachers. After several students expressed the view that teachers do not take time out for students and that most of their classes are boring, the defiant student spun around on his chair to face the group.

With a deadly serious look, he stated flatly, "There's nothin' to do. All the teachers are boring."

"So do you really blame the teachers?" I asked.

"Most of them," he responded.

The female friend at his side concurred, saying, "Yeah."

Although most students participated in the ensuing discussion, the same students who spoke above dominated the conversation. In response to a question about whether there were any classes that interested them, the students mentioned ROTC, gym, a biology class, and an English class. They described the teachers in these classes as making the classes fun and interesting, with a lot of different activities. For the most part, however, students expressed the view that most of their classes were boring. Only one student maintained that she liked all of her classes, "except for this one [Mr. Chilcoate's]," she clarified. "We don't even work [in this class]. We don't do nothin'."

A male student who had not spoken previously offered this opinion about teacher caring: "If you don't want to learn and all that, if you don't want to compete, it's not their [teachers'] fault."

A female student retorted that teachers and students shared responsibility for learning. "It's half 'n half. Like if they see that the kid is failing, why can't they go and try to help him? They don't do nothing with him. Like you're going to kick him out or let him fail and not to do nothin'? They don't want to help him."

In silence, the remaining students tacitly agreed with this young woman's opinion.

I asked the students whether they felt that teachers cared for them. They either shook their heads "no" or they said nothing.

"So, when you say they're boring, do they at least care for you?" I asked.

"No," a female student replied, "if they really cared, they wouldn't be boring and they would show in other ways, too, that they cared."

"Like how?" I questioned.

"Like show us somehow that we are worth their time."

"Like how?" I pressed.

"Like maybe show that they care about our life."

Another student agreed, "I'm tired of teachers telling us about *their* lives. I don't care about that."

"Yeah," chimed in a third, "I got this one teacher who tells all the time about her dog. That's stupid."

As the hour drew to a close, I suggested to the students that they think about a workable solution so that the entire semester would not be lost. Except for a female student's comment that Mr. Chilcoate should apologize to the student he kicked out of class, no other suggestions were voiced. When the bell rang, Mr. Chilcoate stepped in and the students dashed out.

In communicating to Mr. Chilcoate a general summary of what his students had told me, I mentioned specifically that the students thought that dismissing the female student from the classroom was unfair. The students felt that he should have spoken to her first. I gingerly broke the news to him that the students' chief complaints were that they were bored in his class and that they were not prepared to write essays on topics they considered highly personal. I could tell that Mr. Chilcoate felt badly, and I left thinking how difficult it can be to pick up the pieces and go on, especially when you are already trying hard and feel uncertain about what your next step should be. I also knew from previous conversations that Mr. Chilcoate was suffering from an extended illness which had literally slowed him down in the classroom for weeks at a time. I feared increasing his burden but felt obliged to at least provide him with an honest summary.

As I had hoped would be the case, Mr. Chilcoate arose to the challenge. He asked his students to write down on a piece of paper (without their names) a particular criticism they had about the class. He then collected all of the papers, read through them quickly, and arranged them with the most inflammatory comments at the top of the list. This is how he described to me what happened next:

> I told them, "Okay, so the class is boring and another student here says, 'Fuck you.'" Just as I expected, the students immediately reacted, appalled by what some of their fellow classmates had written. One indignant female student said, "We were raised to respect *our* elders and it's not right for anyone to be so disrespectful." Other students chimed in with similar comments. So, as I expected, I wasn't able to get through the rest of their comments. We spent class time discussing how to improve the classroom situation without being rude or hostile.
>
> So, then I continued, "What this communicates to me is frustration." And immaturity, as well, I thought, though I couldn't say [that]. "But the kind of frustration that exists here is not clear, and it needs to be spelled out. What are you frustrated about? About me? The materials we are using? About my approach to teaching? Exactly what kind of frustration do you feel?"

Mr. Chilcoate said that he got excellent feedback from the students. And he apologized publicly to the young woman whom he had offended and dismissed from the class. Though the students were initially uneasy with the process of talking through their problems with the class, Mr. Chilcoate said that the experience "empowered them." He guessed that they had never been in a situation where they were given control over their own learning, communicating their desires, concerns, and wishes. "The students were very constructive in their criticism," he said. Subsequent class periods consisted of varied kinds of activities that galvanized all of the students into greater participation. After several weeks, Mr. Chilcoate felt that the class had moved in a sufficiently positive direction for him to feel tentatively successful. He noted, however, that there was one holdout—one student who insisted on remaining marginal. I could only guess who.

That Mr. Chilcoate chose to try to resolve the problems in his classroom by empowering his students reflects not only his skill as a teacher, but also his commitment to authentic caring. Mr. Chilcoate is well thought of by sophomores, juniors, and seniors who know him. They regard him as one of their most caring teachers. Mr. Chilcoate's point of departure in his teaching is always his students' lives, perspectives, and experiences. His journalism students' writings appear in an impressive school-sponsored student publication, *East End Stories*. Many of the stories are about romance, problems in relationships, and the negative effects of gangs and drugs. The students have also transcribed some of the folklore and legends told to them by adults who reside in their East End community. Through his patient coaching, modeling, and individualized attention, he educates each class of students into an understanding of their own experiences as events of worth and value. Mr. Chilcoate laments his inability to speak Spanish and he admits that bilingualism would draw him even closer to the students in his classes. Nevertheless, he derives much satisfaction from his relationships with students and from observing and nurturing their intellectual growth. It saddened me to hear that he had decided to get out of teaching at year's end. His teaching combined several special qualities that mostly worked well with this community: large doses of patience, a personal concern for each individual student, and an all-encompassing love of the East End community and its stories.

So, how could a teacher like Mr. Chilcoate have had such a dismal classroom experience? What could have gone wrong for a teacher with so much integrity? The answers lie mainly in the structure of schooling. His students did not know him prior to their arrival in his class, partly because as ninth-graders they were new to Seguín, but also because the school's chronic scheduling problems resulted in their not being assigned to *any* English class until several weeks into the semester. That they entered Mr. Chilcoate's class already hostile and disaffected is hardly surprising, given the clear institutional message they had received from Seguín counselors that their education is a secondary concern that can be held hostage to bureaucratic imperatives. Rather than engaging in damage control with his new students, Mr. Chilcoate attempted to make up for lost time. He moved too quickly. As he himself realized—too late—he had not allowed the class sufficient time to develop a trusting relationship with him and with each other before he assigned the personal essays.

In accordance with authentic caring, Mr. Chilcoate's apprehension of "the other"—that is, his appreciation of his students' culture and their *educación* model of schooling—enabled him to successfully navigate through troubled waters. Retaining his own dignity, he made a public apology and then steered his class into a conversation that brought out the best in them. It is thus no accident that one student drew on her collective cultural experience with resounding disapproval at some of the criticism aimed at Mr. Chilcoate, to implicitly silence the extremists among her classmates: "*We* were raised to respect *our* elders and it's not right for anyone to be so disrespectful."

CINCO DE MAYO, 1993

Latina and Latino faculty at Seguín typically organize an annual *Cinco de Mayo* celebration.[2] I have attended several of these programs over the years. The event provides not only an opportunity for emotional release, but also an occasion for a collective expression of traditional Mexican and Mexican American identity. In the 1993–94 academic year, the *Cinco de Mayo* celebration took place on Friday, May 6, in the boys' gym during the late afternoon. Because the air-conditioning in the gym, as in many of the classrooms, was not functioning, the space was extremely hot. Excited and happy, the students did not allow the heat to affect their festive spirit, however. There was lots of horse-play among the young men in the audience.

I observed one small, male student who, as he walked into the gym, was bashed on the back of the head with a notebook wielded by another male student. There were so many students surrounding him and pushing toward the rapidly filling spaces on the bleachers that the student who was struck could not turn around to retaliate physically. He had to settle for hurling an insult.

"*Chinga tu madre!*" ("Screw your mother!"), he yelled.

"*La tuya!*" ("Screw yours!"), his assailant shot back.

I also caught the glance of a young woman holding her nose as she made her entry through the crowd and into the stifling gymnasium. "*Hijo! Huele a sovaco aquí!*" she gasped. ("Man! It smells like somebody's armpit here!")

Notwithstanding the suffocating heat, the crowded conditions, and the smell of daylong sweat, the jam-packed gymnasium
bore testimony to an attendance officer's claim that "*Cinco de
Mayo* is one of our highest attendance days of the year." Many
students were noticeably well dressed in neatly pressed, casual
clothes. I asked several students whom I did not know why everyone was dressed so nicely. They offered a variety of responses:
"*Porque es un día divertido*!" ("Because it's a fun day!") "Today
is a day to look nice on." "Why not?" "Because it's when I get to
wear this shirt." "It's a day for Mexicans to be proud of their culture—who we are and all we have to offer." "*Es un día para estar
unidos, todos, una comunidad*" ("It's a day to be united, all of us,
a community"). *Cinco de Mayo* is thus viewed as a very special
day, and conscientiously selected attire is an important part of the
occasion.

In both assemblies, students who wore T-shirts had chosen
ones that displayed Mexican and Chicano images and statements.
Among the images worn mostly by males were Julio Cesar
Chavez, Pancho Villa, Emiliano Zapata, low rider cars, the Virgin
of Guadalupe, and Aztec warriors. Females typically wore color-
ful T-shirts, or embroidered Mexican and Guatemalan blouses, or
some other similarly dressy apparel. The only embroidered Mexican dresses I saw were worn by Mexican American faculty and
some of the performers in the program. As one faculty member,
wearing a bright-orange, flower-embroidered dress, walked in
front of me, she smiled bashfully and said, "This is the only time
of year I get to wear this!"

"Why the only time?" I wondered, silently.

The program started, as it has most years, with a group of
approximately ten ROTC students performing a drill that features the twirling of wooden rifles. Then the ROTC students
marched around the gym, bearing the Mexican and American
flags. When they arrived at the front of the gym, a whistle
sounded and the students abruptly stopped marching. At the
other end of the gymnasium, an assistant principal bellowed into
a microphone the request that all members of the audience stand.
This was the band director's cue; the band began playing the
Mexican national anthem, followed by the American national
anthem.

During both songs, the majority of students neither placed their hands to their chests nor sang, although presumably because they knew the words, more sang the American than the Mexican national anthem. In contrast, the scores of immigrant youth around me were easy to identify by their vigorous singing of the Mexican national anthem. Overall, most students talked over the music and shifted restlessly in their seats, now uncomfortable in the heat. The din of the crowd offered genuine competition to the blare of the band. During the American national anthem, many students suddenly began to roar with laughter. When I turned to see what had caused this hilarity, I caught sight of ten or twelve students waving tiny, plastic Mexican flags. Others began chanting, "*Viva la Raza!*" "*Viva la Raza!*" ("Long live Mexicans!") Shouts of "*Viva Mexico!*" ("Long live Mexico") could also be heard, intermittently.

There was an immediate response. At breakneck speed, an Anglo school coach wearing green shorts sped to the bottom of the bleachers. Approaching the students, he gestured at them to stop, using the "time-out" hand signal. Evidently confident of their immunity from all school personnel at that moment, the students totally disregarded the coach's message. Their voices booming, they yelled, "*Viva Mexico!*" And others responded, "*Que viva!*" ("May it live!"). Two more rounds of call and response occurred, punctuated by the sound of a long and loud *grito* (yell) from a male student. The *grito* produced much appreciative laughter as other students turned their heads to check out the commotion. Perhaps some two hundred students took notice of this deliberately timed display. I noted that *gritos* and raucous laughter came as easily from the immigrant youth seated around me as from the other students surrounding them.

Administrators and teachers clearly opted for tolerance; they let the incident pass without further note after the red-faced coach turned away from the students he had been attempting to silence. The few faculty I noticed who had caught on to what was happening displayed neither approval nor disapproval, but one African American teacher standing near me was distressed.

"They should have more respect for the American flag! This isn't Mexico!" she said, unhappily.

"They're just having fun," I soothed.

The end of the anthem brought closure to this episode, which had lasted no more than two minutes. The audience then quieted down, eager for the rest of the program to unfold.

After the assembly, I spotted and approached some of the flag-wavers, two male and two female students, all U.S.-born youth. These four told me that they had gotten the flags from another student whose father was on an organizing committee for Houston's *Cinco de Mayo* parade, scheduled for the following day. "About fifteen of us agreed to wave the flags when the American national anthem was going to be played—just for fun," one of the young women explained. I asked her whether everyone who had agreed to wave a flag actually had done so. She thought everyone had. She also said that they had devised a seating strategy whereby several students would sit together while others spread out a bit. They had agreed that after a certain person signaled with a flag, the rest would immediately begin waving their flags.

"Why during the American national anthem?" I asked.

"So what's the big deal?" one of the male students retorted, defensively.

"It's no big deal," I replied, appeasingly. "I just want to know."

"There's a reason," said one of the females. "We just think, hey this is our day, for us Mexicans. *Every* day is American-flag day. This is *our* day."

With the African American teacher's comments in mind, I asked, "So someone might think you don't want to be American. . . ."

"Hey, we're Mexican *and* American and proud of it! It's just that nobody wants to let us be both—which is what we are."

"Nobody?" I probed.

The defensive male student responded, "Not nobody like our parents, but like the school. Our culture is not respected and that's what we tried to show today."

"So why didn't y'all go to the organizing committee—to Mrs. Gomez—with a suggestion?" I wondered aloud.

"Are you joking?" one student asked, incredulously. "She wouldn'ta let us do what we did."

"It was more fun this way," another offered.

In her book, *Borderlands*, Gloria Anzaldúa (1987) writes that there isn't a *Tejana* or *Tejano* alive who does not know that the lands were taken away from them. Anzaldúa argues persuasively that this sentiment operates at different levels of consciousness and is related to Anglo society's rejection and negation of the nation's Mexican past, including its early settlement by Mexican people (Hurtado et al. [1994] also address this issue of how historical events, mediated through family and folklore, become part of individual psychology). What is significant about Anzaldúa's observation is that it helps explain why second- or third-generation Mexican Americans, who are not descendants of the original ten thousand families living in the Southwest during the conquest, lay claim to being charter members of the American Southwest. The second- and third-generation students featured above use the first-person pronouns *we*, *us*, and *our* to at once assert their Mexican cultural identity and to express their collective reaction to the experience of societal exclusion, a macro-drama of which Seguín itself is a part.

Because Anzaldúa traces this sense of ethnic minority identity to the particular experiences that arise out of generations of daily confrontation and coexistence with Anglo culture, she does not ascribe this same sense of identity to Mexican immigrants. An exchange I had with immigrant students after the flag-waving incident, however, suggests that Anzaldúa's concept of identity might be more broadly applicable. I stopped six female immigrant students who were among those who sang all the words to the Mexican national anthem to ask their opinions about the incident that had occurred during the American national anthem. Of all the students whose opinions I solicited after the *Cinco de Mayo* program, these youths provided the most critical commentary.

One small-framed girl with glasses said, "*Pues, no es ningún secreto que esta tierra antes era de México*" ("Well, it's no secret that this land once belonged to Mexico").

Her friend, an even smaller girl, pronounced the flag-waving a harmless gesture and felt that the coach was silly to get angry. With a scornful grin, she asked, "*Que creen? Que ahora les vamos a quitar el Sudoeste?*" ("What do they think? That now we're going to take the Southwest away from them?")

"*Que bien que nos tienen miedo, no?*" ("I'm glad they're

afraid of us. No?") a third member of the group interjected laugh-ingly before they all darted off.

When social, psychic, and emotional distance is the norm between immigrant and U.S.-born youth, what explains these immi-grant students' use of the first-person pronouns *we* and *us* to express solidarity with the rest of the student body, who either are, or who see themselves as, charter members of the American Southwest? An underlying sense of shared history and culture was certainly present, but an emotional understanding of cultural disparagement—a real-ization achievable in and through song—seems to have been the immediate catalyst for the unusual display of unity among the stu-dents that took part in Seguín's *Cinco de Mayo* celebration.

There were no further distractions during the afternoon pro-gram. The rest of the scheduled events were greeted by the audience with an approval so passionate that it sometimes overwhelmed the individual performances. When a female student took the micro-phone and began explaining the significance of *Cinco de Mayo,* the noise in the gym was so loud that all I could hear from where I stood were a few disconnected words—"French," "soldiers," and "Puebla, Mexico" (a state in Mexico). The next student, who read a poem she had written, fared no better. No one in the area in the back where I stood could hear that piece, either.

Then, Seguín's twenty-person, less-than-boldly-voiced chorus sang the first of several songs, "*Cielito Lindo*" ("Lovely Little Heaven" or, more literally, "Beautiful Little Heaven"). That the choir director had spent little time coaching his students to sing the Spanish language tunes that at least some of them held near and dear to their hearts, seemed to make little difference to the packed audience. They readily joined in, making the song's refrain—which begins "Ay! Ay! Ay! Ay!"—sound thunderous.

The highlight was a performance by a couple of singers with guitars. Both were former Seguín High graduates who had been asked to return to perform for the second year in a row. The main singer had a loud, soulful voice that carried well. As he sang, the students sang along, waving their hands and letting out shrill *gritos.* Given the crowd's response, the performers' choice of songs appeared to have been near-perfect. The highly enthusiastic audi-ence needed no urging to join in; they sang all of the choruses to each song. I observed very few students who could not participate because they were unfamiliar with these songs. Among those in attendance, only the Anglo and African American faculty appeared to be "outsiders."

Singing plaintively, the main vocalist aroused the crowd to the highest level of the afternoon with his renditions of the classic songs, "*Pobre de Mi*" ("Poor Me") and "*El Rey* ("The King")." In "*Pobre de Mi*," the lead singer began a cappella. He held the first syllable of the word *pobre* for several long seconds—on key. By the time he got to the second syllable, the crowd was beside itself. The gym reverberated with the sounds of their approval for this selection. The excitement reached an even higher pitch with the singing of the next tune, "*El Rey*." I wrote my impression of this moment in my field notes:

> "*El Rey*" is an interesting song when sung in a situation like this, powerful in its sexism and in its capacity to disintegrate the distance that exists between students. Young men and women alike smile with a satisfied look of self-indulgent pleasure, as if holding onto a secret. The secret may be that the song is as disgusting as it is delightful. (May 6, 1993)

"*El Rey*" ("The King") tells the story of a man who asserts his dominance over a partner (either a wife or lover) who has left him, saying that she will surely cry the day he dies. Though he has neither throne nor kingdom, at home he is the king. With or without money, he does as he pleases because his word is the law. At the point in the song when the singers sang the words "*llorar y llorar*" ("cry and cry"), students in the bleachers on both sides of the gym swayed back and forth to the tune's sentimental refrain, many linking arms with one another at shoulder level.

The notes I took at the *Cinco de Mayo* program are filled with expressions of connectedness and pleasure that contrast markedly with the entries for more typical days, where I tended to record impressions of the students as aloof and dispirited. Not even during pep rallies, where raising students' spirits is the conscious goal, can the entire student body be described as behaving passionately and with single-mindedness. The shared experience of culture—which includes singing the infamous "*El Rey*" (originally made famous by one of Mexico's most beloved classical-era composers and singers, José Alfredo Jiménez)—largely explains this positive, collective, emotional outpouring.

The ceremony continued. Two awards were presented to the winners of an essay competition. The crowd, now in an excellent mood, cheered both recipients as they stepped forward to claim their prizes. (One winner was Rodrigo, whose ideas and experiences are highlighted in chapter 3.) Two senior students (Mely and Sylvia featured in chapter 5) dressed in knee-length white-laced dresses, were next. They performed the *"Jarabe Tapatío,"* also known as the Mexican Hat Dance. A second group of dancers, all male, danced to a marimba tune from Veracruz. They wore white *guayaberas* (tropical, embroidered men's shirts), fitted pants, and black boots, garb that accentuated their agility and finesse. The music was lively and they danced confidently, stomping their dancing shoes in coordinated syncopation. The audience responded with stirring applause. The much louder stomping of this group compared to the previous one elicited an even more soulful round of applause. The widespread feeling of pride was almost palpable as these young people made being Mexican and the color of dark bodies against bright, white clothing look and feel good.

A Mexican American ESL biology teacher spotted me and commented to me with a wide grin on his face, "The *gringos* don't understand us. They think we're savages!" Indeed, Anglos and African Americans in the audience seemed out of their element; faced with phenomena that did not readily resonate with their own experience, these teachers, staff, and students were positioned only to observe, and not to participate. Interestingly, the biology teacher referred exclusively to Anglos when he made his remark; he made no mention of African Americans. Though the emotional distance was experienced by both groups, the teacher's reference to *"gringos"* may have conveyed his own consciousness of the cultural and linguistic domination of whites that songs sung so openheartedly in Spanish implicitly challenge. The relief and release this 45-minute program provided is evident in my own summary of the afternoon's events:

> Whatever meanings each individual attached to *Cinco de Mayo*, it at least meant touching the *Mexicanidad* deep within oneself. It was a healing, joyful moment. A moment when all worries and all divisions were, for a moment, suspended. (May 6, 1993)

THE TALENT SHOW

On February 10, 1995, the dimly lit auditorium was packed to overflowing for Seguín's student talent show. Students were excused from their homeroom period to attend the show if they paid the one-dollar price of admission. Close to a thousand students attended. The school's extremely poor-quality sound system emitted static-filled, muffled sounds from the speakers, but this did not seem to diminish the audience's enthusiasm. Each performance the emcee announced was greeted with applause. After a performance by a Mexican American student who sang a song in English, the school's Anglo female drama teacher jumped on the stage, with an African American male assistant principal in tow. She performed while he played the straight-man, looking embarrassed. He smiled continuously, but he was silent the entire time he was on stage.

Speaking into the microphone, the drama teacher, in outrageous attire—she wore a sexy black dress that was slit high in the middle and sported huge artificial breasts—introduced herself as Dolly Parton. Accompanied by huffing and puffing sounds from male students in the audience, the teacher moved about the stage in a seductive, high-heeled gait. She turned around to a man behind a camera positioned at the front side of the stage. She joked to him about her breasts: "You've been looking at them haven't you?" The audience, especially the male students, roared with laughter. "You're wondering if they're real, aren't you?" The crowd roared again. The group of young men I stood next to in the upstairs balcony began yelling, "*Quítate la ropa! Quítate la ropa!*" ("Take your clothes off! Take your clothes off!"). "They are not!" she responded emphatically, answering her own question. "They're rhinestones!" she continued in a sassy tone, now obviously referring to her necklace. The joke was well received— the students rocked with laughter and cheered. The assistant principal looked more embarrassed than ever; he turned his body away from the drama teacher as she relished the audience's response to her opening lines.

She launched into a song sung to the tune of the Broadway hit, "Mame." As she sang, the drama teacher moved closer and closer to the assistant principal—with her hand approaching his crotch area. She commented, suggestively, that he was "sizzling." Smiling broadly, the assistant principal sprang away from her, as the entire auditorium screamed with laughter. I was slack-jawed with shock, but I noticed the three teachers standing closest to me were laughing along with the rest of the audience. The song finally ended, to be replaced by the frenzied sounds of hoots, hollers, whistles, and barking noises coming from all sides of the auditorium.

The next performance, featuring a young African American woman who sang a song in English I did not recognize, provided some respite. A couple of minutes into this student's performance, however, the audience grew bored and began talking among themselves. The third performer was a young woman who stood on stage preparing to sing and speaking in Spanish only. She wore a midriff and blue denim shorts and a pair of old black tennis shoes. As she spoke, students at the front of the auditorium yelled rudely in English. They apparently did not want her to perform in Spanish only. Other students responded to the hecklers with "Shh" sounds. The singer's appeal heightened suddenly, as she began shaking her hips and sensuously moving her body while she sang the words to a Mexican-rap tune entitled, *"Zapatos Viejos"* ("Old Shoes"). When she finished, she jumped off the stage into the now stimulated and welcoming audience. All kinds of screams filled the air. And again, the male students near me began yelling, *"Quitate la ropa! Quitate la ropa!"* ("Take your clothes off! Take your clothes off!"). With each passing performance, my discomfort grew.

Next in line were three young women and one young man who danced to Mexican rap music. This group made their mark by punctuating their dancing with hip thrusts and by simulating multiple sex-making configurations, all to the beat of heavy, tympanic sounds. The audience reacted with near-hysterical screaming. A male student near me grabbed his pants. The performance culminated with the three young women circling around the young man. One of females jumped on the male, wrapped her legs around his waist, and rode him, making rhythmic motions with her pelvis all the while. With this, the students' screams, unbelievably, ratcheted up to yet a higher pitch. More hysterical laughter followed, assuaged only by a brief break between performances.

An openly bisexual male with multicolored hair took his turn on stage, swinging a small whip to and fro. His performance, it turned out, was a form of erotica. The smooth and graceful movements of his waving fingers and hands and spinning body brought to mind the sensuous seductive motions of a striptease dancer or even a drag queen. Some of the students in the audience booed at him, calling him "*joto*" (queer). A substantial number of other students countered with clapping, urging him to continue. Curiously, the music simply stopped, point-blank, in the middle of his performance. As the performer walked up to the tape player to see what the problem was, the show's emcee (a male student) rudely began to announce the next performance. Some students in the audience protested, booing the emcee. Others began laughing, calling the performer a "freak" and a "*joto.*" The student managed to get the tape player running again and he courageously finished his act.

A female student singing a soft song was next. Students throughout the auditorium start waving their arms to the mellow tune. The voice of the African American artist whose recording the student was singing over sometimes overpowered the student's voice. By now, the crowd had grown about as tough as one at the Apollo Theater in New York City. They quickly lost patience with the performer. "She's lip-singing!" they yelled. "That's not her voice!" "It's not her singing!" The tape player again stopped abruptly, and she, too, had to finish her performance in an increasingly intolerant atmosphere.

The final performance was a metal band consisting of two guitar players, one drummer, and a couple of other members who ended up diving off the stage. After quickly rolling their drum set on stage, they commenced playing. This group produced the best sound heard at the show because they had brought along their own speakers. The band played not more than two-minutes' worth of AC/DC-style heavy metal music when approximately twenty-five young men and a handful of young women seated at the front got up to dance "mush push" in the open area located several feet below the base of the stage. "Mush push" is a high-energy, aggressive dancing style that looks very much like a massive rumble. Flailing arms, fists, and bodies waved violently as scores of more students joined the throng. A wide-eyed audience quickened to its feet, staring at the immense crowd forming at the base of the stage. Students from all parts of the auditorium began pouring out of the aisle seats and heading down to the front.

At least one of the band players on stage fell to the ground as students cheered at his performance. Based on a second band member's successful dive, head first, into the crowd below to an awaiting sea of hands and arms to carry him, his intent was to be similarly caught. Another person got pulled off the stage by the crowd.

For the first couple of minutes, no campus security personnel were present. Confusion and chaos swept the whole crowd, dancers and onlookers alike, into a frenzy. For several seconds, some students in the audience chanted, "Kill!" "Kill!" "Kill!" In the balcony where I stood, a few students described what was taking place below as a gang fight. Several of the young men who had yelled "*Quitate la ropa!*" moments earlier now motioned to other young men to meet them downstairs. Between ten and fifteen students rushed out of the upper-level balcony exits to make their way downstairs, seemingly aiming to partake more fully in the action.

The majority of students, however, remained in a fixed, standing position, staring on, nerves on edge, muscles taut, awaiting any eventuality. My sense that the talent show had been poorly supervised deepened as it became frighteningly clear that there were no administrators or campus security in the immediate area. The students I spoke to afterwards said either that they had felt endangered or that they had thought that something drastic—like someone getting shot or killed—was about to happen. The auditorium was so overcrowded both upstairs and down that any situation producing a mad rush to the exit doors could have proven deadly. The administration had completely lost control—or, more accurately, the administration clearly never had control—over this allegedly school-sponsored event.

As the band finished their tune, the lead band member was called off the stage by the crowd below. His thin, horizontal body was carried a good distance by many hands. Somehow, the procedure was reversed and his body was passed, still held aloft, safely back to the stage. Regrouping, the band members attempted to continue with their next number. At this point, the same assistant principal who had accompanied the "Dolly Parton" act jumped on stage to announce (over the sound system) that the talent show was over. The response, from nearly the entire audience, upstairs and downstairs, came in the form of a single word, *culero*, chanted, hundreds of voices strong, in a measured, trisyllabic cadence: "*CU-LE-RO*." *Culero* is similar in meaning to "asshole," but it is even more negative. When used in fighting situations, another connotation is "sissy" or "homosexual." The intent is to draw out or challenge another who backs down from a fight. The chant lasted a full half-minute and made the entire auditorium reverberate. Those few students not chanting waited in tense anticipation, many with horrified looks on their faces.

The booming quality of the chant reduced the assistant principal's voice to a scarcely audible drone; looking small and isolated on the stage, mouthing words that couldn't be heard, he seemed like little more than a pair of waving arms. Several campus police officers and a second assistant principal finally made their way to the front of the auditorium. With their entry, the house lights went on and the chanting stopped. The authorities broke up the crowd massed at the base of the stage and stopped the band, which had begun to play the opening notes of their next song. Now audible, the assistant principal again announced that the talent show was over and that students needed to get to their next class.

The dispersal of the students milling about near the stage and the curtailment of the band mid-note elicited boos from the audience, even as the students began making their way to the exit doors. It was a high-adrenaline moment. The students spilled through the exit doors looking wide-eyed and anxious. Many seemed to be anticipating some sort of repercussion. Despite this "victory" over the staff, no one was laughing; no one seemed triumphant. The sound of the students' sighs, the deep breaths they drew, and the stunned-looking expressions on their faces revealed their commingled sense of fear and relief as they passed out of the auditorium and into the open hallway spaces.

I conducted several brief exit interviews. I asked one student, a Salvadoran male, what he thought. With his jaw hanging open, he looked like he had seen a ghost, "*No me gustó! Fue horrible!*" ("I didn't like it! It was horrible!"). He then picked up his pace and literally sped off as if he were being chased. A group of female immigrant youths said that they felt very angry with the school because the staff allowed the show to degenerate into chaos or "*desorden*." I asked them if they had participated in the chant. "*Todo el mundo participó, no solamente nosotros.*" ("Everybody participated, not just us.") Their answer confirmed my observation that the students' angry response was so total that it knew no gender or generational distinctions.

In the hallway traffic around the exit doors, I saw several students venting their anger. As if to relieve themselves of pent-up energy and frustration, a group of five males, all apparently friends, swung fist-clenched hands and lunged their bodies only half-playfully at one another. One female who got caught in the crossfire was shoved into a locker. "*Chingao!*" ("Fuck!") she yelled, as her body struck the metal, producing a muffled clang. With an angry look on her face, she flipped a finger at the one male who turned around to look at her. Social studies teachers in nearby classrooms appeared in their doorways to see what the commotion was, but they arrived too late to witness anything. "Let's calm down," one teacher called out as the male students doubled back into an adjoining hallway.

The talent show incident evoked a resounding expression of collectively shared resentment and anger, evident in both the word the students chanted and in the pulsating beat of the chant itself. There are few other words in Spanish, as spoken by Mexicans and Mexican Americans, that are more insulting and disrespectful than *culero*. It is a provocative word reserved for the most serious of moments, such as before or during a fight. In virtually any other situation, the idea of a young person directing this expression toward an adult is unthinkable.

What motivated the audience to use *culero* can be gleaned from students' commentaries about what they saw. I found that the majority of students shared the opinion that the assistant principal and the drama teacher were responsible for what occurred. Consider the following exchange I had with four students, one immigrant and three U.S.-born youths:

AV. Why do you think the students said what they said? Why not some other word?

U.S.-BORN FEMALE STUDENT 1. If he [the assistant principal] would have understood, he would have been really mad and we—all of us—would all be in trouble. *Por eso lo dijimos en español* [That's why we said it in Spanish].

U.S.-BORN MALE STUDENT. Naah, we just said it 'cause everybody else said it. We didn't think about it. We just said what we said.

IMMIGRANT FEMALE STUDENT. Man, he looked like a *pendejo* [like an idiot] with all of us yelling that. And I liked that, *por ser pendejo el cabrón* [for being an idiot that stupid person].

U.S.-BORN FEMALE STUDENT 2. Hey, *no hables así con la señora.* [Hey, don't talk that way with the woman.] Are you a teacher or what?

AV. No, I'm not. I'm writing a book on Seguín. What do you mean?

IMMIGRANT FEMALE STUDENT 2. Yes, the students were disrespectful calling the AP [assistant principal] *cu*— . . . you know, what they called him. But they asked for it and none of us better get in trouble for it.

U.S.-BORN FEMALE STUDENT 2. How could we get in trouble if we were all saying it? I bet you nobody gets in trouble. We're too many. Besides he didn't even know what we were saying.

IMMIGRANT FEMALE STUDENT. *No, pero lo que hicieron no era bien* [No, but what they did was not right], getting up there, acting all sexy *y todo* [and all].

Note how the first-person pronouns *we* and *us* are marshaled once again to express collective solidarity. On the surface, the immigrant female student's comment may sound juvenile. What can also be read in her response, however, is the daring suggestion that administrators and teachers should not succumb to the corrosive influences of the dominant culture. Also noteworthy is how students' *educación* cultural model of schooling surfaces. Even in this agitated exchange, the second female student calls on the other to be respectful in her language toward me. In short, students' disrespect toward the assistant principal felt justified because the assistant principal and the drama teacher were at fault for starting the program with such a sexually suggestive performance.

In light of the resistance earlier in the program to the Mexican-rap tune sung in Spanish, the Spanish language epithet further reveals how language can become a unifying symbol born out of an intense collective experience. Despite the students' differences and the divisions that exist between peers, it is significant that these youth all drew from their cultural and linguistic reservoirs the very same term with which to register their disgust with the system. Specifically, they resisted the double standard: by prematurely bringing the school program to an end, the assistant principal was a "*culero*" for backing down from his established premise of sexual licentiousness. Because it was said in Spanish, the term also doubled as a culturally coded affront and protective shield, immunizing youth from any consequences. (My guess is that the assistant principal is familiar with the term, but students' perceptions are what matter here.) Their greatest source of protection, however, as the second female student suggests, was their successful execution of the "numbers game" (see note 1).

The events associated with the talent show produced the only instance during my research in which I felt morally compelled to express a grievance to the principal. Two days after the incident, I visited him in his office. I indicated that I felt awkward lodging a complaint since I was a guest on his campus, but at the same time, I felt that as a concerned member of the community, I was obliged to speak with him. I told him that the students' parents not only would have been appalled at the talent show itself, they would also have been extremely concerned for the safety of their children during the incident that followed.

The principal looked embarrassed but accepted the criticism well. "Yes," he acknowledged, "a lot of parents have been calling in, and I can assure you that this will not happen again." He said that last-minute changes to the performances had altered the line-up and that administrators had not had time to preview the program. As far as the behavior of his faculty and staff was concerned, he said that he would personally reprimand them. It is my understanding that he did so.

In conclusion, these diverse accounts of student resistance reveal how students' *educación* cultural model of schooling informs their critique of and expectations concerning schooling. Seguín students demand that which the school does not typically provide, namely, trusting, respectful relations between students and the adults who are there to teach and guide them. They further demand an inclusive curriculum responsive to their cultural identity as Mexicans. That these situations all involved large numbers of students underscore the fact that resentment toward subtractive schooling is an ever-present, underlying, and widely shared experience, even if it is not often either visible or consciously perceived. Perhaps it is only in settings such as these where what Raymond Williams (1965) has termed a "structure of feeling"—one rooted in a sense of injustice, deeply felt but not articulated politically—may be found.

CHAPTER 7

Conclusion

Drawing from folk and theoretical traditions, the composite imagery of caring that unfolds in this study accords moral authority to teachers and institutional structures that value and actively promote a search for connection, both between teacher and student, as well as among students themselves. This search for connection takes on added meaning when caring is to be directed toward the culturally different "other." In the case of U.S.-Mexican youth, sensitivity to the "politics of caring" itself is the first step toward a more relevant and authentic pedagogy.

This search for connection is an extremely challenging goal within the context of unfriendly institutional structures. Whenever the leadership is weak or ineffective, as it has been at Seguín, a culture of authentic caring is hard to create. When on a daily basis, several hundred youth violate rules like skipping class and attending all three lunch periods knowing that they are unlikely to get processed even if they get noticed by a teacher or administrator, the school becomes a capricious environment where no one really seems in control. When students are not where they should be by the third week of classes, initiating a structure of caring can easily seem a moot point. And besides, why open pandora's box? What would it mean to really care in such an environment?

This angst is best captured in the words of a former student, a junior female who participated in the October 1989 walkout: "It almost seemed, maybe I'm wrong, like the teachers didn't want to know us, or too much about us. I try to be fair. Maybe it was like the more they knew us, the more they'd be responsible and our problems were so big, big! What would it mean [for them] to genuinely care for us?" (chapter 2). To reverse the deleterious effects of schooling, this student is persuasive with her view that the courage to step outside of one's comfort zone to swim through uncharted, yet no less troubled, waters is what will be required.

For the most part, teachers enter schools with the notion that their central preoccupation is to impart their expert knowledge. Layered over this expectation is a bureaucratically inefficient system that offers no incentives for prioritizing their students' welfare over "the rules." The thought that teachers and other school personnel must find ways to constructively address, rather than wish away, their students' cultural differences is strongly resisted.

Easily overwhelmed are teachers like Ms. Hutchins who resists helping Susana with her disaffectedness: "It's overwhelming to think that this is the level we're dealing at." Or nurturance gets explained away as residing outside of the parameters of their job description as expressed by an algebra teacher: "I'm not here to baby-sit and I'm certainly not their parent. . . ." The mere suggestion that more Latino teachers would make a difference in school climate makes most of these teachers defensive.

The need for more Latino and bilingual school personnel is a major policy issue. Indeed, one study reveals a correlation between Latino student failures and a paucity of Latino teachers (Tomás Rivera Center 1993). As long as those in charge are neither themselves bilingual nor educated on the needs of either Spanish-dominant or culturally marginal, Mexican American youth, schooling will continue to subtract resources from them.

If what students say is true, namely, that they will perform best in a nurturing environment, then the debilitating messages and attitudes to which they are subjected on a daily basis must assume highest priority. As multicultural scholars and practitioners unanimously express, all decision-making should be guided by the goal of narrowing the gap between teachers' and students' social and cultural differences.

Despite the commendable efforts of some individuals like Mrs. Martinez (chapter 5) and others to work toward systemic change in a culturally affirming way, the political will is otherwise absent at Seguín. Problems have to accumulate and stretch beyond certain invisible limits for any alarms to sound off and constructive change to occur. Since parents and community activists seem perennially involved in damage control, proactive grassroots efforts to bring about substantive change have not yet occurred. The curriculum especially remains the sacred cow that not even the October 1989 school walkout could change in any meaningful way. A comfortable, if not callous, fixation on the status quo prevails.

Bereft of power to insert their vision of education into the schooling process, regular-track students, alongside those singular teachers attempting to make a difference, become vulnerable to burnout, disaffection, and the temptation to withdraw mentally and physically from the process altogether. Alternatively, students challenge the status quo either as individuals or as collectivities. While even the collective challenges do little to alter the power structure and, at worst, confirm teachers' and administrators' suspicions that youth really do not care about school, the content of their resistance is what may matter most in the end—if only they will be heard.

So many of the youth I came across were very perceptive. Their insights not only illuminate their critique of subtractive schooling, they also provide guideposts for thoughtful, informed action. Some of their expressions, arranged here from lowest to highest levels of emotional intensity, punctuate the pages of this book:

"I don't expect them [teachers] to visit me, just to know me a little bit. They're always too busy, or if you're like me and like to read, they leave you alone even more."

"Learn the language but stay Mexican."

"Kids have good arguments . . . they have absolutely no argument skills."

"At the end of your four years here, you're going to have a degree and you're going to have two languages. I'll be real lucky if I have a degree—and my Spanish is the pits!"

"I just can't get into my classes this year. They're all so boring and no one seems to care if I show up. And then they talk down to you when you do show up."

"I don't get with the program because then it's doing what *they* [teachers] want for my life. I see *Mexicanos* who follow the program so they can go to college, get rich, move out of the *barrio*, and never return to give back to their *gente* (people). Is that what this is all about? If I get with the program, I'm saying that's what it's all about and that teachers are right when they're not."

"And you're telling me that what I've got on isn't good enough? I don't bother anyone when I go to class. I go to class to learn!

School should be about me learning and not about what I wear!"

How can I even think about going to college when getting out of high school is such a pain in the ass!

"So, in other words, when you [white teacher] ask for parent involvement my parents give you a hard time because they can't speak English? You're acting like it's a sin for us to know our tongue, and if you ask me, it's better for us to speak two languages than just one. And as far as speaking English alone is concerned, that's stupid because that's half the population and you don't make up the [total] population!"

Seguín students clearly state that the school does not sufficiently provide relations premised on authentic caring. They further demand an inclusive curriculum responsive to their cultural identity as Mexicans. Far from affirming their worth as culturally Mexican beings, Seguín subtracts these identifications. An unfortunate by-product of this subtraction is the compromising of students' potential for healthy peer interactions across the generational divide that exists between immigrant and non-immigrants. Additionally compromised is students' folk model of education embedded in the concept of *educación*. In other terms, students come to school with much less than who they are at the same time that the school expects them to shed their perennial "visitor's" status and assume a sense of ownership and belonging.

As Noddings (1984, 1992) suggests, students are objectified by a double standard that calls on them to make sense of schooling when schooling is not attempting to make sense of them. For culturally diverse students like those at Seguín, this objectification is experienced as a forced-choice proposition between being Mexican or American, accounting for the divisions that exist among youth. When the definition of what it means to be educated in U.S. society systematically excludes the Mexican culture, the Spanish language, and things Mexican, the prescription that students "care about" school can be a hard pill to swallow.

There are lessons to learn from those exceptional individuals I either came across or heard about who because of their engrossment in their students' welfare, were able to make sense of their students' lives. For example, Mr. Sosa (chapter 3) responds to the problem of disaffected and poorly nutritioned band members by helping them meet their nutritional needs. We also learn from

Amalia (chapter 4) about her parents' ethic of social responsibility as teachers of Mexico's downtrodden children. Mr. Chilcoate (chapter 6) validates his students' anger and frustration and enlists them into the process of redefining the goals of the course that students had found so troubling. In each instance, the pedagogy that informs their action and that secures the loyalty and commitment of their students reveals a profound respect and awareness of how the problems that students bring with them to school are symptomatic of broader, collective issues. Rather than blaming the students for their poor nutrition, impoverished status, or apparent immaturity, these teachers become champions for their students' rights to a more equal educational opportunity.

Conversations I had with youth also helped me to make sense of their lives. Differences in schooling orientations are linked to differences in the level of social capital that students possess in the context of their friendship networks. Although there are clear exceptions, immigrant youth groups tend to experience the school more positively than their U.S.-born counterparts. Their collective, pro-achievement strategies have even earned some of them the dubious distinction of being the "organized cheaters" on campus. More positively, my findings suggest that the reason they are able to effectively marshal their intellectual resources is because of the benefits they derive from their prior schooling experiences in Mexico. Their academic competence thus functions as a human capital variable that, when marshaled in the context of the peer group, turns into social capital.

There are limits to social capital, however. Even at its most productive levels, as was discovered among the "Urban Youth from Monterrey," it was troubling to see such talent lodged within the regular curriculum track. Social capital is clearly no match against an invisible system of tracking that excludes the vast majority of youth. Strategizing for the next assignment or exam does not guarantee that the exclusionary aspects of schooling will either cease or magically come to light. No student I came across questioned the existence of tracking, not even the "cultural track" within the regular track. Especially for the more socially marginal—like Estéban (chapter 4) whose needs were dismissed by his counselor—the power to circumvent an inappropriate track placement remains an issue.

Enabling immigrant youth to weather the more challenging aspects of schooling is their dual frame of reference. Propelling their present aspirations and efforts is their knowledge of just how difficult life is for the working poor in Mexico. The conditions of schooling and life, generally, are tolerable because the economic well-being of students' families is more secure than it otherwise would be "back home." However, because immigrant youth feel that they should be "*agradecidos*" or "grateful" for the opportunity to attend secondary schools in the United States, their comparative frame also works to mute any criticisms they may have of schooling. Immigrant youth further provide a nuanced view of the dual frame: It can and should be accessible to U.S.-born youth. The enriching experiences that youth in mixed-generation groups enjoyed through family visits and travel to Mexico bear testimony to the incalculable worth of an expanded horizon.

I worry about immigrant youths' frequent mention of feeling too "*calladitos*" ("quiet") and "*humillados*" ("subdued") in Seguín classrooms. They appear to be "learning" to become the silent learners that their U.S.-born counterparts already are. Indeed, silent learning may constitute the basis for the latter's pervasive critique of schooling as boring, as well as for their psychic withdrawal from the schooling process. Whenever I asked students what they thought would be a "fun" thing to do in school, they always told me that "this" is what's fun—that is, my interviewing and connecting with them. Hence when students say that their classes aren't fun, they may be stating in a socially acceptable way their desire for greater connection.

Scarcely manifesting either the esprit de corps or the academic competence of their immigrant counterparts, youth in mixed-generation and U.S.-born groups are socially decapitalized. Inasmuch as they exhibit a pro-school orientation, it is largely due to the efforts of the females in these groups. As an extension of their nurturing role, individual females often become the purveyors of social capital in their groups. That many of these relationships are exploitative, however, suggests some limits or unevenness to the benefits of social capital under such circumstances.

A finding that surprised me is that youth in mixed-generation youth groups appear more like U.S.-born, than all-immigrant, youth in terms of their schooling orientations. Although more in-depth research needs to investigate the significance of such cross-generational alliances, I can tentatively conclude that the concentration of 1.5 generation youth in mixed-generation groups appears to be a moderating influence. Since 1.5 generation youth have schooling and life in the United States as their experiential backdrop, returns to human capital may be less for them than for their counterparts schooled in Mexico. Only future research can tell.

Comparing Mexican to U.S. schooling is probably like comparing apples to oranges. What may be helping students learn the curriculum in Mexico may be its challenging national curriculum at the *primaria* level, as Macías (1990) suggests. That the Mexican government further subsidizes education through the sixth-grade accounts for an accelerated curriculum that can prove beneficial to prospective entrants into U.S. schools. Students' perceptions of the differences between these two educational systems nevertheless shed light on how many of these young people are able to navigate successfully in their new environment. Clearly, additional studies need to be conducted on the kinds of skills, resources, and assumptions about schooling that immigrant youth bring with them to the United States. It would also be important to know about other settings where a collectivist ethos does not exist among immigrants in order to determine the conditions that must hold for its development.

Students in the mixed-generation and U.S.-born groups lack a well-defined and effective achievement orientation. Not only did they seem uninterested in their day-to-day academic responsibilities, they had given little or no thought to their futures. Most consistently expressed a desire to attend college "someday," but they always couched this goal in nebulous and noncommittal terms. I attribute this orientation not only to their antipathy toward schooling, but also to their paucity of social capital. The impact of the state-mandated test as a requirement for graduation also cannot be underestimated, especially when the passing rates are so grievously low. It is unfortunate that this test is used to determine the destinies of students rather than schools, with youth bearing the primary burden of inferior schooling.

By examining the forces of social decapitalization through the analytical lens of subtractive schooling, I sustain a larger argument that the weakened academic status of U.S.-born youth may be understood as a key consequence of schooling. That is, a culturally subtractive schooling process that encourages youth to de-identify from Mexican culture and the immigrants in their midst, results in the latter becoming unavailable as role models for, and co-creators of, achievement. Additionally sacrificed are opportunities to cultivate their bilingual and bicultural competencies. Since I assume that achievement is a social process whereby orientations toward schooling are nurtured in familiar contexts among those with similar dispositions, then the de-identification of U.S.-born youth from those among them who are academically oriented (i.e., immigrant youth) is extremely consequential. As expressed by Adriana in chapter 4, U.S.-born youth foster the pernicious myth that no one at Seguín is "into school." Rather than describing Seguín's empirical reality, such views reveal a profound psychic and emotional distance from the world of Spanish-speaking, immigrant youth.

In the case of immigrant Mexican youth, their social marginality appears less linked to their academic marginality than is the case for their U.S.-born peers. Ironically, immigrants' stigmatized status combines with their criticism of their U.S.-born peers as "too Americanized" to enhance their peer group solidarity. I find that their higher levels of social capital lodged in their peer group relations account for both their higher academic achievement and their collectivist, pro-school orientations vis-à-vis their U.S.-born peers. Nevertheless affecting their academic standing are the numerous institutional structures and practices that compromise their potential.

Immigrant youth must face inordinate challenges to succeed. To begin with, they are regarded as "limited English proficient" rather than as "Spanish dominant" or as potentially bilingual. Rather than as a strength to build on, their fluency in Spanish is construed as a "barrier" that needs to be overcome. Also obstructed is the possibility for fully vested bilingualism and biculturalism because of Seguín's—as well as the state of Texas'—transitional philosophy. That immigrant youth are still able to paddle upward and toward the academic mainstream—albeit within the constraints of regular-track placement—attests to the potency of their academic competence, *empeño* (diligence), and supportive networks. In an era of anti-immigrant hostility, it is important for policymakers to seriously consider the impact of any withdrawal of resources from one of the most promising segments of the Latino school-age community.

From the vantage point of Seguín's culture of caring, an aesthetic or technical definition prevails with devastating consequences to regular-track youth. That is, teachers expect students to demonstrate caring about school with an abstract commitment to ideas or practices that purportedly lead to achievement. This definition departs radically from the composite imagery of authentic caring that unfolds in this work. Aesthetic caring is not only superficial, it also obliges youth to participate in a power-evasive, culturally chauvinistic framework that individualizes students' difficulties with schooling while larger structural issues like the school's subtractive curriculum go unnoticed. It fails to acknowledge that decisions are being made by one group for another. When goals, objectives, and strategies are systematically blind to the experiences of the "other's" history and culture, and especially their folk understandings of education, they are sure to meet with limited success.

What does it mean "to care"? The answer to this question is provided by the students themselves. Teachers and other school personnel are to depart from their penchant for aesthetic caring and embrace a more authentically caring ideology and practice. According to this reformulation, school functionaries are to embark on a search for connection where trusting relationships constitute the cornerstone for all learning. A sincere search for connection will reposition the ill-informed teacher as "student" of the U.S.-Mexican community and its history of subordination. As students of the U.S.-Mexican community, majority teachers (and even minority teachers who adhere to the majority paradigm) will become reflective and arrive at an awareness of their own contradictory position vis-à-vis the community. Their intention of investment and the unintended consequence of divestment becomes their central contradiction. Resolving this contradiction becomes a central concern.

When authentic caring gets ideologically wedded to Mexican Americans' historic struggle for equal educational opportunity, a more useful interpretation of the schooling of U.S.-Mexican youth will have been rendered. A view of cultural assimilation as a non-neutral process will become apparent. It will either involve adding or subtracting a second language and culture, including, possibly, their definition of caring. The patterned divisions that they observe among youth will no longer seem normal but as institutionally contrived. The very concept of investment will get redefined with the idea that youth need to be equipped with the diverse sets of cultural and linguistic skills they need to peacefully inhabit and contribute productively to their diverse social worlds.

While abandoning one's original culture may seem appropriate to the teacher, principal, district-level administrator, or state-level board member for whom the worth of the dominant culture is simply self-evident, it is inherently alienating for Mexican youth whose lived ethnic experience requires that they retain some measure of competence across the varied contexts that characterize their existence. And it is especially alienating for the vast majority of youth who are not located in the privileged rungs of the curriculum. Marginality evolves when children are socialized away from their communities and families of origin. The politics of difference that emerge between immigrant and U.S.-born youth not only reflect but follow from the distancing elements of schooling. While youth indeed enter school with these divisions among them, schooling exacerbates and legitimates these differences through the structure of the academic program.

In a world that does not value bilingualism or biculturalism, youth may fall prey to the subtle yet unrelenting message of the worthlessness of their communities. Regular-track youth are not only prepared for a remote Anglo, middle-class social world that many or most in their group will never experience in any meaningful way, they also get socialized into the belief that leaving their communities through upward and outward mobility is the standard against which their self-worth should be measured. Recall Frank's predicament in chapter 3, which helps illustrate this point.

As bright and capable as he is, Frank finds the aspirations that others have for him as much too compromising. How can he get into "the program" when it manifests such little concern for his community? How can he possibly trust "the program" when his success will not translate into his community's success? He could not be more sociological: if a culturally biased premise is built into the school's definition of success, then the well-being of his community will remain in constant jeopardy. Frank is not saying that he is unwilling to be a productive member of society. He suggests instead his desire for *educación*—that is, to learn how to live in the world as a caring, responsible, well-mannered, and respectful human being. At this point in his life, his world is his *barrio* and he, like Tisa (chapter 3), feels that the goal of an education should be compatible with love of family and community.

At Seguín and other similar places, there always are highly insightful and intuitive practitioners who either have arrived or will arrive at authentic, community-based understandings of caring. However, their numbers are few and the institutional cultures in which these individuals find themselves typically dishearten even the most courageous. At Seguín, such individuals either emanate from similar communities or are well versed in the literature and histories of these communities.

There is much to gain from well-versed understandings. In the best of all cases, practitioners become "honorary members" of the communities they serve. Becoming an "honorary Mexican" should in fact be so treasured that it would constitute the pinnacle of any sincere teacher's or administrator's career. However much coveted, honorary membership status cannot be willed into existence by any single individual. Only members of the community can make this decision. To achieve this type of recognition, much must be demonstrated. That is, the political interests of the community must be embraced. When action demonstrates such awareness, a truly authentic pedagogy will have been set into motion.

Although one does not have to become an honorary member to make a contribution to the Mexican community or any other community in need, a community's interests are best served by those who possess an unwavering respect for the cultural integrity of a people and their history. Since these histories are marginalized in the university curriculum, special efforts need to be undertaken to overcome these deficits in knowledge and understanding. With such shallow understandings of the minority communities that practitioners seek to serve, aesthetic caring and subtractive schooling will continue constituting the rule rather than the exception.

Although my focus has been on Mexican immigrant and Mexican American youth, the concept of subtractive schooling is applicable to the experiences of other U.S. minority youth like African Americans, American Indians, and Puerto Ricans, especially if they come from segregated, low-income, urban communities. They, too, must deal with the derogation of their cultures and histories. Their names and identities also get altered in the process of schooling and the richness and complexity of their linguistic repertoires are also devalued and construed as "barriers" to overcome. Biculturalism or bidialectalism is typically not presented to them as an option.

Rather than expanding opportunity, tracking reinforces their already weak and tenuous position within the academic hierarchy. Despite high failure and dropout rates in their schools, their collective concerns get individualized with the burden of change being placed on the students themselves, as well as on their families and communities. Unfortunately, many are not in schools where more resources are devoted to enhancing the quality of instruction than to maintaining order and discipline. Because of their alienation from schooling, these youth are just as poised as the students I came across to benefit from better relations with adults in their lives who not only hold high expectations for them but who also share in their students' concerns over their families and community (Abi-Nader 1990; Ladson-Billings 1994).

An authentically caring pedagogy would not only cease subtracting students' cultural identities, it would also reverse its effects. It would build bridges wherever there are divisions and it would privilege biculturalism out of respect for the cultural integrity of their students. Even if teachers or other school personnel cannot fully resolve the contradictions or become honorary members of the communities they serve, their repositioning as students, rather than as teachers, of culture will invest them with the dispositions and knowledge that they need to have to maximize their effectiveness as both teachers and purveyors of cultural knowledge. In the case of U.S.-Mexican youth at Seguín and other similar schools, it is entirely accurate to say that we not yet know what it really means to care. Perhaps most heartening is the finding that the mainstream curriculum is demonstrably accessible through a route responsive to students' definition of caring.

EPILOGUE

Some Final Thoughts

For the reader who is perhaps troubled or anxious about some of the study's findings, I conclude by providing a sense of what an "additive schooling" experience might entail. What follows are some thoughts that can serve as a basis for further discussion and exploration.

Most fundamentally, additive schooling is about equalizing opportunity and assimilating Mexicans into the larger society, albeit through a bicultural process. In this world, students do not have to choose between being Mexican or American; they can be both. This pluralistic model of schooling builds on students' bicultural experience—which *all* minority youth bring with them to school—to make them conversant, respectful, and fluent in as many dialects and languages as they can master. The perfect starting point is with those that they already possess (or are on the verge of possessing).

The question of culture is often compromised in bilingual education or dual language programs as if simply teaching in the students' tongue is sufficient for the curriculum to be culturally relevant. While language is a necessary first step toward relevancy, there is more to culture than language. Education still has to be meaningfully tied to children's lives lest they proceed through life aimlessly with little sense of direction. If children do not know who they are or where they are going, the popular maxim that "any road will get them there" has acquired added meaning for me upon the completion of this work.

If we agree that knowledge is imminently cultural rather than neutral, neither is the ability to grasp such knowledge neutral. One's ability to grasp knowledge is determined by one's proximity to the knowledge valued by the dominant society. Since Mexican Americans and other U.S. minorities have been historically distant from the dominant knowledge, their ascendancy remains

269

a piecemeal process with the promise of the good life forever deferred to "the next generation," at least for the vast majority. I by no means suggest that students should not master the dominant knowledge that is customarily embodied in the standard curriculum, but rather that it should be openly recognized as dominant and exclusive so that an additive thought process may supervene to both challenge and counterbalance its undue influence. In an additive school, one's language and ethnic identity are assets and figure precisely in what it means to be educated in U.S. society.

From a practical perspective, additive schooling is about enhancing the labor market status of U.S.-Mexicans (and all other youth) in an increasingly global economy. U.S.-Mexican youth are uniquely poised to become the new kind of worker for which this emerging transborder economy is already in great demand. Because such workers cannot only effectively negotiate a multiplicity of cultures and linguistic codes but are also *bien educados*, the United States stands to benefit both economically and politically from its increased and improved relations with its neighbors in this hemisphere.

Additive schooling is especially about the maintenance of community, which includes improving the home-school relationship, even if this means that the discourse gets politicized. When parents and community call for culturally relevant and sensitive curricula, the status quo is sure to be threatened and possibly upset. However, if such disequilibrium translates into an infusion of people, technologies, and resources that are responsive to the demands of community, progress will have occurred. If relationships within the community—most especially between immigrant and U.S.-born youth—are further mended and healthy and productive peer group interactions take place as a result, this goal will have been worthwhile. Life is fragmented enough without so much of this fragmentation being institutionally contrived such as through nonacademic, "cultural tracking," and other pernicious mechanisms I have identified.

My research suggests that authentic caring can operate within subtractive contexts. However, authentic caring within an additive schooling context is arguably most productive. The concepts of additive schooling and authentic caring—at least the definition that evolves in this work—may ultimately be synonymous. Because both concepts convey a profound respect and love of community as well as an enhanced awareness of Mexican Americans' historic struggle for equal educational opportunity, each unfolds naturally into the other. Thanks to the opinions, thoughts, and expressions of the people who contributed to this work, as well as to the numerous scholars who have thoughtfully considered meanings and dimensions of caring, we may be a step closer in knowing what it means to really care for the U.S.-Mexican youth among us.

APPENDIX

Research Methodology

Little is known about the schooling experiences of immigrant and U.S.-born Mexican youth attending large, inner-city, segregated schools. This study helps fill that gap. It also contributes to a better understanding of the patterns of immigrant achievement and U.S.-born underachievement frequently noted in the literature by building a theoretical framework that specifically addresses each of these phenomena and the interaction between them. The framework draws from three sources: the caring literature (Noddings 1984, 1992); the multiculturalist critique of subtractive assimilation, or culture eradication (Bartolomé 1994; Gibson 1993); and Coleman's (1988, 1990) concern with resource-rich networks—expressed as "social capital" in the sociological literature.

Although my study initially made use of quantitative data, the key modes of data collection are based on participant observation and open-ended interviews with individuals and with groups of students. This approach allowed me to access peer group culture, to examine the nexus between institutional structures and students' behavior and attitudes, and to explore reasons for the social, cultural, and linguistic divisions that I observed among teenagers while they were at school.

Pursuing an inductive, "grounded theoretical" approach (Glaser and Strauss 1967; Strauss and Corbin 1990), I developed themes or categories based on an ongoing analysis of empirical data drawn from several sources and assessed in terms of existing theoretical frameworks. The major themes or categories that emerged over time pertained to conceptions of caring; to social, cultural, and linguistic divisions among youth; to collectivist orientations; and to individuals' orientations toward schooling. These "discoveries" led me to consult two quite different genres: the caring literature, with which I was not familiar at the beginning of the project; and the social reproduction, social capital, and assimilation literatures, which I knew quite well.

My efforts to build—rather than simply test—theory involved me in a highly reflexive process. As I collected my data and evaluated my emerging findings on the schooling experiences of Mexican youth, I simultaneously consulted and considered various literatures. Each major theme or category I identified I also subjected to cross-case analysis (Miles and Huberman 1994). This method entailed examining successive cases (whether of individuals or groups of individuals) to see if later cases matched those found earlier. This in turn led me to develop numerous codes or subcategories that I then used to reduce and organize the data within my major analytical categories. Once the qualitative data from the assorted sources were compiled, I generated displays using Filemaker Pro, a software program that allows for easy retrieval and analysis of textual data. Filemaker Pro enabled me to summarize differences within and between immigrants and U.S.-born Mexican youth. Finally, by triangulating the data I had collected from various sources, I was able to assure the overall validity of the findings. Quantitative survey data (see chapter 1) and group interviews, in particular, provided useful confirmation for some of the major findings from my participant observations.

In the remainder of this appendix, I describe my multifaceted ethnographic approach. I conclude with a discussion of the reasons why I chose Juan Seguín High School in Houston as my site.

PARTICIPANT OBSERVATION

As a participant-observer, I immersed myself in school and community affairs, recording observations over the three-year period from 1992 to 1995. My field notes, recording day-to-day experiences and casual conversations with students, parents, counselors, teachers, administrators, and community leaders, ultimately filled a single three-inch notebook.

I attended, either as an observer or as a participant, numerous school and community functions. School activities included pep rallies, orientation and registration activities, football games, speaker presentations, faculty meetings, Shared Decision-Making

Committee (SDMC) meetings, and Parent Teacher Association (PTA) meetings. Discussions with students, parents, administrators, and teachers occurred most often during the course of normal, everyday activities during school hours. I deliberately sought out students at times and in places where they were likely to congregate. These included the cafeteria area during the lunch hour, the hallways between class sessions, the restrooms (girls), during some physical education (PE) classes, in front of school buildings before and after school, and throughout the day under the stairwells and in other out-of-the-way places students favored, especially when they were skipping classes.

In the community, I attended community functions, political meetings with local leaders, East End area churches, and school board meetings. I do not live in the East End, but my home is located in an adjacent community, so I have easy access to East End area activities and I regularly patronized East End businesses. Involving myself in the community gave me ready access to key institutional players such as school board members, community activists, and local politicians. Discussions with these individuals helped me gain a sense of the community's historic struggle for equal educational opportunity and added a broader perspective to my conclusions.

Each day of participant observation generated a condensed account that, by the end of the day, I expanded into a fuller, more detailed rendering (Spradley 1980). The condensed account consisted of the notes I took either during or after a conversation or event, as well as audiotapes of my impressions and recollections. The latter I made either immediately after a conversation or event, or at the end of the day. I made the tapes in private places (e.g., in my car or in the nearly-always-empty parents' lounge on the school campus) by talking into a microcassette recorder that I carried with me daily. This strategy proved to be a very effective means of accurately recollecting and reconstructing events and conversations with people.

My experiences as a participant-observer enabled me to lay the groundwork for the study as a whole. Findings from my earliest days and weeks of data collection directly shaped the questionnaire I compiled and administered to the entire student body, providing valuable information on student achievement, parental education, and schooling orientations. Participant observation also helped me gain the confidence of many of the students, teachers, administrators, and security guards in the school. Of course, given the large size of the school, I was unable to get to know all school personnel. This meant that occasionally I would be eyeballed with suspicion—especially when I entered the teachers' lounge, where candid discussion of students often took place. School personnel with whom I had not formed any relationship often categorized me either as "the student writing a research paper" or as "the doctoral student working on a dissertation." In some cases, this misperception reflected a simple lack of knowledge or a simple inference drawn from my casual dressing style; in other cases, though, it seemed to stem from status inconsistency.

In the minds of some faculty and staff, my achieved status as a university professor was inconsistent with my ascriptive status as a Mexican American and a woman. This "misalignment" prompted an unconscious—but quite consistent—refiguring of my persona into a more psychologically manageable category. The extent to which I violated social categories or expectations became evident in a number of recurring situations where I had to correct the same individuals who would repeatedly refer to me as "the student from Rice." Dressing up—as I did on numerous occasions for school functions—made little difference in how I was seen by staff. With students, my status as a university professor was not perceived as inconsistent so much as inconsequential. Rice University did not ring a bell for them. Most students came to know me as "the one who was writing the book," since that was how I typically introduced myself to them.

However imperfectly my formal status was perceived, I became a regular fixture on the school's landscape over the course of my three-year study. By the end of the first year, I was able to walk the halls or enter the cafeteria confident that I would run into students I knew. The last time I experienced so much familiarity with so many youth and faculty was when I was myself a student in my hometown high school in a West Texas mid-sized town. Although I never deliberately passed myself off as a high school student, I was often mistaken for one because of my youthful appearance and dress. I typically wore a T-shirt, jeans, and tennis shoes on campus, partly for comfort and partly because such attire helped distinguish me from the students' teachers, with whom I preferred not to be confused as this would have minimized rapport.

In my role as participant-observer, I became attuned to the contradictory and complex social and cultural worlds of immigrant and U.S.-born youth. I followed up on these divisions and contradictions because in my first days of research I had been immediately struck by the distance that existed between these two broad categories of students. In the cafeteria as well as in other gathering places, I noticed how groups divided along language and cultural lines. English-dominant Mexican American youth had little interaction with their Spanish-dominant, immigrant counterparts. Notwithstanding some cross-generational mixing, I observed a pervasive pattern of parallel coexistences. Considering that these individuals are of the same national origin, its extensiveness surprised and disturbed me. While in terms of my own personal experiences, such divisions seemed predictable, the research process of making the familiar unfamiliar helped me to really appreciate the extent of these divisions. My early encounters with highly acculturated immigrant youth, in particular (see chapter 3), impelled me to consider the forces that structure identity.

Teachers and administrators consider these divisions as "normal." Unless asked, most students never questioned or even articulated the divisions that existed among them. This intrigued me. The possibility that these divisions might mark boundaries for orientations toward schooling sparked my interest in conducting a closer investigation. I hoped to learn more about similarities and differences in schooling orientations *within* and *across* groups; I also hoped to find out why the two groups had so little to do with one another. Such divisions might make sense in an integrated setting where pressures to assimilate toward white peers exist (e.g., Olsen 1997), but why would they persist in a segregated setting? What role did institutional factors play in mediating these divisions? And what was I to make of youth who did cross boundaries by forging alliances across generations? Rather than simplifying matters, the research process seemed to complexify the way I looked at young people's social world.

Finally, I wanted to discover how the students themselves felt about the gulf between them. The decision to conduct group interviews followed naturally from these interests. Examining orientations in a friendship group context would allow me to ask students direct questions about their day-to-day social world, such as how they spent their time together, how they identified ethnically, and how they perceived their schooling experiences, both past and present. Insights from social capital theory (especially Coleman 1988, 1990) and from the academic achievement and educational attainment literature comparing immigrant and U.S.-born youth (i.e., the "subtractive assimilation" literature [Cummins 1984; Skutnabb-Kangas and Cummins 1988; Gibson 1988, 1993]) helped shape the questions I raised and provided an interpretive framework for assessing the answers I received. (See especially chapter 5 for a discussion of how subtractive schooling structures and sustains divisions among youth.)

A secondary objective of the group interviews was to extend external validity. As Huberman and Miles (1994) suggest, looking at multiple actors in multiple settings enhances the generalizability of a study's findings while bringing to light key constructs and explanations for the phenomena being investigated.

GROUP INTERVIEWS

Beginning in the fall 1992 semester and continuing through the spring 1993 semester, I conducted twenty-five open-ended interviews during the lunch hour. I spoke with student groups of between two and eight members. Time constraints imposed by academic and family responsibilities limited the total number of group interviews to twenty-five. On average, each group interview lasted between one and one-and-a-half hours. Most of the interviews with immigrants were conducted in Spanish, while most of the interviews with U.S.-born and "mixed-generation" groups were conducted in English or "Spanglish." The latter involves switching back and forth between Spanish and English. These groups are described in Table A.1 according to names that—except for the "Achievement Gang"—were assigned to them. These names were mnemonic devices for easy recall.

TABLE A.1
Composition of Interview Groups

Name	Generational Status	Sex of Members	Grade Levels
English-speaking immigrants	Immigrant (long-term)	2 females; 2 males	All freshmen
Male immigrant study group	Immigrant (long-term)	3 males	All Sophomores
Latina female friends	Immigrant (long-term)	3 females	All juniors
Immigrant females in trouble	Immigrant (long-term)	4 females	All freshmen
Current events, ESL students	Immigrant (recent)	2 females; 2 males	1 freshman; 3 sophomores
Religious immigrant males	Immigrant (recent)	3 males	2 sophomores; 1 junior
Female cousins	Immigrant (recent)	3 females	1 freshman; 1 sophomore; 1 junior
Urban, Monterrey youth	Immigrant (recent)	3 females; 5 males	3 freshmen; 5 sophomores
Preliterate immigrants	Immigrant (recent)	2 females 1 male	All freshmen
Career-minded females	Immigrant (recent)	3 females	All freshmen
"Achievement Gang"	Mixed	2 females; 3 males	2 freshmen; 2 sophomores; 1 junior
Indigenous Mexican American females*	Mixed	3 females	1 freshman; 2 sophomores
Journalism females	Mixed	4 females	All freshmen
ROTC male friends	Mixed	3 males	All sophomore
Cosmetology females	Mixed	3 females	All freshmen
Borderline gang members	Mixed	3 males	All freshmen
Kickers	U.S.-Born	2 females; 1 male	2 freshmen; 1 sophomore

(Continued on next page)

TABLE A.1 *(continued)*

Name	Generational Status	Sex of Members	Grade Levels
Rappers	U.S.-Born	2 females; 3 males	All freshmen
Mixed-race group	U.S.-Born	3 females; 3 males	All freshmen
"We Don't Care" group	U.S.-Born	3 males	All freshmen
"Bad Reps" group	U.S.-Born	3 females	All freshmen
"Wannabe" male toughs	U.S.-Born	3 males	All freshmen
Friends from the 'hood & 1 cousin	U.S-Born	1 female; 3 males	1 freshman; 3 sophomores
Rio Grande Valley students	U.S.-Born	1 female; 3 males	All sophomores
Spanish speakers	U.S.-Born	3 females; 2 males	2 freshmen; 3 sophomores

*Formerly "Social Monolinguals" (see chapter 5)

With respect to individual students' names, if they typically pronounced their names in English, I assigned them an English pseudonym. Spanish-language pseudonyms were assigned names in Spanish. Although most students said that they did not mind the use of their actual names, there were enough who preferred to remain anonymous to prevent me from doing so.

Because the group interviews typically generated additional questions, I also conducted follow-up, informal interviews with individual members of the groups. In some instances, I sought clarification for statements made during the group interview; in other instances, I wanted to know the outcome of a particular problem or issue that had been discussed during the interview.

After several weeks of interviewing, I observed how groups corresponded to the following major categories: immigrant, U.S.-born, and generationally "mixed" friendship groups. To insure variability in these categories, I kept a running count of the number of immigrant, U.S.-born, and generationally "mixed" friendship groups I interviewed. Although I was initially unsure how gender composition would fit into the overall story, a corollary running count of the gender composition of groups enabled me to secure adequate variability to perform gender analyses.

I should interject at this point that because I was concerned with how typical or representative the students I came across in the group interviews were, I dedicated at least two summers conducting semistructured interviews with first-, second-, and third-generation ninth-graders and graduating high school seniors, respectively. (In the summer of 1993, I interviewed their parents as well.) While only a portion of this information found its way into the pages of this book, this experience increased my confidence that the findings generated from my analysis of group interviews were consistent and valid.

I chose the lunch hour to conduct group interviews because this was the part of the school day when students were most likely to associate with their preferred friends—that is, of course, if all had been scheduled for the same lunch hour. I also reasoned (correctly) that in the more relaxed and casual atmosphere in and around the cafeteria, students would be more likely to speak openly, especially if they were in a group.

On a typical group interview day, I would go to the cafeteria and its surroundings during lunch and look for a space where I could stand and casually observe students in groups. Group boundaries were well marked not only through nonverbal cues, but also through the appropriation of certain spaces in and around the cafeteria. For instance, U.S.-born youth tended to either line the perimeters of the cafeteria or they ate outside, either in front of the school or in an adjacent courtyard. ESL students often claimed a space between the cafeteria and "C Hall" where the ESL program was located. Longer-term immigrants, especially the more bicultural youth, occupied central seating in the cafeteria, alongside groups of students who participated in organized school activities like band, choir, football, the pep squad team, and so on.

During my earliest days of observation, I arbitrarily sat either in the perimeter of the cafeteria or somewhere in the adjacent courtyard. This action was perhaps an unconscious manifestation of my own sense of marginality at the time. Not surprisingly, this decision acquainted me with youth located in U.S.-born groups with whom I either conversed or interviewed. This decision was also my first step toward mapping the student population to ensure a generationally diverse set of friendship groups. As I made my way toward the center of the cafeteria, I knew beforehand that I would generate data from youth located in either immigrant or generationally mixed friendship groups. Because my mental schemata of students' friendship cliques did not always conform to my expectation, it also helped to observe whether groups seemed to speak mostly in Spanish or in English.

I deliberately focused on students who looked young because my primary interest lay in meeting and talking with ninth- and tenth-graders. (It is students in these grade levels who have the highest failure and dropout rates). After I had located what looked like a promising group, I would approach the students, introduce myself, and ask them if I could interview them. Once I had confirmed that youth in these groups were all "good friends" and that all were enrolled in regular-track classes (this I determined by simply asking if any of them were in honors), I would begin interviewing them. Interviews took the form of a group conversation that addressed the various themes I asked the students to consider, as well as other issues and ideas that the students raised themselves.

I should note that my research overlapped with my two pregnancies. My twenty-, thirty-, and ultimately, forty-pound bulge often helped open doors into the students' world. Females and males both were very positive, respectful, and affirming of my protruding self. For example, students typically cleared space for me in the school cafeteria despite limited seating. Even among this youthful population, my presence would prompt pictures of younger siblings and relatives, including, occasionally, the students' own children, to spring out of billfolds and notebooks.

I did experience some rejection, but the vast majority of students I approached expressed an interest in being interviewed. I discovered that I had a knack for interviewing students and getting them to open up. I also found that promising to conceal their true identities helped dissolve any lingering suspicion or shyness. Students were motivated to participate in the interviews by two other incentives: so that I would not have to end the interviews as soon as the lunch period was over, the principal had supplied me with signed hall passes. This meant that I could excuse students from whatever class they had immediately after lunch. (I never kept students away from classes if they had assignments due or examinations to take; and no teachers ever indicated to me that they minded their students taking time away from class to be interviewed.) The second factor that attracted students and made them more receptive to being interviewed was the fact that I was writing a book and that they could be in it if they wished.

My views of vexed student-teacher relations were certainly shaped by my own experience of having been tracked and consequently ignored and dismissed by school personnel throughout most of my young life. I expected that I would find general-track teachers to be routinely dismissive of youth. However, because I have had some teaching experience at the secondary level and because of my by now well-versed understanding of the level of university preparation provided to future teachers, I believe that teachers are far from exclusively responsible for their lack of connectedness to youth.

Colleges and universities fail miserably at preparing their students for the urban world in which many will ultimately work. Moreover, because the core curriculum in colleges and universities is Eurocentric and elitist, higher education systematically produces teachers who fail to notice the virtues of a more inclusive approach. Cultural dominance at the university level recreates relations of dominance and subordination at the primary and secondary levels of schooling where urban, minority youth are forced to "learn" what their "place" is in society.

The issues I raise in this study are profoundly systemic. Regardless of how much school personnel say they care, if such caring is not perceived by youth, then their claim that "no one cares" has merit. From these personal and professional experiences, I feel I have done my best to craft a sensitive framework on what it means for faculty and other school personnel to really care for minority youth in schools. Corroborating this sentiment is the openness and nondefensiveness I enjoyed with the vast majority of Seguín faculty, counselors, and administrators I encountered. In other words, most staff saw me (and, I hope, still do see me) as being as much on theirs as on the students' side.

Returning to the interviews, I approached each group with the intention of exploring the following five thematic areas: prior and present schooling experiences; expectations toward the future; how group members spend their time together; and how youth identify ethnically. Implicit social rules made me feel transgressive about asking students about the divisions that existed among them. No matter how I phrased the question, I felt like I had crossed a boundary. In either English or Spanish, it was "impolite" to ask such questions as: "What are your feelings toward immigrants/Mexican Americans in your school?" "Why don't you hang out with *inmigrantes*/Chicanas/os?" "Why don't you have any close friends who are immigrant/Mexican American?"

Indeed, among immigrant and U.S.-born youth alike, whenever negative commentary surfaced, it often came in the form of whispers and lowered voices. Difficulties associated with this line of questioning lead me to focus (in chapter 5) on those groups who, upon reviewing my notes, provided useful, analyzable information. In the case of immigrants, in particular, females' voices stand out in this part of the interview because they turned out to be more willing to discuss these and other sensitive issues.

In addition, I gathered the following personal information from each interviewee: name, sex, generational status, language preference, and current grade level. For the most part, I was able to secure all of the thematic information I needed. Analyses of these group data appear in chapters 4 and 5.

I audiorecorded the first interviews. The noisiness of the cafeteria rendered most of these recordings inaudible, however. When finding a quieter place to talk was not possible, I resorted to taking notes rapidly during the interviews and then writing up the notes immediately after each interview was completed. I also employed the same strategy I used in participant observation. I reconstructed the interviews by talking into my microcassette recorder in a private place. Using my written notes and my taped recollections, I then typed up the interviews. Typically, I used a computer available to me in an office education computer lab at the high school or I returned home for the day to write.

In generating ethnographic records for each interview, I tried to abide by Spradley's verbatim principle, which involves recording speakers' words exactly as they said them. As the students talked, I wrote condensed accounts of the conversation. I then produced expanded accounts (relying on the combination of audio and written notes described above) by late afternoon on the day of each group interview. Whenever I found that a record was incomplete, I jotted down additional questions for a follow-up, informal interview. In most cases, this kind of follow-up conversation involved only one or two of any given group's members. I conducted thirty-five informal interviews, all of which were recorded and transcribed in the same manner as the group interviews. This process of interviewing, recollecting interviews with a tape recorder, and typing up the conversation resulted in an ethnographic record for each interview (Spradley, 1980).

I wrote each ethnographic record into a Filemaker Pro file. Interview data were reorganized into a layout containing categories for the five thematic areas and the students' personal data. The data were then coded within each thematic category according to the empirical patterns which emerged. These included aesthetic and authentic teacher caring, more positive schooling orientations among immigrant youth—of which differential levels of social capital were a subcategory—and student disaffection among U.S.-born youth. Divisions between immigrant and U.S.-born youth, as conveyed in their attitudes, was a final major category.

This analysis alerted me to the possibility that the relationship between higher academic achievement and pro-school orientations among immigrant youth was a function of their greater social capital. A lack of social capital among U.S.-born youth in turn became implicated in the divisions that exist among them. After coding all of the data, I was able to view and analyze the five thematic categories in matrix form by generational status and sex. Where themes overlapped (e.g., in the area of caring teachers), these data were merged with the other textual data generated from participant observation. As the major thematic categories became apparent, these evolved into chapter headings and subheadings as I transitioned from analysis to summarizing my data in prose.

Throughout the duration of the writing and analysis process, I shared my work with Seguín High School students who worked for me as transcribers. I took comfort from their honest, mostly affirming, reactions to my portrayal of their peers and their schooling situation.

I received the best feedback from several Seguín teachers, Mr. Cedillo (Seguín's second principal during my tenure at Seguín), and assistant principal, Ana Luera. Mr. Cedillo made immediate use of my findings at one point. In a faculty meeting, he used my chapter on caring to chastise his faculty for not caring sufficiently for youth. Based on discussions I had with several teachers afterwards, his statements were not taken very seriously.

I also provided very early drafts of the intersecting issues of caring, student resistance, and discipline to a study group comprised of approximately ten teachers who had requested the information from me. They used the information to organize a teacher's workshop on disciplinary issues at Seguín. I understand that the workshop was very well attended and received. This effort evolved into a paper I wrote and made available upon request on the subject of discipline.

In spring 1994, the principal and I tried to arrange a time for me to make a public presentation of my findings during one of the teachers' scheduled workshops. Because the teacher coordinator of these workshops felt strongly that all of their teachers' time needed to be dedicated toward helping teachers improve their students' standardized test scores, it became logistically impossible to squeeze me in.

Since I remained with a persistent desire to present my findings to Seguín's faculty, I embraced an opportunity to invite them to a public address I made one afternoon at a nearby local community college. This effort involved placing invitations in teachers' and administrators' boxes and encouraging faculty I knew to attend via word-of-mouth. Unfortunately, no more than ten teachers attended and neither the principal, nor any of the four assistant principals attended my presentation. This rebuff kept me from pursuing the issue any further.

Both verbally and through my writing, I shared with Mr. Cedillo a number of policy recommendations that were mostly centered around the importance of culture-affirming curricula and nurturing the Spanish language. As a politically conscious Mexican American himself, he understood their importance. He complained, however, that as one of few Mexican American principals within the district combined with an overwhelmingly non-Latino staff in his school placed him in a very delicate position politically. Although he agreed with me "100 percent," he expressed the following concern: "We're [Mexican American principals] not like the Black principals who can do anything they want in their schools because they have people in the administration who will back them up. Me? If I do anything crazy or unusual, I'm out the door." His statements encouraged me not to take matters too personally. Sharing my written work with the above-mentioned individuals became the primary means by which the validity of my findings could be assured.

DOCUMENTARY EVIDENCE

Throughout the three years of the study, I also collected documentary forms of data, including the school memoranda, notices, handouts, archival information, and miscellaneous documents, the bulk of which I received in a staff mailbox that had been assigned to me. Most of these items (which now fill three, three-inch notebooks) were informational, letting me know about scheduled school functions and inviting me to participate in various school-related activities. Additional documentary materials include audiotaped and videotaped interviews with student groups; and copies of students' assignments that teachers shared with me because they shed light on students' lives and experiences. While, as in any ethnography, most of these materials did not make their way into the actual pages of the book, they nevertheless informed the data collection, analysis, and interpretation of the findings.

WHY I CHOSE JUAN SEGUÍN HIGH SCHOOL AS MY SITE

I chose Seguín as a research site for four major reasons. First, I was drawn to the school because three years earlier, in October 1989, it had been the site of a massive student walkout involving most of the school's three thousand students, all demanding a better education (see chapter 2 for an overview of this event). I was finishing my dissertation at Stanford University in Palo Alto, California in 1989, but I made numerous trips to Houston that year in order to visit Rice University, where I had already been hired. Partly because I lived in an apartment only several blocks away from Seguín, I learned of developments at the school that October and later. As an attendee at numerous community meetings called to address the problems at Seguín, I became increasingly well acquainted with city politics and with Houston Independent School District politics.

By the time I arrived at Seguín as a researcher (fall 1992), the excitement of the walkout had subsided significantly. While glimpses of the collective grievances that were voiced during and after the walkout appear in this book (especially in chapter 6), I discovered that memory of the walkout had already faded from most students' active consciousness.

Second, Seguín's location within an historic Mexican community guaranteed not only a high concentration of Mexican youth, but also generational diversity. This diversity made Seguín a natural laboratory for exploring my hypotheses about cultural assimilation. The student body reflects the community's combination of recent- and long-term residents (including, in the latter category, a significant portion whose origins date back to the 1910s). Third, I chose Seguín because it mirrors several national trends in the schooling of Mexicans. Seguín is an inner-city, virtually all-Mexican school and thus represents the trend of increasingly segregated schooling for U.S. Mexicans (Donato et al. 1991). The school also conforms to a nationwide pattern among Mexicans and other Latinos who tend to be schooled in large, comprehensive public schools (Fine 1991; Patthey-Chavez 1993). According to *Education Week*, May 14, 1986, the majority of students are now minorities in each of the twenty-five largest school systems in the country. Also, as is true at the national level, Latino, Spanish-speaking teachers are few in number at Seguín (Valencia 1991; Tomás Rivera Center 1993).

Whereas the high school's three head principals since 1989 have been Mexican American, most of the staff at Seguín are non-Mexican and non–Spanish speaking. Most reside outside of the East End area. This contrasts with the makeup of the predominantly Latino, mostly Mexican, student body—which grew from

95 to 97 percent over the course of this study. According to Seguín's 1992–93 master schedule, 16 percent of all courses were taught by Latinos, compared to 29 percent and 55 percent among African American and Anglo American faculty, respectively. In practical terms, Latino teachers' low numbers, combined with their tendency to work as teachers in the English as a Second Language (ESL) curriculum, translates into few U.S.-born students having the experience of being taught by a Latino high school teacher, especially for later-generation youth.

The final reason why I chose Seguín is that the school's record of achievement is bleak. I hoped that if I could find out what worked within an abysmal schooling context, I would then be able to shed light on some of the most important factors contributing to achievement generally among Mexican, inner-city adolescents. My ground-level approach led to an understanding of how Seguín is organized in ways that subtract resources from youth.

NOTES

CHAPTER 1. INTRODUCTION

1. Throughout this study, I use the terms "immigrant" and "first-generation" to refer to Mexico-born persons. I use the self-referents "Mexican American" and "Chicana/o," and the term, "U.S.-born" to refer to second- and third+-generation persons. (Fourth-generation youth [i.e., those whose parents and grandparents were born in the United States] were combined with third-generation youth because of their shared resemblance in all analyses.) I use the term, "Mexican," another popular self-referent, to refer to all persons of Mexican heritage when no distinction based on nativity is necessary.

2. Steinberg et al.'s (1996) study of school achievement in nine Wisconsin and Northern California schools is heartening inasmuch as it, too, utilizes students' self-reported grades as the key dependent variable. In their experience (also see Valenzuela and Dornbusch 1994), students provide candid and accurate responses *under conditions of anonymity and confidentiality*. Meeting these conditions and arriving at findings similar to those obtained in previous studies, combined to help me feel confident that the data I collected were valid. Administering the survey the day after report cards were issued further makes these data sufficiently reliable. Though the generational differences in grades were not large, they were consistently statistically significant in all analyses. (See Table N.1.)

3. See Table N.2.

4. See Table N.3.

5. Although external factors like the economy and broader political struggles over language, race, and immigration clearly influence the process of social reproduction for Mexicans (especially see Ogbu 1978, 1991), this study highlights the institution of schooling as a central agent of reproduction (Bourdieu and Passeron 1977a, 1977b; Willis 1977). Because of the determining influence of structural variables like tracking and other curricular biases on students' academic trajectories, ground-level ethnographic studies often invoke a reproduction theory perspective (e.g., Willis 1977; Fine 1991; Olsen 1997). In a similar fashion, this study emphasizes that variation in student achievement and schooling

orientations for which the school and educational policies and practices are largely responsible.

6. A caveat is that studies have thus far focused on "survivors' populations." These by definition do not include those students for whom school constituted an experience of blocked opportunity either because of a language barrier, irreparable culture shock, or institutional negligence (for example, see Romo and Falbo 1996).

7. Academic adeptness is formally referred to as Cognitive Academic Language Competence or CALP in the sociolinguistic literature (for example, Cummins 1984).

8. "Traditional values" must be understood in the context of the Mexican immigrant community itself, a highly select group. They

TABLE N.1
Generational Differences in Self-Reported Grades
among Regular-Track Youth at Seguín by Sex

Generational Status	Males and Females Combined Mean GPA sd (n)	Males Mean GPA sd (n)	Females Mean GPA sd (n)
First Generation	2.66*** .89 (600)	2.52 .93 (286)	2.82*** .76 (288)
Second Generation	2.50 .87 (430)	2.33 .88 (235)	2.75*** .80 (184)
Third Generation	2.44 .93 (373)	2.32 .91 (180)	2.56* .95 (186)

Significance levels: * = ≤.05; *** = ≤.001

Note: The analysis is a multiple comparison where all pairs were tested for significance. This variable combined self-reported grade-point averages (GPA) in English, Math, Social Studies, and Science and ranges from 0.5 to 4.0, with the latter equaling an A average. Ideally, I would have had access to students' actual grades. I did request the information from the school several times and they seemed willing but technically unable to meet my request. This task became impossible when the most knowledgeable person I could deal with on this matter was transferred to another school.

Analysis of Variance of Teacher Caring and
School Climate Items by Generational Status (Total Sample)

Gen 1 $\bar{x}$ (n) sd	Gen 2 $\bar{x}$ (n) sd	Gen 3+ $\bar{x}$ (n) sd	F-Ratio	Survey Items
			Teacher Caring	
2.92 (643) .68	2.78 (485) .67	2.72 (362) .79	11.8***	My teachers give me the moral support I need to do well in school.
2.67 (635) .77	2.58 (479) .70	2.49 (355) .76	7.10***	I rely on my teachers for advice and guidance in making important school-related decisions.
2.49 (625) .71	2.40 (477) .70	2.37 (352) .72	4.17*	My teachers are sensitive to my personal needs.
2.67 (623) .73	2.67 (474) .68	2.68 (351) .69	.03	My teachers are good in helping me solve school-related or academic problems.
2.55 (606) .78	2.32 (458) .73	2.24 (341) .76	22.3***	My teachers are good in helping me solve personal problems.
2.89 (615) .79	2.77 (472) .80	2.78 (348) .80	3.65*	I have a friendly and trusting relationship with at least one teacher.
			School Climate	
2.75 (694) .66	2.58 (505) .63	2.56 (375) .60	15.7***	Students get along well with teachers.
2.69 (684) .70	2.54 (506) .68	2.56 (378) .72	8.1**	There is real good school spirit.
2.74 (675) .70	2.64 (506) .67	2.63 (379) .69	4.60*	Discipline is fair.

(continued on next page)

TABLE N.2 *(continued)*

Gen 1 $\bar{x}$ (n) sd	Gen 2 $\bar{x}$ (n) sd	Gen 3+ $\bar{x}$ (n) sd	F-Ratio	Survey Items
2.08 (670) .66	2.10 (505) .63	2.09 (379) .67	.29	Other students often disrupt class.*
2.92 (671) .68	2.75 (502) .66	2.72 (370) .66	13.6***	The teaching is good.
2.84 (654) .70	2.72 (489) .69	2.74 (367) .65	5.1**	Teachers are interested in students.
2.78 .75 (667)	2.63 (494) .70	2.63 (369) .70	7.9***	When I work hard on schoolwork, my teachers praise my effort.
2.87 (652) .70	2.73 (492) .66	2.76 (369) .66	6.1**	Most of my teachers listen to what I have to say.

Significance levels: * = ≤.05; ** = ≤.01; *** = ≤.001

Note: Response categories ranged from "Strongly Agree" = 1 to "Strongly Disagree" = 4; the one-asterisked item was not reversed. A high score thus signifies either high teacher caring or a positive school climate. Except for one item, "Discipline is fair," gender differences were not statistically significant.

emanate largely from the interior of Mexico and their average education levels are higher than the national average for Mexico. They are risktakers able to delay gratification by accumulating capital to effectuate their passage across the border. They further exhibit a progressive orientation toward mainstream U.S. society (for reviews, see Buriel 1987, 1994).

9. Similar proportions of immigrant and U.S.-born youth are located in the regular and college-bound (honors and magnet school) track, respectively. Whereas 42 percent of immigrants and 58 percent of U.S.-born youth are in the regular track, 43 percent of immigrants and 57 percent of U.S.-born youth are college-bound.

10. Only a small fraction of the entire student population is located in the college-bound honors and magnet programs. Many of the honors students are also located in the advanced-level courses in Seguín's highly

TABLE N.3
Generational Differences in Parental Education,
Males and Females Combined
(Total Sample)

	Mean PARED *sd* *(n)*	*Parental Education Level*
First Generation	3.22** 2.88 (813)	"finished elementary school" (or 6 years)
Second Generation	3.57** 3.11 (600)	"some middle school" (or 7–8 years of school)
Third Generation	4.75*** 3.23 (514)	between "some middle" and "some high school" (or 9 years of school)

Significance levels: ** = ≤.01; *** = ≤.001

Note: The analysis is a multiple comparison where all pairs were tested for significance. Whereas immigrant parents of Seguín High students average a little over six years of education, parents of U.S.-born youth average around nine. In Texas, Chapa (1988) found that third-generation Mexican Americans complete an average of 9.3 years of education and that the dropout rate is 56 percent. According to Chapa, the comparable figures for Mexicans in California and the nation are 11.1 and 10.4 years of schooling completed and dropout rates of 39 and 48 percent, respectively. Mexicans from Texas are thus faring even more poorly than their underachieving counterparts nationwide.

selective Career and Technology Education (CTE) program. Hence, the overwhelming majority of youth at Seguín are located in the regular track.

11. "Cholo" is a term used often by Mexican nationals to refer to U.S. Mexicans who, in many instances, also drive lowrider automobiles (see Matute-Bianchi [1991] for her examination of Cholos in her ethnographic account). Also see Buriel (1984), whose analysis of reasons for gang membership support this finding. For contrary evidence, however, see O'Connor (1997) and Mehan et al. (1994, 1996). O'Connor provides evidence from several case studies that show how achievement orientations among African American high school youth are compatible with collective orientations embedded in group identities that challenge the dominant achievement ideology. Mehan et al. similarly find that Latino and African American youth participating in a detracked enrich-

ment program are able to develop academic identities without sacrificing their ethnic identities.

12. Darder's (1991) framework on adaptational strategies sheds additional light on how historically subordinate students negotiate the dominant culture. Through "cultural negotiation" and "cultural dualism," academically oriented minority youth can respond to racism and discrimination in a constructive manner. Akin to the students in the O'Connor study (see previous note), successful "cultural negotiation" entails retaining one's primary cultural identity while developing a critical consciousness toward inequality in society. Another response or adaptation is "cultural dualism," with youth perceiving an existence of two separate and nonnegotiable identities. Away from school, youth in the Mehan study (see previous note) lead separate lives in their homes and neighborhood, retaining friends whose schooling experiences differ vastly from their own. According to Darder, cultural dualists adopt mainstream institutional values, including those wedded to the logic of domination, citing minority entrepreneurs as an example. In a parallel manner, though aware of discrimination, students in the Mehan study attribute their success to their own individual hard work. According to Darder, "cultural negotiation" and "cultural dualism" strategies affirm the worlds of students whose lived experience is bicultural.

Two final responses advanced by Darder are "cultural separatism" and "cultural alienation." That is, individuals may either reject the dominant culture and retreat to the primary culture, or they may become reactionary, demonstrating a decided preference for the dominant culture and denying the existence of racism in U.S. society. "Cultural separatism" comes closest to what Fordham and Ogbu (1986) and Matute-Bianchi (1991) have in mind when they suggest that involuntary minorities adapt to schooling by rejecting it because they correlate academic achievement with "acting white." However, if secondary culture more accurately characterizes the culture of involuntary minorities as Ogbu suggests, then youth in the Darder model retreat not to a primary culture, but rather to a *version* of the primary culture, that is, secondary culture.

Unfortunately, Darder does not engage Ogbu's framework so it is impossible to know how the four responses to mainstream cultural dominance play out generationally. It is nevertheless safe to say that of the four, "cultural alienation" has been the least observed in ethnographic studies on immigrant and U.S.-born youth. Rodriguez's (1982) well-known autobiography, however, serves as an important reminder that such a response is experienced by some members of the Mexican American community. While "cultural separatism" is probably observed more among U.S.-born than immigrant youth, "cultural negotiation" and "cultural dualism" can operate among both, especially if secondary culture is allowed to substitute for Darder's concept of a primary culture. Ogbu's cultural-ecological framework and Darder's theory of biculturalism are both useful because of their attention to how students adapt to racial inequality in U.S. society. Underemphasized in both accounts is how students' varied responses are themselves implicated in a subtractive schooling framework. For example, what may appear as "cultural separatism," may actually reflect students' disaffection from *schooling* rather than education.

13. The "Mexican American" category of student that Matute-Bianchi (1991) came across was represented at Seguín, but were mostly located in the honors track or magnet program. These were average- to high-achieving U.S.-born, English-speaking youth who tended to participate in mainstream activities and had parents who were involved in the school (either as active members of the PTA, supporters of the student band, choir, pep squad, football team, or other extracurricular organizations on campus). Many of these parents had themselves attended Seguín in their youth and are long-time residents of the surrounding community. Some are even sons and daughters of East End politicos and activists. While visible because of their achievements and involvement, this segment constitutes a small share of the entire student population. As my focus is on regular-track youth herein, I scarcely address this segment.

14. With his discussion of subtractive and additive bilingualism, Lambert (1975) used a variant of this term. Also see Portes and Rumbaut (1990) who apply these concepts to the assimilation experiences of immigrants. They argue that Anglo monolinguals are threatened by the advantages that a liberal policy on bilingualism could establish for "non-natives" in a competitive labor market. Herein lies the basis for "linguistic nativism" (p. 211).

15. Some critics of bilingual education (e.g., Ravitch 1985) insist that since the United States is an English-speaking country, school programs need to focus on helping youth achieve fluency in English only. Others argue that programs that promote maintenance of Spanish could lead to the development of separatist movements. The latter concern is, according to Hernández-Chávez (1988), a false issue. Spanish-speaking people typically seek integration into society on their own terms, as empowered bilinguals, with a masterful command of their two languages and communication styles (Darder 1991; Stanton-Salazar 1997). Ironically, there is evidence that separatist sentiments can be fueled by the denial of the Spanish language, rather than by its promotion (Sanchez 1993; Rosales 1996).

16. This division is reminiscent of the division that existed between

the predominantly white "Hallway Hangers" and the predominantly African American "Brothers" in MacLeod's (1987, 1995) study of working-class high school youth in Clarendon Heights. Because the Hallway Hangers' racist ideology blinded them to the possibility of class-based solidarity with their African American peers, they inadvertently perpetuated their own status within the larger social division of labor. In a similar fashion, U.S.-born youth fail to articulate either a sense of shared interest or fate with their immigrant peers. This undermines the productive potential that solidarity with immigrants could bring. Because unlike MacLeod, my study examines variation *within* a national origin group, the school emerges as a chief architect in the production of ethnic minority status and identities.

CHAPTER 2. SEGUÍN HIGH SCHOOL IN HISTORICAL PERSPECTIVE

1. The "East End" is actually comprised of several *barrio* (neighborhood) communities.

2. The presence of Mexicans in the periphery of modern-day Houston may be traced back to the Spanish/Mexican colonial period, beginning with Alvar Núñez Cabeza de Vaca's expedition in 1528. This period ended in 1836 when General Sam Houston defeated the Mexican forces led by General and President Antonio Lopez de Santa Ana in the decisive battle at the San Jacinto River/Buffalo Bayou battlefield. This resulted in Texas' independence from Mexico (DeLeón 1989).

3. Unless otherwise noted, the early history of Houston and its Mexican American society is gleaned from the following sources: Rosales (1981), DeLeón (1989), Zamora (1992), and San Miguel (forthcoming). Other more general sources that treat the history of Mexicans in the United States and Texas include Montejano (1987), San Miguel (1987), Meier and Ribera (1993), Zamora (1993), and Rosales (1996).

4. Even before the 1920s, white Houstonites did not have a history of friendly relations with Mexicans. As far back as 1839, a local newspaper editor complained that unemployed or underemployed Mexicans were a "degraded class, a miserable remnant of our conquered enemy" (DeLeón 1989, 5–6). His suggestion was that the city simply expel its Mexican population. Although there is no record of an actual government order to that effect, by the 1880s less than ten Mexicans lived in the area.

5. The failure to achieve occupational mobility at the same rate as white workers was a trend evident throughout the Southwest. Barrera (1979) argues that, even today, while Mexican Americans hold positions throughout the occupational structure, they constitute a subordi-

nate segment within each class (i.e., working, petty bourgeois, professional-managerial, and capitalist classes).

6. Poor school attendance rates among Mexican American children in the Houston public school system were not a new development. Mexican children began attending Rusk Elementary in the city's second ward during the first decade of the 1900s. By the 1920s, Mexican children were attending four other elementary schools in the first, fifth, and sixth wards located on the north and northeast side of downtown. Despite the growing numbers of school-aged Mexican children, attendance levels were low. District officials seldom discouraged absenteeism among Mexican children who attended white schools. Additionally, poverty-stricken families often depended on the income of young adults and consequently discouraged them from attending beyond the elementary grades. A de facto practice of excluding Mexican children from predominantly white middle and high schools also discouraged their attendance. Lastly, a rigid policy of Americanization that devalued Mexican culture and enforced punitive measures against children who spoke Spanish on school grounds caused great resentment among parents. Many opted to simply keep their children at home (San Miguel forthcoming).

7. Between 1982 and 1987, when Houston was in the throes of a recession, a significant in-migration of people from Latin America and Asia occurred, reinforcing Mexicans' bottom position in the occupational structure (Rodriguez 1993). The 1990 Census reported a continuation of this trend.

8. While some of the decline is attributable to students who transfer to other schools, it is also the case that Latino youth typically transfer to other predominantly Latino schools that also register relatively higher dropout rates than non-minority schools.

9. Until the doors of a ninth-grade relief school were opened in fall 1997, no systematic effort existed at Seguín to address these youth who are mixed into the same classes with "regular" ninth-graders. The school serves 150 entering ninth-graders from the two middle schools in its feeder pattern.

10. According to Chapa (pers. com. 1995), third-generation Latino parents statewide average a ninth-grade education. Comparable schooling data for Houston demonstrate the persistence of low attainment levels. In 1950, Mexicans over twenty-five years of age had completed 5.2 median years of schooling, while whites had finished 11.4 grades, and African Americans 7.6 grades (DeLeón 1989). A 1994 survey of Houston adults revealed that 34 percent of Latinos attained eleven or fewer years of schooling. Whites and African Americans attaining eleven years or less, on the other hand, registered 4 and 10 percent, respectively. Among adults with a bachelor's degree or higher, 43 percent were Anglos, 25 percent

were African American, and 15 percent were Latino (Klineberg 1994).

11. See *Brown et al. v. Board of Education of Topeka et al.*, 347 U.S. 483 (1954).

12. See *Ross v. Eckels*, 434 F. 2d 1140 (1970).

13. According to the HISD Attendance Boundaries and Transfer Department (1996), the attendance zone for Seguín High School is roughly similar to what it was before *Ross*.

14. Apart from the specific issue of correcting racial integration, the demands called for the hiring of more Mexican American administrators, proportional representation of Mexican Americans on all HISD public school committees, programmatically correcting the serious shortage of Mexican American teachers, counselors, and other personnel, and textbook and curriculum development reflecting Mexican Americans' cultural heritage.

15. The figure of 1,000 students is the official count reported in the *Houston Chronicle* (October 21, 1989). Interviews with numerous students and teachers suggest a much higher figure, ranging from a low of 85 to a high of 95 percent of the student body.

16. An investigation conducted after the walkout revealed that Seguín was receiving an amount equal to that of other HISD high schools. A school board member representing Seguín later made the argument that equal funding for unequal needs perpetuates inequality ("Time to Move Ahead at Seguín, Trustee Says," *Houston Chronicle*, November 4, 1989).

17. Quoted from "A Report on Students to the Task Force" (no date) by a former Seguín teacher and task force member who wished to remain anonymous. Containing fifteen major grievances, the report highlighted teachers' lack of caring. However, only three are mentioned as only the second page containing these grievances was salvaged from her personal archive.

18. At a fall 1990 education summit that brought Seguín students, parents, and community members together on the campus for an entire day, I listened to several discussions that revealed students' and parents' view that the hoped-for fundamental changes in schooling that inspired the walkout had not yet occurred. Except for ever-increasing enrollments, little had changed by the time I began my study in fall 1992.

CHAPTER 3. TEACHER-STUDENT RELATIONS AND THE POLITICS OF CARING

1. This moment of community activism was a singular high point since the October, 1989 walkout. It resulted in the demand for a ninth-

grade relief school and a bilingual counselor, both of which were granted by the district. Seguín went without a bilingual counselor for a semester after the one they had was terminated (see chapter 5).

2. Reducing the school's dropout rate and increasing the graduation rate are other state-wide accountability criteria.

3. In exchange for Channel 1 television programming, every classroom boasts a television monitor on which movies and special programming are broadcast.

4. A social worker at Seguín told me that although she is somewhat hesitant to do so, she often counsels youth to leave the high school and enroll in GED programs so that they might eventually enter the community college system. In her words, "The traditional, factory-model of schooling simply does not work for most of these kids. Especially for many of the over-aged ones, high school is a waste of their time."

5. Anzaldúa (1987) provides a sociohistorical perspective on the complexities of a *mestiza* identity.

6. Because I entered the field with a theoretical concern about the widely observed contradiction that often exists between minority students' aspirations and their actions, I asked scores of students this question. Until I came across Tisa in the spring 1994 semester, it had not occurred to me that my question was not only about whether students understand the significance of higher education in today's world, especially its role in securing a toehold into the middle class. It can also be interpreted as privileging an Anglo, middle-class definition of success that is ultimately subtractive. According to this definition, minority youth are asked to eschew their cultural and working class identities and to measure their self-worth against their ability to "escape" the *barrio*. At this point, I stopped asking this question and engaged in sober reflection on how I as a researcher, through my questioning, may have inadvertently contributed to the reproduction of power relations.

CHAPTER 4. EVERYDAY EXPERIENCES IN THE LIVES OF IMMIGRANT AND U.S.-BORN YOUTH

1. Willis (1977) and Ogbu (1991) provide additional insights that help explain why an *esprit de corps* does not exist among U.S.-born youth.

2. I utilize HISD's definition of "short-" versus "long-term" immigrants. "Short-term" immigrants have been in the United States for three years or less.

3. In fact, at times there may be a fine line between cheating and

cooperation. The ESL teachers in particular view some of their students' behaviors with suspicion, accusing youth of "organized cheating." The fine line is evident in one ESL teacher's assessment:

> My immigrant students tend to help each other out so much that it's sometimes hard to tell where one student's work begins and the other ends. I have to be crystal-clear with them on what's permissible. There's lots of tough calls, but I would call "cheating" what many of them would probably call "working together."

4. The SEP administers the schooling that most students in Mexico (65 percent) receive, from preschool through higher education. Despite recent efforts to decentralize, the complexity of the SEP's management system often translates into the kind of snail-paced change at the local level that Cuahtemoc describes (Gutek 1993; Martin 1994).

5. From an array of thirty labels, respondents were allowed to choose as many self-identifiers as they wished. This produced dichotomous labels (self-descriptive or not) for an analysis of how they clustered together. The authors found that while Mexican immigrants possess five distinct identities ("working class," "middle class," "family cultural identity," "binational," and "Panraza"), Mexican Americans possessed seven, adding "farmworker" and "political Raza" as self-identifiers. This differentiation occurs by virtue of facility with the English language, many generations of U.S. residence, and greater geographic and occupational dispersal. In separate regressions, Mexicans' and Chicanos' social identities were then related to their views toward extended family orientations, cultural retention, Spanish media preferences, and approval of bilingualism.

6. Fito's situation approximates Coleman's (1988, 1990) optimal schooling situation, namely, one characterized by "intergenerational closure." Under such circumstances, youth are embedded in family and school networks of obligation that enable normative control of their actions. Fito's story also raises the question of whether "intergenerational closure" can transcend geopolitical boundaries like the U.S.-Mexican border.

7. Depending on one's perspective, American urban youth culture may appear as either black or white.

8. In March of 1993, 19 percent of the senior class had passed all three portions of the TAAS test. A year later, slightly more students (21 percent) had passed all three portions, resulting in a ranking that made Seguín one school above the worst school in the district at the high school level. Consequently, I also interpreted students' reluctance to discuss their futures as a logical, if not necessary, coping mechanism against such odds.

9. In chapter 3, I criticize myself for this line of questioning. Though inconclusive, students' depressed responses may have been conditioned in part by the question itself.

10. Except for the "Achievement Gang," which exhibited at best a lukewarm orientation toward school, no mixed-generation group was aggressively pro-school.

11. This analysis regressed achievement on a set of background, acculturation, and school-based variables that included school climate, teacher caring, and students' aspirations and expectations. Despite a lower rating of teacher caring among U.S.-born youth (see chapter 1), it emerges as an important, independent predictor of their academic achievement. This contrasts with its lack of predictive power among immigrant youth. (Table available upon request.)

CHAPTER 5. SUBTRACTIVE SCHOOLING AND DIVISIONS AMONG YOUTH

1. Broader societal forces certainly affect the attitudes that immigrant and U.S.-born youth hold toward each other. For example, Rodriguez and Nuñez's (1986) research among adult Mexican Americans and undocumented workers in the labor force shows the impact of each group's distinctive location in the occupational structure on the social distance between them and on their mutually critical perceptions.

2. For example, the Texas Bilingual Education Code (Sec. 29.051 State Policy) rejects bilingualism as a goal: "English is the basic language of this state. Public schools are responsible for providing a full opportunity for all students to become competent in speaking, reading, writing, and comprehending the English language." See also chapter 2 for a review of some of the most important historical and contemporary social, political, and economic factors shaping students' experiences at Seguín High.

3. For Mexican American girls, gender becomes an additional basis for marginality, although that issue was not raised during the classroom discussion. On average, females outperform males academically in each generation. However, as discussed in chapter 1, they are no more likely than males to see teachers as caring or to describe the school climate as favorable. Hence, good grades do not necessarily forestall marginality among regular-track youth.

In my research, it was females' withdrawal in the classroom that emerged as the primary indicator of their marginality. Indeed, Mexican American girls' silence and their hesitancy to speak up was a common complaint among Seguín teachers. Faculty often attributed this withdrawal either to the presence of males in the classroom or to Mexican culture, which allegedly inculcates passivity. Regardless of what they saw as the basis for their female students' disengagement, some teachers, as Linda's account (see chapter 4) makes clear, take advantage of the girls' compliance. However, since I did not focus my inquiry on gender and classroom dynamics, my findings in this area are somewhat limited (but see Orenstein [1994] and Olsen [1997] for an investigation of Latina female marginality).

4. Immigrants tend to refer to Mexican Americans as either "Chicano" or "Chicana," depending on whether they are male or female, respectively. "*México-Americano*" is another term immigrants used. As an identifier *for* Mexican Americans, "Chicana/o" may be popular among immigrants because the Mexican media popularized the term after it appeared in the title of several movies.

5. Rumbaut (1997) observed a correlation between self-esteem and being labeled "limited English proficient." Olsen's (1997) ethnographic data also reveal the powerful, negative impact of being an "ESLer" on immigrants' self-esteem.

6. Beginning in fall 1995, the mission statement was inserted into the teachers' handbook. Revised by Assistant Principal Ana Luera, the statement now reads: "The mission of Juan N. Seguín High School is to provide students with academic and technological excellence and social and emotional support in preparation as twenty-first century Americans." Note how the original reference to a multilingual world was subtracted.

7. The history of the school's mission statement helps account for its wording. It was drafted in the aftermath of the 1989 walkout due to the efforts of Ms. Martinez, a Mexican American Spanish teacher who headed the curriculum committee at the time. The walkout gave her and several other sympathetic faculty the political leverage necessary to write the statement. In light of Ms. Martinez's persistent efforts to alter the school's curriculum, the mission statement doubled as her critique of Seguín, on the one hand, and her emancipatory vision of education, on the other.

8. Because of limited school resources, many teachers are forced to draw from their personal reserves to enhance their ability to teach. An interesting question for future research is whether such spending varies according to the extent to which teachers perceive schooling as subtractive. A corollary question is whether a teacher's perception of schooling as subtractive is mediated by her/his academic field's location in the curriculum. It is conceivable that Spanish or ESL teachers not only see schooling as more subtractive than do their counterparts in other departments, but that they also spend more of their money as a percentage of their total income.

9. Partly following from Ms. Martinez's efforts, five classes of Spanish for native speakers (of Spanish) were eventually offered in 1991. In 1996, Honors Spanish was offered at Seguín for the first time in its history.

10. In 1993–94, for example, following the advice of the Math Department chair, the head counselor and head registrar in charge of the master schedule took it upon themselves to eliminate all ESL-Math courses. The chair's advice and the administration's response infuriated the two Latina math teachers, who ended up getting many of the ESL students rerouted to their classes anyway because the non-ESL math teachers were at a complete loss in having to contend with unprecedented numbers of students with whom they could not communicate (see Valdés [1998] for a comparable situation she came across in her research).

11. The Spanish and ESL clubs are the only exceptions to this rule.

12. I have visited many East End churches and have observed in each the same kind of divisions between immigrants and U.S.-born members. In fact, one large church I belonged to for several years dissolved along generational lines. This is a ubiquitous issue in Latino churches. Half of the church congregation prefers an exclusively Spanish service while the other half prefers either a bilingual or an exclusively English-speaking service. Moreover, the latter two options are often preferred within the context of Mexican or Latino church membership for cultural reasons. That is, they can more easily impart their religious beliefs and values to the next generation when members' experiences and cultural values are shared. However, there are also many people like these young women who attend either predominantly Anglo or integrated churches.

CHAPTER 6. UNITY IN RESISTANCE TO SCHOOLING

1. As mentioned in chapter 3, many students—mostly U.S.-born—violate rules like skipping class and attending all three lunch periods. They do so knowing that the numbers are on their side and that they are unlikely to get processed even if they get spotted. A common scenario is the presence of several administrators in the school cafeteria alongside scores of students whom they know are skipping class. The sheer amount of time, paperwork, and effort that would be required to process every offender discourages massive administrative action. A coach on the school's discipline committee has articulated this problem as students playing and beating the "numbers game."

2. May 5 marks the defeat of the French by Mexicans in the battle of Puebla in 1862. Puebla is a central state southeast of Mexico City.

REFERENCES

Abi-Nader, Jeannette. 1990. A house for my mother: Motivating Hispanic high school students. *Anthropology and Education Quarterly* 21: 41–58.

Althaus, Dudley. 1995. "Twilight's Children," *Houston Chronicle*, special report, December 17, 1995, pp. 1–12.

Anzaldúa, Gloria. 1987. *Borderlands/La Frontera: The New Mestiza.* San Francisco: Aunt Lute Books.

Barrera, Mario. 1979. *Race and Class in the Southwest: A Theory of Racial Inequality.* Notre Dame: University of Notre Dame Press.

Bartolomé, Lilia I. 1994. Beyond the methods fetish: Toward a humanizing pedagogy. *Harvard Educational Review* 64: 173–94.

Batalla, Guillermo Bonfil. 1996. *México Profundo: Reclaiming a Civilization.* Austin: University of Texas Press.

Bean, Frank D., and Marta Tienda. 1987. *The Hispanic Population of the United States.* New York: Academic Press.

Bean, Frank D., Jorge Chapa, Ruth Berg, and Katherine Sowards. 1994. Educational and sociodemographic incorporation among Hispanic immigrants to the United States. In *Immigration and Ethnicity: The Integration of America's Newest Arrivals,* edited by Barry Edmonston and Jeffrey S. Passel. Washington, D.C.: Urban Institute Press.

Blau, Peter M., and Otis D. Duncan. 1967. *The American Occupational Structure.* New York: The Free Press.

Bourdieu, Pierre. 1986. The forms of capital. In *Handbook of Theory and Research for the Sociology of Education,* edited by John G. Richardson. New York: Greenwood Press.

Bourdieu, Pierre and Jean-Claude Passeron. 1977a. Cultural reproduction and social reproduction. In *Power and Ideology in Education,* 487–511. New York: Oxford University Press.

———. 1977b. *Reproduction in Education, Society, and Culture.* London: Sage.

Brandstetter, John and Charle R. Foster. 1976. "Quality integrated education" in Houston's magnet schools. *Phi Delta Kappan* 57 (8): 502–6.

Buriel, Raymond. 1984. Integration with traditional Mexican-American culture and sociocultural adjustment. In *Chicana/o Psychology,* edited by Joe L. Martinez Jr. and Richard Mendoza, 2d ed. Orlando, Fla.: Academic Press.

——. 1987. Academic performance of foreign- and native-born Mexican Americans: A comparison of first-, second-, and third-generation students and parents. Report to the Inter-University Program for Latino Research, Social Science Research Council.

——. 1994. Immigration and education of Mexican Americans. In *The Educational Achievement of Latinos: Barriers and Successes*, edited by Aida Hurtado and Eugene Garcia. University of California Latino Eligibility Study. Santa Cruz, Calif.: University of California, Santa Cruz.

Buriel, Raymond and Desdemona Cardoza. 1988. Sociocultural correlates of achievement among three generations of Mexican American high school seniors. *American Educational Research Journal* 25: 177–92.

California Tomorrow. July 20, 1998. *Proposition 227 Update*. San Francisco: California Tomorrow.

Callahan, Raymond E. 1962. *Education and the Cult of Efficiency*. Chicago: University of Chicago Press.

Chapa, Jorge. 1988. The question of Mexican American assimilation: Socioeconomic parity or underclass formation? *Public Affairs Comment* 35 (1): 1–14.

——. 1990. The myth of Hispanic progress. *Harvard Journal of Hispanic Policy Issues* 4: 3–17.

——. 1991. Special focus: Hispanic demographic and educational trends. *Ninth Annual Status Report: Minorities in Higher Education*. Report for the American Council of Education. Office of Minorities in Higher Education.

——. 1995. Telephone conversation with author.

Chapa, Jorge and Richard R. Valencia. 1993. Latino population growth, demographic characteristics, and education stagnation: An examination of recent trends. *Hispanic Journal of Behavioral Sciences* 15 (2): 165–87.

Chavez, Linda. 1991. *Out of the Barrio: Toward a New Politics of Hispanic Assimilation*. New York: Basic Books.

Coleman, James S. 1988. Social capital in the creation of human capital. *American Journal of Sociology* 94: 95–120.

——. 1990. *Foundations of Social Theory*. Cambridge, Mass.: Harvard University Press.

Collier, Virginia P. 1995. Acquiring a second language for school. *Directions in Language and Education* 1 (4): 2–14.

Cox, Barbara, ed. 1993. *Resolving a Crisis in Education: Latino Teachers for Tomorrow's Classrooms*. Claremont, Calif: Tomás Rivera Center.

Cummins, Jim. 1981. The role of primary language development in promoting educational success for language minority students. In *Schooling and Language Minority Students*, 3–49. Sacramento: California Department of Education.

———. 1984. *Bilingualism and Special Education: Issues in Assessment and Pedagogy*. Clevedon, Canada: Multilingual Matters 6.

———. 1986. Empowering minority students: A framework for intervention. *Harvard Educational Review* 56: 18–36.

Darder, Antonia. 1991. *Culture and Power in the Classroom: A Critical Foundation for Bicultural Education*. New York: Bergin and Garvey.

———. 1995. Buscando America. In *Multicultural Education, Critical Pedagogy, and the Politics of Difference*, edited by Christine E. Sleeter and Peter L. McLaren. Albany: State University of New York Press.

DeLeón, Arnoldo. 1989. *Ethnicity in the Sunbelt: A History of Mexican Americans in Houston*. Houston: Mexican American Studies Studies Monograph Series No. 7.

Delgado-Gaitan, Concha and Henry Trueba. 1991. *Crossing Cultural Borders: Education for Immigrant Families in American*. New York: Falmer Press.

Delpit, Lisa. 1995. *Other People's Children*. New York: The New Press.

DeVillar, Robert A. 1994. The rhetoric and practice of cultural diversity in U.S. schools: Socialization, resocialization, and quality schooling. In *Cultural Diversity in Schools: From Rhetoric to Practice*, edited by Robert A. DeVillar, Christian J. Faltis, and James P. Cummins. Albany: State University of New York Press.

Donato, Ruben, Marta Menchaca, and Richard R. Valencia. 1991. Segregation, desegregation, and integration of Chicano students: Problems and prospects. In *Chicano School Failure and Success: Research and Policy Agendas for the 1990s*, edited by Richard R. Valencia. London: Falmer Press.

Eaker-Rich, Deborah, and Jane Van Galen, eds. 1996. *Caring in an Unjust World: Negotiating Borders and Barriers in Schools*. Albany: State University of New York Press.

Fine, Michelle. 1991. *Framing Dropouts: Notes on the Politics of an Urban Public High School*. Albany: State University of New York Press.

Fisher, Bernice, and Joan Tronto. 1990. Toward a feminist theory of caring. In *Circles of Care: Work and Identity in Women's Lives*, edited by Emily K. Able and Margaret K. Nelson. Albany: State University of New York Press.

Fix, Michael, and Jeffrey S. Passel. 1994. *Immigration and Immigrants: Setting the Record Straight*. Washington, D.C.: The Urban Institute.

Flores, William V., and Rina Benmayor. 1997. *Latino Cultural Citizenship: Claiming Identity, Space, and Rights.* Boston: Beacon Press.

Foley, Douglas E. 1990. *Learning in Capitalist Culture: Deep in the Heart of Tejas.* Philadelphia: University of Pennsylvania Press.

Fordham, Sygnithia, and John U. Ogbu. 1986. Black students' school success: Coping with the "burden of acting white." *Urban Review* 18 (3): 176–206.

Frankenberg, Ruth. 1993. *White Women, Race Matters: The Social Construction of Whiteness.* Minneapolis: University of Minnesota Press.

Freire, Paolo. 1985. *The Politics of Education: Culture, Power, and Education.* South Hadley, Mass.: Bergin and Garvey.

Galindo, D. Letticia. 1992. Teaching Spanish to native speakers: An insider's view. *The Journal of Educational Issues of Language Minority Students* 11: 207–18.

Gans, Herbert J. 1992. Second-generation decline: Scenarios for the economic and ethnic futures of post-1965 immigrants. *Ethnic and Racial Studies* 15 (2): 173–92.

Gibson, Margaret A. 1988. *Accommodation without Assimilation: Sikh Immigrants in an American High School.* Ithaca, N.Y.: Cornell University Press.

———. 1993. The school performance of immigrant minorities: A comparative view. In *Minority Education: Anthropological Perspectives,* edited by Evelyn Jacob and Cathie Jordan. Norwood, N.J.: Ablex.

Gilligan, Carol. 1982. *In a Different Voice.* Cambridge, Mass.: Harvard University Press.

Giroux, Henry A. 1992. Resisting difference: Cultural studies and the discourse of critical pedagogy. In *Cultural Studies,* edited by Lawrence Grossberg, Cary Nelson, and Paula A. Treichler. New York: Routledge.

Goffman, Erving. 1977. *Asylums: Essays on the Social Situation of Mental Patients and Other Inmates.* Garden City, N.Y.: Anchor Books.

Gold, Raymond L. 1969. Roles in sociological field observation. In *Issues in Participant Observation,* edited by George J. McCall and J. L. Simmons, 30–39. Reading, Mass.: Addison-Wesley.

Gordon, Milton M. 1964. *Assimilation and American Life: The Role of Race, Religion and National Origins.* New York: Oxford University Press.

Gutek, Gerald L. 1993. *American Education in a Global Society: Internationalizing Teacher Education.* White Plains, N.Y.: Longman.

Hayes-Bautista, David E., Werner O. Schink, and Jorge Chapa. 1988. *The Burden of Support: Young Latinos in an Aging Society.* Stanford, Calif.: Stanford University Press.

Hellman, Judith Adler. 1994. *Mexican Lives*. New York: The New Press.

Hernández-Chávez, Eduardo. 1988. Language policy and language rights in the United States. In *Minority Education: From Shame to Struggle*, by Tove Skutnabb-Kangas and James Cummins. Clevedon, Canada: Multilingual Matters 40.

Holland, Dorothy C. and Margaret A. Eisenhart. 1990. *Educated in Romance: Women, Achievement, and College Culture*. Chicago: University of Chicago Press.

Horswell, Cindy. 1989. "Cafeteria Woes at Seguín," *Houston Chronicle*, October 26, 1989, pp. 1A and 12A.

———. 1989. "Seguín High: Textbook Example of Confusion," *Houston Chronicle*, October 29, 1989, pp. 1C and 2C.

Horswell, Cindy and Melanie Markley. 1989. "High School Students Stage Mass Walkout: Scheduling Chaos Cited as 1,000 Leave Campus," *Houston Chronicle*, October 21, 1989, 1A and 12A.

Houston Independent School District. 1951. Board Member Services archive.

———. 1993. Pupil Accounting Department.

———. 1993–94. District and School Profiles (also 1996–97).

———. 1995–96. Academic Excellence Indicator System Report.

———. 1996. Attendance Boundaries and Transfer Department.

Hurtado, Aida, Patricia Gurin, and Timothy Peng. 1994. Social identities—A framework for studying the adaptations of immigrants and ethnics: The adaptations of Mexicans in the United States. *Social Problems* 41 (1): 129–51.

Kagan, Spencer, and M. Madsen. 1970. Experimental analysis of cooperation and competition of Anglo American and Mexican children. *Developmental Psychology* 6: 49–59.

Kao, Grace, and Marta Tienda. 1995. Optimism and achievement: The educational performance of immigrant youth. *Social Science Quarterly* 76 (1): 1–19.

Keefe, Susan E., and Amado M. Padilla. 1987. *Chicano Ethnicity*. Albuquerque, N.M.: University of New Mexico Press.

Klineberg, Stephen. 1994. *Houston's Ethnic Communities: Findings from the Thirteenth Year of the Houston Area Survey*. Houston: Rice University Press.

Kozol, Jonathan. 1991. *Savage Inequalities*. New York: Crown Publishers.

Ladson-Billings, Gloria. 1994. *The Dreamkeepers: Successful Teachers of African American Children*. San Francisco: Jossey-Bass.

Lambert, Wallace E. 1975. Culture and language as factors in learning and education. In *Education of Immigrant Students*, edited by A. Wolfgang. Toronto: O.I.S.E.

Lareau, Annette. 1989. *Home Advantage: Social Class and Parental Intervention in Elementary Education*. New York: The Falmer Press.

LeCompte, Margaret, and Anthony Dworkin. 1991. *Giving Up on School: Student Dropouts and Teacher Burnouts*. Newbury Park, Calif.: Corwin Press.

Lindholm, Kathryn J., and Zierlein Aclan. 1991. Bilingual proficiency as a bridge to academic achievement: Results from bilingual/immersion programs. *Journal of Education* 173: 99–113.

Lipsitz, George. 1995. The possessive investment in whiteness: Racialized social democracy and the "white" problem in American studies. *American Quarterly* 47 (3): 369–87.

Loewen, James W. 1995. *Lies My Teacher Told Me*. New York: The New Press.

Lopez, David E. 1976. The social consequences of Chicano home/school bilingualism. *Social Problems* 24 (2): 234–46.

Lucas, Tamara, Rosemary Henze, and Ruben Donato. 1990. Promoting the success of Latino language-minority students: An exploratory study of six high schools. *Harvard Educational Review* 60: 315–40.

Macías, José. 1990. Scholastic antecedents of immigrant students: Schooling in a Mexican immigrant-sending community. *Anthropology and Education Quarterly* 21: 291–318.

———. 1992. The social nature of instruction in a Mexican school: Implications for U.S. classroom practice. *The Journal of Educational Issues of Language Minority Students*. 10: 13–25.

MacLeod, Jay. 1987, 1995. *Ain't No Makin' It: Leveled Aspirations and Attainment in a Low-Income Neighborhood*. Boulder, Colo.: Westview.

Madsen, Millard C., and Ariella Shapiro. 1970. Cooperative and competitive behavior or urban and Afro-American, Anglo-American, Mexican American, and Mexican village children. *Developmental Psychology* 3: 16–20.

Markley, Melanie. 1989. "Time to Move Ahead at Seguín, Trustee Says," *Houston Chronicle*, November 4, 1989, p. 31A.

———. 1998. "Walkout Leader Says HISD Must Keep Bargain Vow," *Houston Chronicle*, October 23, 1989, pp. 9A and 12A.

Matute-Bianchi, María Eugenia. 1991. Situational ethnicity and patterns of school performance among immigrant and nonimmigrant Mexican-descent students. In *Minority Status and Schooling: A Comparative Study of Immigrant and Involuntary Minorities*, edited by Margaret A. Gibson and John U. Ogbu. New York: Garland Publishing.

McCarthy, Cameron. 1993. Beyond the poverty of theory in race relations: Nonsynchrony and social difference in education. In *Beyond*

Silenced Voices: Class, Race, and Gender in the United States Schools, edited by Lois Weis and Michelle Fine. Albany: State University of New York Press.

McIntyre, Alice. 1997. *Making Meaning of Whiteness: Exploring Racial Identity with White Teachers*. Albany: State University of New York Press.

McLaren, Peter. 1995. *Critical Pedagogy and Predatory Culture*. New York: Routledge.

McNeil, Linda M. 1988. *Contradictions of Control: School Structure and School Knowledge*. New York: Routledge.

McQuillan, Patrick James. 1998. *Educational Opportunity in an Urban American High School: A Cultural Analysis*. Albany: State University of New York Press.

Medina, Marcello Jr., and Shitala P. Mishra. 1994. Relationships among Spanish reading achievement and selected content areas. *Bilingual Review* 19(2): 134.8.

Mehan, Hugh, Lea Hubbard, and Irene Villanueva. 1994. Forming academic identities: Accommodation without assimilation among involuntary minorities. *Anthropology and Education Quarterly* 25 (2): 91–117.

Mehan, Hugh, Irene Villanueva, Lea Hubbard, and Angela Lintz. 1996. *Constructing School Success: The Consequences of Untracking Low-Achieving Students*. New York: Cambridge University Press.

Meier, Matt S., and Feliciano Ribera. 1993. *Mexican Americans and American Mexicans: From Conquistadors to Chicanos*. New York: Hill and Wang.

Mejía, Daniel. 1983. The development of Mexican American children. In *The Psychosocial Development of Minority Group Children*, edited by Gloria Johnson Powell. New York: Brunner/Mazel.

Merino, Barbara J., Henry T. Trueba, and Fabián A. Samaniego. 1993. Towards a framework for the study of the maintenance of the home language in language minority students. In *Language and Culture in Learning: Teaching Spanish to Native Speakers of Spanish*, edited by Barbara J. Merino, Henry T. Trueba, and Fabián A. Samaniego. Washington, D.C.: The Falmer Press.

Miles, Matthew and Michael Huberman. 1994. In *Handbook of Qualitative Research* edited by Norman K. Denzin and Yvonna S. Lincoln. Thousand Oaks, Calif.: Sage Publications.

Montaño-Harmon, María Rosario. 1991. Discourse features of written Mexican Spanish: Current research in contrastive rhetoric and its implications. *Hispania* 74 (March): 418–25.

Montejano, David. 1987. *Anglos and Mexicans in the Making of Texas, 1836–1986*. Austin: University of Texas Press.

National Center for Education Statistics. 1992. Are Hispanic Dropout Rates Related to Migration? Issue Brief.

Neidert, Lisa and Reynolds Farley. 1986. Assimilation in the United States. *American Sociological Review* 50 (6): 840–50.

Noblit, George W. 1994. The principal as caregiver. In *The Tapestry of Caring: Education as Nurturance*, edited by A. Renee Prillaman, Deborah J. Eaker, and Doris M. Kendrick. Norwood, N.J.: Ablex.

Noddings, Nel. 1984. *Caring: A Feminine Approach to Ethics and Moral Education*. Berkeley: University of California Press.

———. 1992. *The Challenge to Care in Schools: An Alternative Approach to Education*. New York: Teachers College Press.

O'Connor, Carla. 1997. "Dispositions toward (collective) struggle and educational resilience in the inner city: A case analysis of six African-American high school students. *American Educational Research Journal* 34: 593–629.

Ogbu, John. 1974. *The Next Generation: An Ethnography of Education in an Urban Neighborhood*. Orlando, Fla.: Academic Press.

———. 1978. *Minority Education and Caste: The American System in Cross-Cultural Perspective*. Orlando, Fla.: Academic Press.

———. 1987. Variability in minority responses to schooling: Nonimmigrants vs. immigrants. In *Interpretive Ethnography of Education: At Home and Abroad*, edited by George and Louis Spindler. Hillsdale, N.J.: Lawrence Erlbaum Associates.

———. 1991. Immigrant and involuntary minorities in comparative perspective. In *Minority Status and Schooling: A Comparative Study of Immigrant and Involuntary Minorities*, edited by Margaret A. Gibson and John U. Ogbu. New York: Garland Publishing.

———. 1993. Frameworks—variability in minority school performance: A problem in search of an explanation. In *Minority Education: Anthropological Perspectives*, edited by Evelyn Jacob and Cathie Jordan. Norwood, N.J.: Ablex.

Olsen, Laurie. 1997. *Made in America: Immigrant Students in our Public Schools*. New York: The New Press.

Orenstein, Peggy. 1994. *School Girls: Young Women, Self-Esteem, and the Confidence Gap*. New York: Doubleday.

Pack, William. 1989. "Disgruntled Students Await Changes," *Houston Post*, October 22, 1989, p. 1B.

Paley, Vivian G. 1995. *Kwanzaa and Me: A Teacher's Story*. Cambridge, Mass.: Harvard University Press.

Patthey-Chavez, G. Genevieve. 1993. High school as an arena for cultural conflict and acculturation for Angelinos. *Anthropology and Education Quarterly* 24 (1): 33–60.

Pedraza-Bailey, Silvia. 1985. *Political and Economic Migrants in America: Cubans and Mexicans*. Austin: University of Texas Press.

Peshkin, Alan. 1991. *The Color of Strangers, The Color of Friends: The Play of Ethnicity in School and Community*. Chicago: University of Chicago Press.

Phelan, Patricia, Ann Locke Davidson, and Hahn Cao Yu. 1993. Students' multiple worlds: Navigating the borders of family, peer, and school cultures. In *Renegotiating Cultural Diversity in American Schools*, edited by Patricia Phelan and Ann Locke Davidson. New York: Teachers College.

Platt, Anthony. 1992. Defenders of the canon: What's behind the attack on multiculturalism? *Social Justice* 19(2): 122–41.

Population Reference Bureau. 1989. *America in the 21st Century: Human Resource Development*. Washington, D.C.: Population Reference Bureau.

Portes, Alejandro, and Rubén G. Rumbaut. 1990. *Immigrant America: A Portrait*. Berkeley: University of California Press.

Portes, Alejandro, and Min Zhou. 1993. The new second generation: Segmented assimilation and its variants. *Annals of the American Academy of Political and Social Sciences* 530: 74–96.

———. 1994. Should immigrants assimilate? *The Public Interest* 116: 18–33.

Prillaman, A. Renee, and Deborah J. Eaker. 1994. The weave and the seaver: A tapestry begun. In *The Tapestry of Caring: Education as Nurturance*, edited by A. Renee Prillaman, Deborah J. Eaker, and Doris M. Kendrick. Norwood, N.J.: Ablex.

Putnam, Robert D. 1995. Bowling alone: America's declining social capital. *Journal of Democracy* 6 (1): 65–78.

Putnam, Robert D. 1993. The prosperous community: Social capital and public life. *The American Prospect* 13 (Spring): 35–42.

Ramirez, J. David, Sandra D. Yuen, Dana R. Ramey, David J. Pasta, and David K. Billings. 1991. *Final Report: Longitudinal Study of Structured Immersion Strategy, Early-Exit, and Late-Exit Transitional Bilingual Education Programs for Language-Minority Children*. Executive summary. San Mateo, Calif.: Aguirre International.

Ravitch, Diane. 1985. Politicization and the schools: The case of bilingual education. *Proceedings of the American Philosophical Society* 129: 121–28.

Reese, Leslie, Silvia Balzano, Ronald Gallimore, and Claude Goldenberg. 1991. The Concept of *Educación*: Latino Family Values and American Schooling. Paper presented at the Annual Meeting of the American Anthropological Association, November, Chicago, Illinois.

Rivera, Tomás. 1987. The teacher was surprised. . . . . . . *Y No Se Lo Tragó la Tierra*. Arte Público Press.

Rodriguez, Luis J. 1994. *Always running: La vida loca, gang days in L.A.* New York : Simon & Schuster.

Rodriguez, Nestor P. 1986. The growth of Houston's Hispanic population. In *Hispanics in Houston and Harris County: 1519–1986*, edited by D. Caram, A. G. Dworkin, and N. Rodriguez, 49–54. Houston, Tex.: Houston's Hispanic Forum.

————. 1993. Economic restructuring and Latino growth in Houston. In *In the Barrios: Latinos and the Underclass Debate*, edited by Joan Moore and Raquel Pinderhughes. New York: Russell Sage Foundation.

Rodriguez, Nestor P., and Rogelio T. Nuñez. 1986. An exploration of factors that contribute to differentiation between Chicanos and indocumentados. In *Mexican Immigrants and Mexican Americans: An Evolving Relation*, edited by Harley Browning and Rodolfo de la Garza . Austin: CMAS University of Texas Press.

Rodriguez, Richard. 1982. *Hunger of Memory, The Education of Richard Rodriguez, An Autobiography*. Boston: David R. Dodine.

Romo, Harriett D. 1985. The Mexican origin population's differing perceptions of their children's schooling. In *The Mexican American Experience: An Interdisciplinary Anthology*, edited by Rodolfo de la Garza et al. Austin: University of Texas Press.

Romo, Harriett D., and Toni Falbo. 1996. *Latino High School Graduation: Defying the Odds*. Austin: University of Texas Press.

Rosales, F. Arturo. 1996. *Chicano! The History of the Mexican American Civil Rights Movement*. Houston, Tex.: Arte Público Press.

————. 1981. Mexicans in Houston: The struggle to survive, 1908–1975. *The Houston Review: History and Culture of the Gulf Coast* 3: 224–48.

Rumbaut, Rubén G. 1994. The crucible within: Ethnic identity, self-esteem, and segmented assimilation among children of immigrants. *International Migration Review* 28: 748–94.

Rumberger, Russell. 1995. Dropping out of middle school: A multilevel analysis of students and schools. *American Educational Research Journal* 32 (fall): 583–625.

Sanchez, Rosaura. 1993. Language variation in the Spanish of the Southwest. In *Language and Culture in Learning: Teaching Spanish to Native Speakers of Spanish*, edited by Barbara J. Merino, Henry T. Trueba, and Fabián A. Samaniego. Washington, D.C.: The Falmer Press.

San Miguel, Guadalupe. 1987. *"Let All of them Take Heed": Mexican Americans and the Campaign for Educational Equality in Texas, 1910–1981*. Austin: University of Texas Press.

———. Forthcoming. *"Brown, Brown, We're Not White, We're Brown": Identity and Activism in the Politics of Chicano School Reform in Houston, Texas, 1965–1980*. College Station: Texas A & M Press.

Skutnabb-Kangas, Tove, and James Cummins. 1988. *Minority Education: From Shame to Struggle*. Clevedon, Canada: Multilingual Matters 40.

Smith, Frank. 1995. Let's declare education a disaster and get on with our lives. *Phi Delta Kappan* 76 (8): 584–90.

Spindler, George, and Louise Spindler, eds. 1994. *Pathways to Cultural Awareness: Cultural Therapy with Teachers and Students*. Thousand Oaks, Calif.: Corwin Press.

Spradley, James. 1980. *Participant Observation*. New York: Holt, Rinehart and Winston.

Spring, Joel. 1997. *Deculturalization and the Struggle for Equality: A Brief History of the Education of Dominated Cultures in the United States*. 2d ed. New York: McGraw-Hill.

Stanton-Salazar, Ricardo. 1997. A social capital framework for understanding the socialization of ethnic minority children and youths. *Harvard Educational Review* 67: 1–39.

Stanton-Salazar, Ricardo, and Michael Bressler. 1997. Recasting social integration as social embeddedness: How social networks facilitate academic persistence among high school students of color. Paper presented at the Annual Conference of the Pacific Sociology Association, April 16–19, San Diego, California.

Stanton-Salazar, Ricardo, and Sanford M. Dornbusch. 1995. Social capital and the social reproduction of inequality: The formation of informational networks among Mexican-origin high school students. *Sociology of Education* 68 (2): 116–35.

Steinberg, Laurence, B. Bradford Brown, and Sanford M. Dornbusch. 1996. *Beyond the Classroom: Why School Reform Has Failed and What Parents Need to Do*. New York: Simon & Schuster.

Stone, Merlin. 1981. *Three Thousand Years of Racism*. New York: New Sibylline Books.

Suárez-Orozco, Marcelo M. 1989. Psychosocial aspects of achievement motivation among recent Hispanic immigrants. In *What do Anthropologists Say About Dropouts?*, edited by Henry T. Trueba and George and Louise Spindler. New York: The Falmer Press.

———. 1991. Hispanic immigrant adaptation to schooling. In *Minority Status and Schooling: A Comparative Study of Immigrant and Involuntary Minorities*, edited by Margaret A. Gibson and John U. Ogbu. New York: Garland Publishing.

Suárez-Orozco, Carola, and Suárez-Orozco, Marcelo M. 1997. *Trans-*

formations: Immigration, Family Life and Achievement Motivation among Latino Adolescents. Stanford, Calif.: Stanford University Press.

Suro, Roberto. 1998. *Strangers among Us: How Latino Immigration is Transforming America.* New York: Alfred A. Knopf.

Thomas, Wayne P., and Virginia P. Collier. 1996. *Language Minority Student Achievement and Program Effectiveness.* Fairfax, Va.: Center for Bilingual/Multicultural/ESL Education, George Mason University.

Trueba, Henry T. 1993. The relevance of theory on language and culture with pedagogical practices. In *Language and Culture in Learning: Teaching Spanish to Native Speakers of Spanish,* edited by Barbara J. Merino, Henry T. Trueba, and Fabián A. Samaniego. Washington, D.C.: The Falmer Press.

Twine, France Winddance. 1996. Brown skinned white girls: Class, culture and the construction of white identity in suburban communities. *Gender, Place and Culture: A Journal of Feminist Geography* 3 (1): 205–224.

U.S. Census Bureau. 1989. *Current Population Reports,* Series P-20.

Valdés, Guadalupe. 1998. The world outside and inside schools: Language and immigrant children. *Educational Researcher* 27: 4–18.

Valdivieso, Rafael. 1986. *Must They Wait Another Generation? Hispanics and Secondary School Reform.* Hispanic Policy Development Project, August, Washington, D.C.

Valencia, Richard. 1991. *Chicano School Failure and Success.* London: The Falmer Press.

Valencia, Richard, Marta Menchaca, and Angela Valenzuela. 1993/94. The educational future of Chicanos: A call for affirmative diversity. In Special Issue: Challenges of Diversity. *The Journal of the Association of Mexican American Educators* 1993/94: 1–13.

Valenzuela, Angela. 1997. Mexican American youth and the politics of caring. In *From Sociology to Cultural Studies,* edited by Elizabeth Long. Second Volume: Sociology of Culture Annual Series. London: Blackwell.

———. 1999. Subtractive schooling: U.S.-Mexican youth and the politics of caring. *Reflexiones 1998: New Directions in Mexican American Studies.* Center for Mexican American Studies, University of Texas.

———. 1999. "Checkin' up on my guy": Chicanas, social capital, and the culture of romance. *Frontiers: A Journal of Women Studies* 20 (1) (Spring). In press.

Valenzuela, Angela, and Sanford M. Dornbusch. 1994. Familism and social capital in the academic achievement of Mexican-origin and

Anglo high school adolescents. *Social Science Quarterly* 75 (1): 18–36.

Velez-Ibañez, Carlos, and James B. Greenberg. Formation and transformation of funds of knowledge. *Anthropology and Education Quarterly* 23 (4): 313–35.

Vigil, Diego. 1997. *Personas Mexicanas: Chicano High Schoolers in a Changing Los Angeles.* Fort Worth, Tex.: Harcourt Brace College Publishers.

Vigil, James D. 1988. "Group processes and street identity: Adolescent Chicano gang members," *Ethnos* 16 (4): 421–445.

Vigil, James Diego, and John M. Long. 1981. Unidirectional or nativist acculturation: Chicano paths to school achievement. *Human Organization* 40: 273–77.

Watson, James B., and Julian Samora. 1954. Subordinate leadership in a bicultural community: An analysis. *American Sociological Review* 19: 413–21.

Webb-Dempsey, Jaci, Bruce Wilson, Dickson Corbett, and Rhonda Mordecai-Phillips. 1996. Understanding caring in context: Negotiating borders and barriers. In *Caring in an Unjust World,* edited by Deborah Eaker-Rich and Jane Van Galen. Albany: State University of New York Press.

Williams, Raymond. 1965. *Marxism and Literature.* New York: Oxford University Press.

Willis, Paul. 1977. *Learning to Labour.* New York: Columbia University Press.

Wilson, William Julius. 1987. *The Truly Disadvantaged: The Inner City, the Underclass, and Public Policy.* Chicago: University of Chicago Press.

Yeo, Frederick L. 1997. *Inner-City Schools, Multiculturalism, and Teacher Education: A Professional Journey.* New York: Garland Publishing.

Zamora, Emilio. 1992. The failed promise of wartime opportunity for Mexicans in the Texas oil industry. *Southwestern Historical Quarterly* 95: 323–68.

Zamora, Emilio. 1993. *The World of the Mexican Worker in Texas.* College Station: Texas A & M Press.

Zsembik, Barbara A. and David Llanes. 1996. Generational differences in educational attainment among Mexican Americans. *Social Science Quarterly* 77: 363–74.

INDEX